An Accidental Daughter

An Accidental Daughter

a novel by

AMANDA RAYNER

RICHARD COHEN BOOKS · London

British Library Cataloguing in Publication Data:
A catalogue record for this book is available from the British Library

Copyright © 1996 by Amanda Rayner

ISBN 1 86066 036 3

First published in Great Britain in 1996 by
Richard Cohen Books
7 Manchester Square
London W1M 5RE

1 3 5 7 9 8 6 4 2

Typeset by Rowland Phototypesetting Ltd,
Bury St Edmunds, Suffolk

Printed in Great Britain by
Clays Ltd, St Ives plc

For Colin M

Acknowledgements

Michaela Economides for the help with all things Greek; Russell Jones for an understanding of the stock market; Liz McCarthy for her typing services; Stuart McInnes of Pannone and Partners, Pritchard Englefield, for legal brainstormings; Claire Rayner for matters medical; Linden Stafford for her patient editing; Ken Tweedie of the MG Owners Club; Matthew White of the Rover Club of Great Britain and Dee Remmington for the kick-start.

Staff of St Catherine's House, London; the Library for Hellenic Studies, University of London; the National Tourist Organisation of Greece; the Turkish Information Centre; and other sources too numerous to mention.

Part One

Alex was puzzled. It did not make sense. The given names were correct, as were the surname and place; even the occupation, bio-chemist, was right. But that was all. Admittedly the year – 1952 – was as it should be, but the actual date was wrong. Her birthday was 14 November but this certificate showed 23 October and the entry under 'NAME, SURNAME AND MAIDEN NAME OF MOTHER', instead of 'Elizabeth Deirdre Ghillyand formerly Rouget', read 'Sally Pauline Ghillyand formerly Chambers'.

Dr Alexandra Ghillyand sat hunched forward in the high-backed leather swivel chair and stared at the document in her hands. Straightening up, she slowly turned the seat round so it faced the large old desk and with equally deliberate movements smoothed the wide piece of paper across its polished surface. She put her elbows on its top, pleated her fingers together and rested her chin on her hands.

At that moment Alex was assailed by a mixture of bewilderment, curiosity, numbness and anger – intense, simmering anger – that even after he had died her father had once again forced her to question herself.

She kept reading the birth certificate over again, her thoughts increasingly confused. Outside, the grey February afternoon grew darker. Inside, the clock ticked, and the sound of Barbara clattering away on the ancient typewriter in the adjoining office filtered through the door. ('I'm not having one of those PC things. I'm a secretary, not a computer programmer,' Barbara would tell the office services manager whenever he tried to get her to update her equipment. 'Besides, if it's good enough for Dr Ghillyand, it's certainly good enough for me!')

'Barbara?' Alex called sharply, lifting her head and running her fingers through her short brown hair.

'Yes?' The door opened and Barbara came in, switching on the light.

Alex blinked in the sudden glare and looked across the vast office at the woman who had been her father's secretary for more years than she cared to remember. Holding her notebook, Barbara stood there in her plaid skirt, toning blouse and polished court shoes, as neat and as precise as everything else in the office. This had once been the billiards-room of the Manor House; it was still lined with oak panels, and a high ornate ceiling supported a magnificent chandelier. The tall glass-fronted cabinets with her father's books methodically arranged according to size within the subject categories reflected the rest of the room: from the desk and chair perfectly positioned to create the greatest impact on anyone entering the office, to the impeccably straight prints and certificates that adorned the walls.

Thinking how tatty she looked in the comfortable sweater, leggings and scuffed boots, and aware of the contrast between herself and Barbara, Alex spoke sharply. 'When did you last look in the bottom drawer?' She tilted her head to indicate the one she meant.

'I have *never* looked in that drawer,' Barbara replied crisply, obviously affronted. 'Dr Ghillyand – I mean your father – always kept it locked. He held the only key – the one you received with his other things when he passed on . . . Why?' With a casual air she asked, 'Is there anything interesting in it?'

Mentally Alex kicked herself: her aggressive question had aroused the woman's curiosity. Out loud she said, 'No, it's only that some of the papers in there were quite old.'

Pushing the chair back and rising to her feet, she flexed her shoulders against her tiredness. She gave Barbara a tight smile, tucked the birth certificate into the top of a bulging folder and walked across the washed Chinese carpet to the coat-rack, to collect her wrap.

'I'm going to call it a day, though there's still a lot to be sorted out. I'm not sure exactly when I'll be back. But I've got a full set of keys and can let myself in – so you don't have to worry about being here . . . Oh, and by the way . . .' Alex turned as she reached the door. 'My father was a doctor and I am a doctor. One thing we did have in common was calling a spade a spade. He did not "pass on". He died.'

With that she opened the door and swept out past Barbara who was standing just inside the office with a hurt expression on her face. Alex shut the door behind her with a firm bang and walked a couple of yards down the corridor before stopping to lean against the wall. She sighed deeply, and closed her eyes.

Why? Why does that woman always bring out the worst in me? Christ, Alex, you virtually accused her of going through Father's things. It's not her fault he kept personal stuff under lock and key in his desk. Though heaven knows why. You know you should go back and apologise; after all, she's got a right to be there. Poor cow, she probably doesn't know what's going to happen now that he's dead. Oh, but she's so ingratiating and irritating. Alex Ghillyand, if you had any . . .

'It's never easy, is it?' A friendly male voice broke into her thoughts.

Alex opened her eyes quickly and pushed herself away from the wall. She stared at Dr Bratby with a puzzled frown.

'Clearing out someone's things when they've died,' he explained softly. 'I had to do it for my mother and it took for ever. It's amazing how many useless bits of paper people keep, isn't it? Trouble is, if you're like me, you keep stopping and remembering all sorts of nice things about them – which slows it down, when really you should just chuck it all in the bin.'

Alex remained silent, while Bratby continued.

'Anyway, I shouldn't be rabbiting on like this . . . I only wanted to say, your father was a highly respected man here at the Corporation. We're going to miss his input on a number of current projects. And if there's anything I can do, to help get you through what must be a difficult time, let me know. OK?'

'Thank you, Dr Bratby. I'll do that.' She gave him a polite smile as she flicked her wrap over her shoulder and fled down the stairs, leaving her pass at reception, and out into the car park.

By now it was getting dark. She had spent more time than she had intended in her father's office and realised she would probably hit the traffic on her way back into town. Nevertheless, as she sat in the car catching her breath, disjointed thoughts tumbled through her head.

He's a nice old boy, Dr Bratby . . . not that old, actually . . . practical, down to earth . . . Lucky him to have nice things to remember about his mother . . . Wish I could feel like that . . . Why was it always so revolting when I was with my father? . . . Why can't I tell Bratby what it was really like being David Ghillyand's daughter? . . . Funny how he only said he'd miss my father's work, and nothing

5

about him ... He's right. I should have dumped all that paper in the bin. Wouldn't have found that stupid birth certificate then, would I? Whose is it? Not mine. Is it? ... You didn't like him much either, did you, Bratby? ... I wonder what projects he's been working on.

Alex looked up at the façade of the elegant Georgian house that was the UK headquarters of the Rouget Corporation. It was odd to recall that the splendid building had once been someone's home. Now it was the cornerstone of a multi-million-pound business that had offices, manufacturing plants and research laboratories worldwide. The security lights were on, giving an eerie glow to the pale brickwork. Where people had not bothered to draw the blinds they stood out clearly against the darkness as they finished off their day's work.

Barbara's back was upright as she sat at her typewriter thumping out thank-yous to all those people who had written to send their condolences. *I must phone and apologise,* thought Alex. Dr Bratby, one floor up over the other side of the porch, obviously preferred a single desk lamp to the overhead fluorescent strips. He had his feet up on his desk, leaning back in his chair dictating something – probably the day's report on his work. People were going about their jobs, thinking about going home.

Alex liked the fact that, despite its hard commercial core, the Corporation's public face was represented by this elegant building, nestling in its own vast acreage. She knew that one of the reasons her long-dead grandfather had bought the Manor House in Elstree back in 1927 was that it had allowed for the expansion that now included the sprawling laboratory wing at the back of the house. It had been typical of him to leave it all to the Corporation when he died, thus ensuring his ideals were maintained long after he'd gone.

Cecil Rouget, founder of the Rouget Corporation, had always insisted on having the most modern, best-equipped resources anywhere in the world, arguing with his board of directors, when they demurred, 'How can we attract the top medical men, biochemists and technicians – not to mention their funding – if we don't offer them the best to work with and on?' As a result the Rouget Corporation now had leading scientists queuing to bring their research projects to one of the six centres that made up the Corporation in Europe, America and Japan.

Alex shook her head. 'It's a hell of an inheritance,' she said wryly

6

to herself as she started up the engine and swung the car round the gravel forecourt. As she'd expected, the traffic was heavy and by the time she turned off the A41 on to the North Circular it was nose-to-tail. For once she could not even be bothered to be irritated by her stop–start progress. She turned on the radio, half listening to *Newsnight* on Classic FM. *Pictures at an Exhibition* was just finishing and the next item was being introduced.

'*I'm sure many people will have been sad to hear of the recent death of Dr David Ghillyand.*'

Alex turned it up slightly. '*His work at the Rouget Corporation has been recognised across the world. He was nominated for the Nobel Prize in Medicine in 1957 and during his lifetime was involved in many findings which still have a bearing on the way we think and look at medicine today. With me in the studio is Professor Lockton, who worked closely with Dr Ghillyand . . .*

'*Professor Lockton, what would you say was Dr Ghillyand's greatest contribution to modern science?*'

'*That's very difficult to answer. But I would say, in my opinion, it was the work he did in the fifties on the whole subject of pain control. You have to appreciate that in those days . . .*'

Alex couldn't bear it any longer. She snapped off the radio, thumped the steering wheel and muttered aloud through gritted teeth, 'My bloody father!' The man in the next car raised a bemused eyebrow. Now, fully rattled, she slammed the car into second gear and pushed across into the outside lane, ignoring the irritated horns behind her.

For the rest of the journey Alex tried to concentrate on the traffic, pushing all other thoughts to the back of her mind until she arrived home. In Notting Hill she managed to find a vacant resident's parking bay right outside her garden flat. As she locked the car, she had to admit she was more than a little pleased to be back. It had been a long day.

Letting herself in, she tossed her wrap and the file with her father's papers on top of the pile of magazines by the telephone. Then she sat down and pressed the button to collect the two messages flashing away on the answering-machine. As the tape rewound she began pulling off her boots.

'Hello, Alex, it's Sam.' Sam Baldock was Alex's junior houseman at the Queen Victoria Hospital – Vickie's – where Alex was senior consultant in oncology. 'I know you're on compassionate. But I thought you'd want to know . . . Ruth Cunningham died today. In the end it wasn't too bad. Her husband and eldest daughter were with her. She regained consciousness and was quite lucid for about five minutes. So they were able to say their goodbyes. As I say I realise you're on leave, and I hope it's not a bit tactless to call you about this . . . but knowing how you always like to talk to families yourself, and Ruth had been one of your patients for a long time, I thought you'd want to know. Hope I've done the right thing? Just in case you want to call them before you come back, the number is . . .' The tinny voice gave her the phone number, which Alex hastily scribbled down.

BEEP. The machine went on to the next message. 'Hi, hon,' came a cheery female voice. 'Jen here, in case you hadn't guessed. I thought I'd give you a buzz as I knew – at least I think I've got it right – that today was the day you were going over to the Corporation to start going through his stuff. If I've got it wrong then ignore this call. If I've got it right (and I think I have) and you fancy a bit of company this evening then give me a buzz. Talk to you soon. Byee!'

As Alex listened she could see Jenny in her mind's eye – a mass of wild spiky hair, startling make-up and large glasses. It was a deceptive image. Behind it was a shrewd businesswoman who had turned one rather tatty dance class into a number of highly success-ful keep-fit and beauty sanctuaries. Jen had told Alex in one of her more candid moments that she would actually like to tone it down a bit, with contact lenses and neat suits, but the image would be bad for business, so Lycra and craziness it was.

Alex laughed a little and gave the answering-machine an affec-tionate pat. When she came in all she wanted to do was have a hot bath and an early night, but hearing Jen's lively voice she decided a bit of undemanding company might be a good idea. She picked up the phone and dialled her friend's number.

'Yes, Jen, it *was* a bit depressing and there *was* something else,' she replied when asked how it had gone. 'But rather than go over it all on the phone, why don't you come over here and pick up a Chinese on the way? I'll talk about it when I see you.'

'Don't tell me, you've unearthed the secret of your father's dim and distant past,' Jen joked. 'You've discovered he had a love child tucked away somewhere and you're not an only child after all!'

'Not quite. At least, I don't think so.' Alex sounded cautious.

'Look, I'll explain when I see you. About eight then? Don't forget the seaweed,' she finished in an attempt to lighten her tone.

By the time Jen arrived, Alex had bathed and was wrapped in an oversized towelling robe. As soon as she opened the door Jen could see that something was wrong, so she busied herself removing the lids from the foil containers of steaming Chinese food. Alex was normally in tight control of her feelings and tended to be on the serious side, despite a streak of dry humour. Tonight, though, she was decidedly fidgety. Jen had more sense than to ply her with questions, knowing she would tell her what was the matter in her own good time.

They settled down to their supper, catching up on each other's news and gossiping about mutual friends. Alex helped herself to a pancake and slowly spread it with plum sauce, not sure how to start her conversation with Jen. She concentrated on picking up the bits of glistening crispy duck and sticks of cucumber and spring onion. It was as she was carefully rolling it all into a fat parcel that she finally began to tell Jen about the birth certificate she had found hidden in her father's drawer.

'So you see, maybe you weren't that wrong when you suggested I had a sibling tucked away somewhere. The silly thing is, I have the oddest feeling that this birth certificate is mine.'

'Oh, come on! That's a bit far-fetched. I mean, how can it be? From what you've said, half the details on it aren't yours at all.'

'I know. But half of them are – or close enough to be more than coincidence. You've got to admit it's odd, haven't you?'

'No,' said Jen firmly, nibbling a prawn cracker. 'Not until I've seen it. I take it you did bring it home with you?'

Alex licked her fingers and went to rescue the certificate from her file. Once again she spread it out in front of her. The two women looked at it in silence.

'Alex, where is *your* birth certificate? I mean the one with the correct stuff about your parents and the date and whatnot?'

Alex shrugged.

'You must have it somewhere. What about when you got your passport?'

'I don't know. I've never seen my birth certificate – never had to use it. My father sorted out my first passport and since then I've just renewed it when the time came. I never thought I'd say this, but I wish the miserable sod were here so I could ask him about it.' She stood up and moved towards the kitchen. 'I can't tell you how odd it's making me feel. I mean, I've spent all my life celebrating my birthday on one date and suddenly it looks as if I'm a month out. Just think, all these years I've been looking at Scorpio and I'm actually the sign before . . . whatever that is,' she finished lamely.

'It's Libra and you'd be on the cusp.' Jen dismissed that as she hurried on. 'Don't you think you're rather jumping to conclusions? I'm sure there's a perfectly logical explanation. Why not go along to St Catherine's House and look yourself up in the register?'

'I could, couldn't I?' Alex answered thoughtfully from the kitchen. 'You know,' she continued as she brought in two mugs of coffee and sat down, 'I always forget they record births as well as deaths there. I guess it goes with the job.'

'Sometimes I think you're more like your bloody father than you realise. That's the sort of morbid comment he'd have made,' Jen said in a derisive tone. 'I know I shouldn't say this, hon . . . not speaking ill of the dead and all that . . . but on the few occasions I met him he seemed such a cold man. I wondered if it was a sort of shyness.'

'No, it wasn't that,' responded Alex, curling up in the corner of the comfortable settee and tucking her feet up underneath her. 'He was always so precise and stern, wanting everything just so. My earliest memory of him is being told off when I was about three and a half. I don't know where I was . . . I just remember sitting on the floor, playing with coloured building bricks. I was having a lovely time, singing away to myself. Then he came in and yelled at me for making a noise. Scared me something rotten.' She paused, wrapping her hands round the mug of coffee.

'You know, it carried on like that . . . Most of the time he only ever spoke to me to have a go at me or criticise my school reports. You know something? I found all my reports when I moved in here eight years ago and they weren't that bad. In fact I was pretty much a straight B-plus student, with a few A grades thrown in for good measure. I always thought I was such a lousy scholar too.'

'But you got the gold medal at medical school,' Jen reminded her.

'Oh, sure. I worked my butt off for those finals and even then it wasn't enough. Best passes in the country, that was me. Not just

London but the whole bloody country. And did he utter so much as a word of congratulations? Not on your life. I got summoned to the Corporation, where he sat me down and went through my papers, scolding me for dropping a few marks.'

Jen shook her head. 'Not much fun.'

'The awful thing is, Jen, that people are commiserating with me . . . Offering their condolences, telling me what a brilliant and respected man he was . . . And I don't want to know. I want to scream at them, tell them what a bastard he was. Tell them I'm glad he's dead. Then all I feel is guilt.'

Alex stopped suddenly and let out a sob. Jen scrambled to her feet and removed the coffee mug from her friend's shaking hands before wrapping her arms around her. Crooning quietly, Jen rocked her gently backwards and forwards.

'Ah, hon, you have got yourself into a pickle, haven't you? Have a good cry. You'll feel better for it. I know, I know: you hate self-pity. But if it's any consolation I didn't like your father much either. Come to think of it, he was a first-class shit! How he ever got such a smashing daughter as you I'll never know!'

Alex gave a sniff and raised a blotchy face from Jen's jumper. 'I don't know what I did to deserve a friend like you. Sorry for making such a fool of myself.'

'Belt up! You haven't, and I don't want to hear another word. In fact you're going to bed.'

'Jen, you may be the nearest thing to a mother I've got, but may I remind you I'm older than you. So stop clucking round me like a hen!'

'I'm not listening to another word. Look at you – you're knackered. Just leave all this and I'll deal with it. Tomorrow you can come up to Covent Garden, pop into St Catherine's House and sort out that stupid birth certificate. Then come and have lunch with me at the Beauty Spot and tell me what you've found. Which I'm sure will be nothing. Tell you what, I'll even let my top aromatherapist loose on you.'

'You and your smelly oils!' Alex snorted, trying to keep the banter going.

'Say what you like, a good massage is still a good massage. And you're so strung up I could . . .' Jen glanced round the room, looking for inspiration.

'You could what? Play a violin concerto on me?'

'Exactly. Now, *bed*!'

Finally Alex didn't argue.

'BBC Radio News. It's five minutes past six and here is today's financial news.

'Following the sale of a large block of Rouget Corporation stock earlier today, rumours have been rife in the city about management problems with the company. Sir John French, International Executive Chairman of the Rouget Corporation, issued a statement denying that any such problems exist. He also stated that the sale of stock has come from a private international shareholder who is yet to be identified, although a full DTI investigation has been initiated.

'The statement did little to allay fears, and shares have closed 37 per cent down at 799.6 amid speculation that all dealing in Rouget Corporation shares will be temporarily suspended on the international market tomorrow.'

'I just have a gut feel that there's something in it, that's all. First the old boy Dr Ghillyand pops his clogs, then shortly afterwards the Rouget Corporation stock takes a nose-dive overnight, virtually wiping itself out. Three days later everything's hunky-dory again – shares almost back where they were, as if nothing unusual had happened! Come on, Peterson, even you ran a front-page leader on it. And it's not often you move financial news from the back of the spread.' Daniel Westbury banged his fists on the desk to emphasise his point.

Russell Peterson, editor of the *Citadel*, looked at Dan over the top of his half-moon glasses, watching him in his careful way as he considered the matter. Dan, in turn, slouched back in his chair and crossed his arms defensively while he waited for Peterson's verdict, worried that this time he had gone too far.

Although he could be insistent when he wanted to be, it was not often that Dan presented himself at his mentor's door positively clamouring to be let in to discuss an idea. Like most freelance journalists he was usually happy to wait until he was summoned, preferring to submit ideas through the relevant section editor and wait for the go-ahead or the rejection.

12

Dan always made sure that a feature had more than one angle so he could offer it to another publication. Even if it had to be rewritten in a different style, one way or another the Dan Westbury byline would appear on it eventually. Of course, if he was really clever he would sell a story first to the *Citadel* and then at a later date, crediting the paper, sell the second rights to a magazine or tabloid. If anyone ever commented that his name bobbed up in a lot of places, he simply joked about being 'a prostitute to his art' before reminding people that his first loyalty was to the *Citadel*, which he always gave first refusal – providing it was their type of story.

Which was why he was now sitting in the office on the fifteenth floor waiting for Russell Peterson to make up his mind. Dan knew there was no point in rushing him; he was renowned for weighing all questions carefully before answering. It was one of the things that made him such a good editor. Moreover Dan respected the man who had not only given him his first big break on Fleet Street but also taken a mediocre broadsheet paper like the *Citadel* and turned it round to fulfil his pledge to put it back 'on top of the bloody pile'!

It had been a long haul, due in part to the type of solid journalism at which Dan excelled. As the reading public noticed that an increasing number of important stories were first reported in the *Citadel*, gradually more people began to buy it instead of one of the other 'heavies'. Slowly the circulation figures had climbed until the '*City*' – as the paper was nicknamed on the street – was winning readers from the tabloids as well as other broadsheets. People liked its style, and its blend of major news items and substantial features. A number of those key reports had been filed by Dan; he seemed to have a sixth sense about where good stories could be found. His forte was articles about big business written with a human angle, the sort of idea he had just presented to Peterson. Dan knew that with so little to go on this proposal would be harder than most to get accepted but his gut feeling (which had yet to let him down) told him it was worth pushing for.

Peterson obviously agreed with him. 'OK, Dan. You've got your commission. But if you look as if you're getting too close to any-thing, or into deep water, for Chrissake let me know. Last thing I need is Rouget Corporation lawyers breathing down my neck. When d'you think you can let me have copy?'

'Hang on a minute!' exclaimed Dan. 'I've got a few ideas where to begin, but until I start digging I don't know what I'm actually going to find – or which leads will be worth following. I'll keep you informed. But if this is as big as I feel it is it could take some time. I assume it's the usual deal on expenses?'

'Christ. Bloody freelancers. Yes, within reason. Now go and get on with it before I change my mind.'

Dan heaved himself out of the low-slung chair and walked quickly across the room. As he opened the heavy smoked-glass door Peterson called after him, 'Dan, if you're right, then this could be great for our figures. Good luck!'

Clutching his battered old briefcase under his arm Dan called the lift. He had not exactly lied when he told Peterson he had a few ideas; nor had he quite told him the truth. The place he was going to start was where every journalist who worked for the Affiliated Newspaper Publishing Company began, and that was the library.

Previously housed in the basement of the old ANPC Fleet Street building, the library had retained its old nickname of 'The Crypt', even though it now occupied the whole of the third floor of the new Docklands building. Not surprisingly, Tom, the chief librarian, who had been there for over forty years and was now close to retiring, was known as Dracula, or 'The Count'. The entire library had been computerised when the offices moved a few years ago and ANPC now boasted one of the most up-to-date cross-referencing systems available. Which, as everyone said, was fine if you knew what you were looking for and how to use it. If not, you spoke to the Count.

Tom's memory for the contents of the ancient leather-bound volumes that had filled the old library was astonishing. He could tell you which newspapers had covered which important stories in depth, those that had taken one side of a debate against another, and whether or not 'The Morgue' (the old photographic library) held certain pictures.

Dan walked up to the desk and greeted Tom warmly. ''Morning, Count. How's things in the Crypt today?'

'Bit quiet for my likin'. Nobody wants anythin' real interestin'. It's all political intrigue, no real scandal. What you after, Dan?' Tom always liked it when young Westbury visited him as his searches were usually a bit different and gave Tom something to get his teeth into.

14

'The Rouget Corporation. I'm not sure exactly what I need. It's probably the business stuff. Annual reports, share info, stock-holders . . . that sort of thing. You know. Oh, and anything on Dr David Ghillyand. He's just died, and was one of their shining lights – had been for years apparently. So that might help.'

Tom moved across to the computer terminal and eased himself in behind the desk. 'I 'spect you'll need stuff on the social side as well. You know he married Rouget's daughter?'

He logged on and began by entering, from memory, the various names under which the Rouget Corporation operated, from the Rouget Foundation through to Rouget Pharmaceuticals. After scanning the files he instructed the computer to make a printout of all relevant references. A long list began to rattle off the machine. It gave a one-line abbreviation of each file's contents, and its location by date, page and column number. Tom checked how far back Dan wanted to go before calling up the list of shareholders and finally the diary and social reports.

Dan was amazed at the number of column inches the Rouget Corporation and Cecil Rouget himself had accumulated over the years. He began to realise that this job was going to be far more complicated than he had first anticipated.

It took about ten minutes to print out all the lists. Dan thanked Tom and stuffed all the paper into his briefcase. There was so much that he had to struggle to fasten its buckles and it was a dead weight in his hand as he left the Crypt. Deciding not to use the freelancers' desk in the corner of the bustling features room, Dan headed for home, where it would be easier to study those lists and make notes undisturbed.

Home for Dan was two floors of a large Edwardian house in Chiswick. Although he had converted the third bedroom into a study, in the early stages of his research he often worked in his living-room; it gave him more space to spread his notes around him, and get his thoughts into an order that enabled him to shape his features. He retreated to the study only when he was ready to start writing.

Dan made himself a pot of coffee and prepared a large pile of toasted cheese sandwiches before settling down to open his brief-case and start examining the lists the computer had spewed out for him. He kicked off his shoes and sprawled on the couch.

Laboriously he studied each entry in the hope that something would catch his eye. As the afternoon went by, the coffee in the pot got lower and lower. Occasionally Dan put down his mug and marked something on one of the lists with a highlighter pen.

After a few hours he felt he had learned enough about the financial make-up of the Rouget Corporation to be able to telephone the Count and ask for the various full reports to be retrieved from the files. When Dan warned him there would be more, the Count said that if he could fax the remainder to him by nine the next morning then all the documents could be biked to him.

Dan stretched as he hung up the phone, and was surprised to see that it had already gone six o'clock. Nevertheless he decided to carry straight on. He exchanged his coffee-pot for a cold beer from the fridge and got back to work. This time he inspected the diary and social lists. Initially these contained little more than a record of Mr and Mrs Cecil Rouget's social engagements. 'Cecil and Helena Rouget attend gala dinner at the Café Royal', 'Mr and Mrs Cecil Rouget at fund-raising ball at the Savoy', and so on. There was a reference to the death of Helena Rouget – 'Mrs Cecil Rouget killed by Café de Paris bomb, April 1941' – followed by a list of the events that Cecil had supported during the war. Dan was beginning to get bored when the entries began to change: 'Mr Cecil and Miss Elizabeth Rouget attend opening night', 'Mr Cecil and Miss Elizabeth Rouget at the Derby'; 'Miss Elizabeth Rouget buys Dior's "New Look"'; 'Miss Elizabeth Rouget announces engagement to Dr David Ghillyand'.

Dan put down his beer bottle. Here was the first link in a chain that would lead him . . . to what? Still he was not sure, but he ran his pen across the entry and carried on reading, this time with greater urgency. He began to feed the long printout through his fingers as he looked for a reference to their marriage. Sure enough, there it was: 'Society wedding for Miss Elizabeth Rouget and Dr David Ghillyand'. The date was June 1951. Again he marked it and carried on, this time searching for any mention of children. He was in luck: 'Daughter born to Dr David and Mrs Elizabeth Ghillyand, Nov. 1952'.

Well, they didn't waste much time! he thought to himself, bemused as he did the sums in his head. *If she was born in 1952, she'd be . . . well, not much older than me. The question is, how do I find her? The cutting should give me her name; then it's the electoral*

16

register. Shit! What happens if she's married? It'll just have to be the Rouget Corporation. They must know where she is.

It was going to be harder than Dan had imagined.

When he received the bundle of cuttings the next day, he flicked through to find the one recording the birth of David and Elizabeth's daughter. It was very small, just four lines in the 'Society' column.

To Dr David and Mrs Elizabeth Ghillyand (née Rouget) a daughter. Born at the Rouget Clinic, Elstree, 14 November 1952. Names not yet announced.

Dan looked at the brief announcement. *Big bloody deal! Now what? Call the Rouget Corporation and let them know they're being investigated? Do it now and you won't be able to go to them later, when you have serious things to ask. Call yourself a journalist, when you're prepared to blow a story before you've started it? Huh!*

He put down the pile of cuttings and thought for a moment. There had to be a way round this particular problem. It could not be that difficult to track down a child born in 1952. He had the date and surname; that should make it easier. Grinning to himself and whistling between his teeth, he picked up a fresh notepad and slid it into his jacket pocket before running downstairs, slamming the front door behind him.

It was probably because she was so exhausted that Alex slept surprisingly well after her outburst. She got up at a leisurely pace and found she was hungry, glad that for once she had time for breakfast. Feeling calm and relaxed, almost lethargic, she ambled into her small kitchen. True to her word, Jen had cleaned up the debris from the night before, leaving everything tidy.

Alex went to get orange juice from the fridge and saw the scrawled note Jen had left under one of her fridge magnets. 'Hope you slept well. Don't forget we have a lunch date. See you there about 1. Love, J.'

Instantly her languor evaporated as she remembered the events of the day before, and more to the point her promise to look up her records in the register before meeting Jen. Her appetite suddenly disappeared. Maybe she could turn up to lunch without going to St Catherine's House. It was worth a try.

Alex shook her head, dismissing the idea. If she did that, Jen would frogmarch her there herself. Alex knew that if she had to go she would rather go by herself, not knowing what she might find. As much as she loved her friend, this was one occasion when Jen would probably be more of a hindrance than a help.

By the time she was ready to set off it had turned into one of those crisp winter days with the hazy brightness that suggested spring was not so far away. As a concession to the watery sun, Alex decided to travel to St Catherine's House by bus rather than by Underground. She told herself that the fact it would also take longer this way had nothing to do with her decision. Even as she stood at the bus stop waiting for the number 15, she knew she was lying to herself.

When the bus arrived Alex found a seat downstairs at the front and spent the journey absent-mindedly gazing out of the window. She was vaguely aware of the bus swaying and rattling as it lurched along Westbourne Grove towards Paddington and into the Edgware Road. At Marble Arch she glimpsed early crocuses; shop windows in Oxford Street announced 'MASSIVE SALES!' Trafalgar Square had passed in a blur before she realised, with regret, that they were coming to the end of the journey when the bus swept into the Strand and round into the Aldwych. Alex's mouth felt dry as she walked up the steps to St Catherine's House.

Despite its imposing external appearance, inside the building was rather shabby, with a subdued air. Alex watched people heave large volumes off the shelves and look up entries before replacing the books with a thud. The area devoted to births was on the right-hand side of the room; slowly she walked towards the section for 1952.

All the books were neatly lined up on two levels, each labelled with the year, the quarter and the part of the alphabet from which they were drawn. She began looking for the 1952 volumes. On the bottom shelf, where 'BIRTHS, E–K, 1952' should have been, there was a gap.

Alex frowned as she stood up, hearing the clunk of the metal-edged books as other researchers slid them in and out of their allotted spaces. At that moment she became aware of the only other person with her in that section. He was a tall man with a mop of thick brown hair. She noticed he was wearing jeans that fitted well without being too tight, with a navy sweater over a cream shirt; on top of this was a battered leather jacket. In his hand was a pen and propped next to the book in front of him was a notepad. He had obviously just pulled the book from the shelf, since he was flicking through it, searching for the page he wanted.

Alex sidled a little closer, feeling impatient; it was obviously the volume she needed. He had settled on a page and was using his pen as a pointer as he ran it down the list of names. She hovered and surreptitiously glanced over his shoulder, curious to know what the man was trying to find in her book. He was peering down at a page headed 'GHI' and his pen had stopped a third of the way down – at 'GHILLYAND'.

'Why are you interested in my family?' Alex asked sharply.

'Sorry?' The man looked up at her and then down at the page, before looking up again, clearly puzzled.

'My name is Ghillyand and I want to know who the hell you are and why you're interested in us.'

The man bristled. 'I'm so sorry. I didn't realise you owned these books. I was led to believe they were public records which anyone could use. I must have been mistaken. But as you're so damn proprietorial about your book Mrs – or is it Miss? – Ghillyand, be my guest and have a look.' He stood to one side, waving his hand magnanimously over the volume.

Alex inhaled through her nose deeply, dipped her head in mock thanks, and moved to stand in front of the book. Resting her hands lightly on the rim of the reading desk, she cast her eyes down the list until she reached 'GHILLYAND'. Then she gave an involuntary start and slid her hand up the page so that her fingers were splayed out beneath the entries. There were two of them, one under the other. Below the headings 'NAME', 'MOTHER'S MAIDEN NAME', 'DISTRICT', 'VOLUME', 'PAGE', she read:

GHILLYAND

	NAME	MOTHER'S MAIDEN NAME	DISTRICT	VOLUME	PAGE
–	Alexandra M	Chambers	Watford	5f	455
–	Alexandra M	Rouget	Watford	5f	631

'Curious, isn't it?' the man said smoothly. Then 'Hey, are you OK?' as she went very white and gripped the edge of the desk.

Dan sprang up the steps of St Catherine's House. It did not take him long to find the section he wanted, two aisles down on the right. Identifying the relevant book, he grabbed it firmly by its canvas handle to swing it unceremoniously up on to the reading desk. He took out his notepad and began to flip through until he found 'GHI'. Flattening out the pages, he used his pen to guide his eye as he looked down the list. There it was – 'GHILLYAND' – except there was not one entry, but two. And the only difference was the mother's maiden name and the page number of the volume where both entries would be given in full.

He was about to make a note of the references so he could fill in the forms to order full copies of both birth certificates when he was interrupted.

The question threw him for a moment and he glanced first at the indignant woman and then back at the page, double-checking to see what he was doing that was so wrong. The tone of the woman's voice was presumptuous and made him feel as if he were a schoolboy. She was talking again, asking more stupid questions. Why didn't she just go away? He made a suitable retort and stepped aside to let her get a better look at the page.

As she studied the page, Dan studied her. She was about five foot seven with short, reddish-brown, wavy hair. Although not thin, neither was she fat, and he could sense the curves under her clothes. She was well turned out in a calf-length green wool skirt clinched in at the waist by a large black belt. Tucked into this was a black cotton shirt that was half undone, revealing a lighter green T-shirt underneath. She was wearing black boots, and over the top, hanging open, was a Burberry raincoat that was obviously much loved. Her make-up was neat but not overpowering, unlike that of so many of the women with whom he came into contact on his regular round of magazines and newspapers. Under different circumstances Dan might have been tempted to chat her up, but she had been so frosty with him that he had decided not to bother turning on the charm.

Stuck-up bitch, he thought. He wanted to get back to work. She was gawping at the page, her hand spread out, clearly looking at the same double entry he had found so interesting. He drew her attention to it in a casual manner. He was about to be even more acerbic in his comments in an attempt to get rid of her when he noticed that she had turned very pale and was gripping the edge of the desk so tightly her knuckles had gone white.

Dan moved across and put a steadying hand on her arm. 'Hey, are you OK?'

'Yes . . . yes . . . I'm fine,' she said shakily. 'I'm sorry for being so rude. It's just that I got myself geared up to walk in here and look this up . . . It's quite important . . . And when I found you here . . . ' Alex tailed off, her excuses sounding lame even to her.

Alex, why are you babbling away to this man? He's not interested. Shut up, she told herself.

'Don't worry, I wasn't too polite myself. Sorry, but you startled me. You did say your name was Ghillyand?'

'Dr Alexandra Ghillyand.' And she held out a still trembling hand.

As Dan introduced himself in turn, he realised that, without even having had to try, he was experiencing one of those wonderful coincidences that you read about but never expect to happen in real life. Only last night he had been struggling to work out how to trace David Ghillyand's daughter, and here she was! Or was she? She looked about the right age, but of course she could be the other one. After such a dodgy start he did not want to scare her away.

She was speaking to him again, asking how she could get hold of the right forms to order copies of the certificates.

'You need the pink ones to apply for a full birth certificate.' Dan pointed to where the forms were stacked in boxes at the end of the bookcases. 'You still look a bit pale. I don't like to leave you in this state . . . Look, by way of an apology, may I buy you lunch? I've got a couple of applications to do myself, so how about both of us sorting out our paperwork and meeting at the entrance in a few minutes?'

Alex hesitated; it was obvious that he was the type of man whose invitations were usually accepted. She was still embarrassed by her silly behaviour, but she had to admit that he was at least trying to make amends and she was feeling hungry. She was about to agree when she remembered her lunch date with Jen.

'Oh, my God! It's one fifteen and I was meant to be meeting a friend at one. No, it's not a brush off, honestly. If it weren't for my friend I'd have loved to have lunch with you. But she'd kill me if I didn't show. Which forms did you say I needed?'

Once again Dan pointed at the boxes. 'Look, if you're that pushed for time, fill them out and I'll hand them in for you. Don't worry . . . I promise I'll do it and get them posted to you. In case you want to check up on me here's my card.' He opened his wallet and held out one of his cards. It gave just his name, address and phone number; he had discovered early on in his career how people mistrusted him once they discovered he was a journalist.

Alex made her mind up and rummaged in her bag for her purse. 'OK. Thank you. Here's twenty quid – that should cover it, I hope . . . I'll get the forms done.' She grabbed them from out of their boxes and quickly filled them in, checking in the book for the right references. Like so many other people she gave 'family research' as her reason for wanting the copies. She also scribbled down her address, so that Dan could organise the postal dispatch for her. Apologising yet again for her behaviour, she thanked him for his help and smiled when he said, 'Don't forget, I still owe you lunch', before she quickly walked out of the building.

Dan was delighted. Not only had he obtained her address but he had an excuse to get in touch with her. Alex had given him far too much money and he would have to give the change to her somehow. He was also quite pleased that she had gone, since he could now fill in his own forms without arousing her suspicions again. Thoughtfully he completed them and handed them in. The clerk was a little surprised at the duplication but accepted Dan's explanation about a race with his cousin to complete their mutual family tree and processed the forms.

Dan knew he would have to wait about a week before he could contact Alex; but waiting was something he was used to in his job.

Alex spent the rest of that week in her father's office, finishing the job of clearing his room. Since all his notes and research material, regarded as the property of the Rouget Corporation, had been removed the day after he died, she only had to worry about his personal belongings. Emotionally it proved to be a difficult task – not because, as Malcolm Bratby had said, of the pleasant memories but because of her total lack of any type of feeling at all. Alex thought she should at least have felt regret or remorse, but she was only aware of an enormous sense of relief.

Relief that he was dead; relief that he was no longer around to make her feel inferior; and relief that, at last, the vague disappointment that she had always sensed he felt towards her would no longer be a part of her life. The relief made her feel guilty. Alex knew what to expect from bereavement; she had treated too many families and experienced their genuine grief not to recognise it in all its forms, and she knew hers was not what was usually experienced by a child when a parent died.

She worked quickly, trying to analyse her feelings, but it did not help; touching all his books and papers still meant nothing to her. To Alex Ghillyand, Dr David Ghillyand had become little more than a name; a name that belonged to a man who had once worked for the Rouget Corporation and now ceased to do so. It was all very remote.

She was also trying to keep her mind off her findings at St Catherine's House, not just the entries in the register but the fact that someone else was interested in her family. Since meeting Dan Westbury she had reproached herself on more than one count; first for being stupid enough to get light-headed over something written in a book; secondly for not finding out more about him and why he was looking up the Ghillyands. Thirdly, she had trusted a total stranger with twenty pounds and her home address. She was already anticipating the non-arrival of the certificates and consequently the return trip to reorder them. It was annoying, especially as she was due back at work on Monday, but it would teach her not to trust strangers.

Barbara was keeping her distance, just sliding in and out of the room with a fresh mug of coffee, which Alex did her best to accept graciously. Knowing that she would be coming into contact with Barbara, Alex had made a point of dressing in smarter clothes for her journeys to Elstree. It was a childish defence but it made her feel more in control of the situation, in the same way as wearing her white coat at the hospital. Alex also knew that if she had any sense she would apologise to Barbara, try and make a friend of her, and have a good talk with her about her father.

It was not until his death that Alex realised how little she actually knew about him as a person. Indeed, she knew little more than the facts the papers had reported in their obituaries; his pre-eminence as a biochemist, his appointment in 1947 at the Rouget Corporation as Director of Development, his Nobel Prize nomination ten years later. All this was public knowledge – as were the details of his marriage to Elizabeth Rouget, in 1951. Some of the papers had alluded to her parents' fifteen years' age difference ('a spring and autumn alliance'); all had commented on her mother's death in an accident in Greece, yet none had offered a glimpse of David Ghillyand the man.

The procession of nannies, boarding-schools and childhood holidays spent with friends meant that all her life Alex had been kept at arms' length. She had learnt very early on that her father was not an affectionate man. That is to say, he had showed her no affection. For the first time Alex found herself wondering about his relationship with Barbara. Then the thought of stolid Barbara having an affair with her equally staid father brought a brief smile to Alex's lips. Yet it was probably this idea that stood between her and the much-needed conversation with Barbara.

With a slight shake of her head Alex decided all she could do was return to work on Monday and hope that Daniel Westbury had indeed been honourable and put through the forms for her. As much as she hated to admit it, the birth certificates had become extremely important to her; she wanted to stop the theories from rushing round in circles inside her head. After all, there might simply have been some clerical error.

After her visit to St Catherine's House, Alex had run virtually all the way to the Beauty Spot in Long Acre to meet Jen. When she arrived, half an hour late, she was flustered and breathless.

'Whoa, slow down!' Jen had laughed at her as she burst through the door. 'Come and get a fruit juice. Catch your breath before lunch.'

Alex had not been allowed to say another word until she was sitting down with a lemon *pressé* in her hands. Jen listened as Alex made her excuses and then castigated her.

'You are unbelievable! A gorgeous man asks you out for lunch and you turn him down?'

Alex flushed at Jen's description of Dan; but she had certainly said he was good-looking.

'I've spent heaven knows how long trying to set you up with every eligible male I know,' Jen continued, 'and when one falls into your lap you turn him down. Ye gods!'

Alex gave a feeble smile. 'Don't start that again. I'm not ready for another boyfriend. After being with Peter for five years I want time to be by myself.'

It was old ground between the two friends. Jen felt fourteen months was more than long enough for Alex to have finished licking her wounds after her split with her ex; while Alex could still feel them smarting. As the two women made their way to the restaurant, they carried on talking about the various men Jen had paraded in front of Alex during the last year.

Over lunch the conversation turned to the double entry in the register of births. Ghillyand was an unusual name. Yet Alex could not remember any other Ghillyand living in Watford – except, of course, David's brother Robert, but he had died before she was born and, as she was rapidly discovering, he was yet another subject to add to the list of topics she had never discussed with her father.

Remembering her lunch with Jen made her realise she was hungry, which was hardly surprising; she had been sorting and packing books since nine that morning without a break. That was four and a half hours of putting books into piles and boxes marked for either herself or the second-hand shop. Her shoulders ached. The dust that had been stirred up made her feel grubby; Alex was now regretting the pride that had led to her wearing good clothes. It would be easiest to get lunch in the staff canteen. She didn't bother to tell Barbara she was going, just leaving her jacket and the mess behind to show she would be back.

The canteen was in an annexe joined to the old house by a covered walkway. It was meant to protect people from the elements when they crossed from one building to the other but, as Alex found out, it didn't do a very good job and the blustery March winds that had been blowing all day cut through her.

She was concentrating on where she was going, dodging the stream of people who were going back to work after having eaten. Suddenly she heard half a comment in her ear, the wind snatching the other half away. She turned to see that Dr Bratby had fallen into step beside her.

'I said, one day they'll cover this in properly . . . oh, sorry.' He had bumped into a woman wearing a lab coat. 'And make it wider . . . If you're going to the canteen may I join you?'

Alex would have preferred to sit by herself but he had asked so pleasantly it would have been churlish to say no, particularly since Bratby would have seen her sitting alone. 'With pleasure,' she said, trying to sound as if she meant it, and let him lead the way.

She selected a rather grey-looking lasagne and a lank salad, with a cup of coffee. 'The prices are good . . . At least it fills you up, if nothing else,' Bratby remarked from behind her in the queue. The next few minutes were spent with Alex objecting while he paid the ninety pence for her subsidised meal and found a table.

'Busy, isn't it?' she remarked as they sat down, more for something to say than out of any interest in starting a conversation.

'It usually is. There's about three thousand people here, all told.'

'Good God! I didn't realise it was so big.'

'Well, don't forget there's five different divisions based here. There's all the Foundation people – and I don't care what you read in the papers about cutbacks in medical research. As far as we're concerned, it's still a huge part of what we do. That sort of links to Rouget Pharmaceuticals, which includes branded and OTC medications – we produce those on site.'

Alex looked puzzled, and Bratby twisted round to point out the large low buildings they could see through the trees.

'Old man Rouget thought it more economical to manufacture here.' He shrugged, indicating neutrality, before carrying on. 'Then there's Rouget Agricultural doing all that food development stuff . . . and its sister division, Rouget Chemicals, working in the oil and petrochemical industry. Of course, over the whole lot is the Rouget Corporation itself . . . But why am I telling you about your inheritance? I'm sorry, my dear. I must be a terrible bore, talking about things you already know.'

'Actually I've never really known that much about the Rouget set-up. I mean, I knew it was big, but I've never bothered to find out exactly how big.' She paused, trying to decide whether to ask him what she wanted to discover. 'Dr Bratby –'

'For goodness sake, call me Malcolm,' he interrupted.

'Malcolm, then.' She began again. 'How well did you know my father?'

'What an odd question . . . very odd question. I worked with him on a number of projects . . . and although we burnt the midnight oil on more than one occasion I wouldn't say I genuinely knew him. Not the sort of chap you'd have a drink with after a day's work, your father. As a chemist he was quite brilliant, but I don't recall . . . No, I can't say I've ever had a conversation with him that wasn't about work. Why do you ask?'

Alex hesitated for a moment before replying, 'I just wondered, that's all . . . What with being away so much of the time, I never really got to know him.'

It was a comment that did not encourage further talk and they both sat looking at their plates, playing with their food. Alex traced patterns with her fork in the remains of the lasagne sauce, unaware that Malcolm was watching her. Gently he began speaking again.

'I wasn't here at the time – I didn't join the Corporation until '67 – but even then people who remembered used to say your father wasn't the same after he came back from Greece. Some of the staff described him as having a "hunted air", which I said was romantic nonsense. Very practical chap, very practical, your father – definitely the head-ruled-heart type. But I don't deny he missed your mother. When I joined, her portrait was still hanging in what is now the reception . . . Very beautiful woman . . . But David would have just got on with things. Anyway, he had you to care for, didn't he?'

Alex nursed her coffee-cup in her hands and gazed out of the window beyond Malcolm's head. She was aware of traffic in the distance, as light reflected off the windows of cars snaking fast along the M1. More to herself than Malcolm, she said out loud, 'I'm so busy thinking about my father, I forgot about my mother. And that's something else I know very little about – my parents' relationship. Crazy, isn't it, how much you take for granted until it's too late to find out?'

Malcolm Bratby was about to answer what was essentially a rhetorical question, so Alex decided that lunch was over. Quickly she rose to her feet, thanking him for his company and for buying her lunch and, after joking that the next one was on her, went back to her father's room to finish packing his books.

After his visit to St Catherine's House, Dan had returned home to Chiswick to continue reading the copies of cuttings the Count had sent over from the Crypt.

Most of these related to the business transactions of the Corporation, but Dan was interested in those that detailed the shareholders. There had been a few profile pieces about Cecil Rouget that gave Dan a sketchy history of the Austrian who had inherited his father's pharmacy business during the First World War and built it into a multinational concern. Dan had only glanced at these, concentrating instead on articles that featured David Ghillyand and Elizabeth Rouget.

Elizabeth appeared in a few photographs from the late 1930s –

a pretty child with large eyes and curly hair who apparently never went through a plain stage. It was clear she was growing up in the rarefied atmosphere of the very rich.

As Dan flipped through the photocopies he could see her growing up and taking over as her father's escort, photographed with him at one social event after another. The pretty child became a shapely teenager (who despite rationing was immaculately dressed), who grew into a stunning woman. Dan was not surprised to read she had been named as Débutante of the Season in 1950. Slowly he became aware of another person appearing in the shots – first as a shadowy figure in the background, just out of range of the flash guns, then increasingly in focus until, at last, he was allowed to be seen in the foreground and acknowledged as 'Fiancé Dr David Ghillyand'.

Dan found himself wondering what sort of man David Ghillyand was. He looked like most society men of that era, well turned out and wearing the right suit with the right tie and the right shoes for whichever event he was seen entering or leaving. His hair was slicked back; everything about him was precise. Unlike the images of his fiancée very few of the shots showed him smiling, but in those that did he displayed a tight-lipped upwards turn of the mouth. He was slim and a little taller than average, so many of the photographs showed Elizabeth with her perfect little chin gazing up at him. Maybe it was the adoring look in her eyes that made Dan decide he did not like the man.

According to the reports of her wedding, it was one of the big social events of the year. The spread in the *Daily Mirror* revealed not only the splendid spectacle of the Bride and Groom, but also pictures of their immediate families and various well-known faces of the time as they stood around outside St Albans Cathedral. The diary columns recorded their honeymoon plans; there were a few shots of them mounting the gangplank of the *Queen Mary* as they left on their cruise.

After that the photographs and mentions grew fewer. Dan found it interesting that, while he was prepared to gad around town with his fiancée, Dr Ghillyand was obviously not so happy to entertain his wife in such a public and lavish manner.

And that brought Dan back to his starting-point – the four-line birth announcement. At least he now knew her name, Alexandra M. He looked at the cuttings one last time, scribbling notes that might be useful later on, once he had received copies of the certificates, which with a bit of luck would arrive the next day.

Dan was still in bed but only half asleep when he heard the letter-box rattle as his post dropped on to the floor. He was about to roll over to have an extra half hour's doze when he remembered that the packet he wanted could be in the pile waiting downstairs. He flung back the duvet and reached for his dressing-gown, tying it round his middle as he leapt down the stairs two at a time to scoop up his mail. In anticipation he stood there and flipped through it. Two bills, a mail shot, a couple of cheques, a trade paper and a large brown envelope with a WC2 postmark.

He bent down again to pick up the newspapers and tucked these, with the rest of his post, under his arm as he made his way into the kitchen, opening the package as he went. He hooked the documents out, discarding the envelope with everything else on the table. With one hand he opened the fridge and took out the orange juice, at the same time flicking his other wrist so that the birth certificates spread out. Leaning on his work-top, swigging from the carton of juice, he eagerly compared the two documents, noting the details of the first one.

WHEN AND WHERE BORN: Twenty-Third October 1952. The Rouget Clinic, Elstree. NAME, IF ANY: Alexandra Marie. SEX: Girl. NAME AND SURNAME OF FATHER: Dr Robert Henry Ghillyand. NAME, SURNAME AND MAIDEN NAME OF MOTHER: Sally Pauline Ghillyand formerly Chambers of The Rouget Foundation, The Manor House, Elstree. OCCUPATION OF FATHER: Biochemist. SIGNATURE, DESCRIPTION AND RESIDENCE OF INFORMANT: Rose Haggerty. Midwife. The Rouget Clinic, Elstree. WHEN REGISTERED: Twenty-Ninth October 1952.

Dan then looked at the other certificate. He felt a frisson of excitement as he realised he had found the first thin thread that would help him shape his story. The details on this paper were surprisingly close to those on the first.

WHEN AND WHERE BORN: Fourteenth November 1952. The Rouget Clinic, Elstree. NAME, IF ANY: Alexandra Marie. SEX: Girl. NAME AND SURNAME OF FATHER: Dr David Rodney Ghillyand. NAME, SURNAME AND MAIDEN NAME OF MOTHER: Elizabeth Deirdre Ghillyand formerly Rouget of The Manor House, Elstree.

OCCUPATION OF FATHER: Biochemist. SIGNATURE, DE-SCRIPTION AND RESIDENCE OF INFORMANT: Edith Jones. Mid-wife. The Rouget Clinic, Elstree. WHEN REGISTERED: Seventeenth November 1952.

This had to be more than coincidence. The likelihood of two girls being born to fathers with the same surname in the same place and given the same names within a few weeks of each other – with all the people involved connected in some way to the Rouget organisation – was very remote. And both fathers had the same occupation.

What on earth went on at that place in 1952? Dan asked himself as he took another swig of juice. *Now I have to get in touch with Alexandra; but which one is she – David or Robert Ghillyand's daughter – and what if anything does she know about the Rouget Corporation shareholders?*

Back upstairs, Dan showered, shaved and dressed, trying to work out the best way of approaching Alexandra Ghillyand without scaring her away. His encounter at St Catherine's House suggested he should move carefully; she was obviously a prickly character who did not like people poking about in her personal history.

Fair enough, thought Dan as he yanked the belt on his jeans, *especially if you've got a family skeleton to hide. But I'm sorry, darling, if you're hiding something I intend to find out what it is, with or without your consent!*

Alex was not so gleeful when she read her copies of the birth certificates, which arrived on a day that started badly and grew steadily worse. She overslept and woke with a banging headache she could not shake off and by the time she set off for work it was obvious it would be with her all day. She grabbed her post on the way out and stuffed it in her briefcase, telling herself she would look at it after she arrived at work. When she reached her car she saw that, yet again, it had been vandalised overnight and the aerial snapped off. Because of the delay, the traffic was heavier than usual, and to make matters worse when she got to Vickie's someone had pinched her designated parking space. Furiously Alex ran into the building to locate the culprit and make them move the offending vehicle. Added together the morning's events made her extremely late for her first appointment and pushed the rest of her clinic late.

By early afternoon not only had she forgotten about the post but her headache felt like a tight metal band round her head, with the tension running down her neck and across her shoulders. The over-running of her clinic meant that lunch was an apple and a Mars bar, gobbled on the hoof. Alex did not even have time to go to the consultants' lounge before her ward rounds. These were also drawn out, since one of her patients had finally plucked up the courage to ask all the questions that had been bothering her about her illness. Having ensured the patient's family were present, Alex found their questions very direct (which she always preferred), demanding precise details about the operation, post-operative care and the possible effects of the chemotherapy. Although Alex had already discussed these matters with them in some detail, the family had been unable to take it in while they were coming to terms with the illness. Patiently she went over it all again but found herself having to concentrate hard, ensuring she said the right thing and gave the right amount of information and reassurance.

After the ward round she was aware she had a pile of files to wade through, in order to catch up on the progress of her cases while she had been off work, as well as write up notes from that morning's clinic. She walked back from the wards, deep in conversation with her surgical registrar, Edward Maklin, and her junior houseman, Sam Baldock. In the corridors people made way for them when they saw the white coats, yet none of the trio acknowledged this, accepting it as their right. Edward left her at the lift to go back down to theatre, while Sam continued along the corridor to Alex's tiny office, still arguing a point with her.

'OK, Sam, we've agreed we'll reduce the chemo, so let's leave it at that, shall we?'

Sam stopped, bringing Alex to a halt. 'Christ, Alex, you're hell when you're like this. Look, do us all a favour and take a five-minute breather. You haven't stopped all day.'

'Sorry, Sam . . . It's been really shitty lately. I shouldn't take it out on all of you. I've also got a head like an arse split down the middle.' Sam smiled at the old hospital joke. 'And you're right – I could do with a sit-down. But on one condition. You get me a decent coffee – not that muck from the machine.'

'You got it. See you in a few minutes.' And he scuttled off to raid the nurses' common room.

Alex sank wearily into the old armchair, adjusting her bottom to fit the lumps in the sagging cushion. Her head was still thumping away. She had taken her last paracetamol at midday; as it was now close to four-thirty, she could take another dose. It might at least stop the headache getting any worse. Although she was not supposed to carry any drugs, like everyone else she ignored this rule, and always kept a small bottle in her briefcase. As she took the bottle out she found that morning's mail, so took it back to her chair to open.

By the time Sam returned with a steaming mug of strong coffee Alex was sitting with her head in her hands, her elbows propped on her knees, with a couple of long papers across her lap.

'You look bloody awful! You OK?' Sam was concerned to see her face so grey and pinched. He thought she had been looking peaky all day, but had put it down to emotional strain. It could not have been easy to come back to Vickie's and face the huge backlog of work, combined with another management rejection of funds for the new equipment.

Alex stared at him and blinked, as if trying to get him into focus. 'Yes, Sam, I'm fine.' Hastily she folded up the papers and stuffed them back into their envelopes. 'This morning's post. I didn't get a chance to open it until now . . . and something threw me a little, that's all.' She held out her hand for the mug Sam was holding. 'Great, I needed that.'

Sam was still unpersuaded. 'If you're sure . . .' He looked doubtful. 'It won't do you any harm to bung some extra sugar in it. Here you are.' He dug his hand into his pocket and pulled out a few sachets.

Alex did as she was told, stirred in three spoonfuls and took a grateful sip. For a few hours she had forgotten about the forms and St Catherine's House, and the two certificates had caught her unawares. The information that had delighted Dan earlier in the day had shaken her badly.

Although it was still not clear from the register entries, it now seemed obvious that the other Alexandra Marie was some sort of relative. But why had her father kept that baby's certificate? What had he done with hers? Alex knew her father had a younger brother, Robert, but he had rarely referred to him, and then only obliquely as 'my brother', seldom by name.

As she had studied the two certificates one question after another tumbled through her head. Who and where was this other Alexandra Marie? When had Robert Ghillyand died? Was his wife Sally still alive? She buried her head in her hands and tried to control the surge of panic. It was at this point that Sam walked in and restored a bit of sanity.

Stifling her confused thoughts, she kept working steadily as the day ground relentlessly on. By the time she left she was exhausted. But driving home she cautiously decided that the last dose of painkillers had finally taken effect. Gratefully Alex let herself into her flat, kicking off her shoes as usual to pad through to the kitchen. It was not that she was hungry, but common sense told her to eat something. The phone rang as she was about to set the microwave. For a moment she considered letting the machine answer it but knew she would only have to return the call. She pushed the start button, so that she could use its *ping* four minutes later as an excuse for a short conversation, and picked up the phone.

'Hello. Is that Dr Alexandra Ghillyand?' It was a man's voice she could not identify, but warily she confirmed it was. 'I don't know if you remember me . . . it's Daniel Westbury. We met the other day at St Catherine's House,' he added, to jog her memory.

'Yes, Mr Westbury. I remember you. The certificates arrived today. Thank you for organising that for me – I'm most grateful.'

'Good, I'm glad you received them. You know, you gave me far too much money. I've got the change, and was hoping you might let me take you out for that meal I owe you – so I can give it to you in person?'

The question hung in the air. If Dan had called at any other time Alex would probably have accepted, but right now the last thing she wanted was to arrange to meet a man she did not know.

'That's very kind of you – but there's no need. Anyway, thanks for calling to see if I got the certificates.' A thought occurred to her. 'How did you get my number?'

'Well, I had your address, so I just looked you up in the phone book. There's not many Ghillyands in there, you know. Look, if you change your mind . . . you've got my card . . . call me.' And without giving her the opportunity to comment he rang off, leaving Alex holding the receiver as it buzzed in her ear.

It was about a week later that Alex thought of Dan Westbury again.

Since receiving the certificates she had done nothing with them other than prop the envelope on the mantelpiece behind a vase of daffodils. She had not forgotten about them – far from it. The thought of their contents was constantly with her during the day, and disturbed her sleep night after night with vivid dreams. But catching up with work at Vickie's as well as trying to clear out her father's rooms at the Corporation had allowed her no time to do anything about them.

On one of her days off, as she opened her living-room curtains the spring sunlight burst into the room. When she turned round, the first thing she saw was the vase of now dead daffodils on the mantelpiece, and the sight of the withered yellow trumpets upset her. Alex decided there and then to take herself down to Portobello Market and buy armfuls of fresh flowers to fill every vase in the flat. As she scooped up the vase the envelope behind it fell on to the floor. Picking it up in her free hand she took it with her into the kitchen. She dumped the flowers in the bin and as she rinsed out the vase told herself that she had probably been, yet again, rather rude to Dan Westbury when he phoned. After all he was only trying to be friendly. She decided to dig out his card and call him. If he offered again, this time she would accept his invitation.

Having made the decision, she still put it off for a couple of hours and when she did phone him she got his answering machine.

' "This is Dan Westbury. I'm sorry I'm not here right now, but if you leave a message . . ." I'm here, I'm here . . .' A breathless voice cut into the recorded one. 'Hang on – I'll just turn it off.' The machine clicked.

'Hello, it's Alex Ghillyand.' Suddenly she felt shy. 'Ummm . . . I wanted to apologise if I sounded rude the other day. I didn't mean it, but you caught me on a bad day.'

'That's OK. Forget it. I don't suppose you've changed your mind about getting together, have you?'

'Well, yes, actually, I have. It would be nice.'

At his end of the phone Dan triumphantly punched the air but his voice remained calm. 'Great. How about tonight, if you're free?'

Alex was surprised that he responded so rapidly, but since she had just planned to stay in and watch TV she accepted. They arranged to meet at Ari's, a small Greek restaurant in Chiswick. Alex assured Dan that it was no trouble for her to come over to his part of town. The truth was, she felt safer that way, as if she still had the upper hand and could escape if she wanted to.

Later that day Alex spoke to Jen, dropping into the conversation that she was meeting Dan for supper that evening.

Jen was delighted. 'Hallelujah! The woman comes to her senses at last! It's about time you got back into circulation . . . I think it's great you've finally got your eye on someone at last. Let me know when I can arrange a dinner party so we can meet him.'

Alex laughed. 'Hey, Jen, slow down! All I'm doing is having a bite to eat . . . No need to start planning which hat you're going to buy. If I'd known you'd make such a fuss I wouldn't have told you.'

Jen's teasing made Alex question her own motives, and eventually she had to admit there was something about Dan that she did find appealing. She was also surprised to find herself feeling a bit nervous as she got ready to meet him; she even changed her top a couple of times before she was satisfied with her appearance. She then rebuked herself for this show of vanity as she drove to Chiswick and as a result was quite miffed when she walked into the restaurant to discover that Dan had left a message to say he would be late.

The message was delivered by a short, round man in neatly pressed black trousers, and an open-necked white shirt with a bright blue scarf tied at his throat. He had come bustling over to her and his thick black hair and moustache seemed to gleam with the effort he was putting into his movements. Alex guessed, correctly, that he must be the owner.

'Ah, you 'ave dinner wiv Mr Dan?'

She nodded and was escorted to a table in the corner.

'Mr Dan, 'e phone to say 'e be late, but 'e tell me – Ari – to see you hokay.'

Taking his instructions very seriously, Ari made a fuss of settling Alex into her seat and fetching her a glass of wine.

As she waited for him to return, she looked around. The restaurant held about twenty tables, closely set together, each with a blue tablecloth placed over a white one. A low light glowed from among bowls of flowers arranged in the centre of each table next to blue and green ceramic salt and pepper pots. Blue cushions were tied to the seats of all the wooden chairs. The general air of cosiness was also partly due to the cluttered bar at the back of the room. Apart from the usual range of bottles and optics there was also a lot of Greek brandy, including the biggest bottle of Metaxa she had ever seen. All around the white walls hung worry beads – small wooden ones, large plastic ones, tiny metal ones and even some made out of shells. Photographs and paintings of obviously Greek subjects also proliferated; artists' impressions of white tavernas and villas with blue shutters competed with lush islands thrusting out into vibrant aquamarine waters; peaceful churches and fishing boats jostled with lively photographs of bazouki players. Alex was still gazing at these when Ari returned with her glass of wine and a plate of olives.

'Ahh, you look at my pictures? You like Greece?' he asked her, his chest expanding with pride in his home country.

'I don't know,' she replied feebly. 'I lived in Greece for a while, until I was a few months old. But I was too young to remember it . . . and I've never been back.' Alex felt almost ashamed as she watched Ari visibly deflate.

Before he could start to re-educate her, Dan arrived, out of breath and full of apologies.

'Sorry I'm late, but I take it Ari has been looking after you?'

Alex confirmed she had been in good hands and that they had been talking about Greece.

Dan laughed, a full and throaty chuckle. 'Get him going on his beloved Greece and you'll be here for at least a week. Now, Ari, don't look like that, you know I love the islands almost as much as you do. Be a good man, will you, and get me a beer?'

Ari hurried away to fill the order.

'I'm really sorry you had to wait for me – but Ari's a great host and serves the best kleftiko outside his precious homeland.' Dan brought out four pound coins and put them on the table. 'I almost forgot why I wanted to see you,' he said lightly. 'Here's that four quid I owe you.'

'Thank you. And thanks again for dealing with that for me. I'm very sorry I was so rude to you – twice. I'm not usually that bad. Sorry.'

'Will you stop apologising? We all have our off days.'

Alex laughed, feeling surprisingly comfortable in Dan's company. Ari reappeared with Dan's beer and the menus but Dan waved them away, checking first that Ari's special *meze* and his own choice of wine would be acceptable.

The formalities agreed, Alex and Dan began to chat, first about nothing in particular in the way that is peculiar to people getting to know each other – safe subjects such as the glorious day it had been; the day's news; how appalling the roadworks were in town – and as they talked Alex felt increasingly at ease with Dan. When the starters arrived she became aware of how very hungry she was.

As they helped themselves to taramasalata and tsatsiki, Dan reckoned it was time to start turning the conversation round or the opportunity might be lost. 'By the way, what do you do?' He tried to make the question sound light.

Alex began to tell him about Vickie's, and it was easy for Dan to use his skill as an interviewer to keep her talking about her training and how she got into medicine in the first place. One thing led to another and soon Alex was broadly touching on the subject of her family and the Rouget Corporation. Then suddenly she seemed to realise how much she was saying and quickly turned the tables on him.

'But this is boring. What about you. What do you do?'

Dan considered her not unreasonable question and decided the time had come to be honest. Taking a deep breath, he admitted that for his sins he was a journalist. He waited for Alex's reaction, almost expecting her to get up and walk out.

She tipped her head on one side and scrutinised him over the top of her wineglass. 'I knew the name was familiar. You do a lot of stuff for the *Citadel*, don't you?'

Dan agreed that he did and mentally gave himself a point; it was clear she was not bothered. In fact, far from being bothered, she was now asking him about his background. Alex too was a good interviewer because of her experience in talking to patients, putting them at their ease before examining them or explaining a diagnosis. As the starters made way for the main courses, Dan found himself telling her about the letters and features he had fired off to various editors including Russell Peterson at the *City*. His timing had been good. Peterson's new broom had caused many of the old hacks to leave: the long lunches, elastic expense accounts and the days of maximum return for little effort were clearly over. Their departure had created space for bright new talent. The story Dan had submitted on JCBs was not exactly riveting, but Peterson had noticed it was well researched and, more to the point, written in a lively, readable style. He had offered Dan a junior job on the diary. Soon Dan had begun coming up with his own ideas – and was on his way.

'The trouble was, I got the Newspaper Association award as "The One to Watch", and Peterson fired me!'

'Why?' Alex pushed away the empty dish of grilled squid and turned her attention to the famous lamb kleftiko.

'It's not as bad as it sounds,' Dan continued. 'Peterson took me out for a slap-up lunch, and told me I had a lot of talent which would be squashed if I stayed at the *City*. He told me to get out and build a freelance career. He reckoned the award still meant something in the industry – that I'd get some good commissions. He's a canny old bugger, because he made me promise that once I'd stopped hating his guts I'd give him first refusal on my work.'

Dan paused, picking at the pork stifado. 'Well, he was right. It took me two years to forgive him . . . That night I remember I went out and got so bombed I slept in the bath because my girl-friend wouldn't let me near her.'

Alex was aware of a tremor of disappointment when she heard Dan mention a girlfriend. She sipped her wine.

'But Peterson was right. I think it was a sort of "I'll show him" attitude that pushed me on. Mind you, I won't hear a word against him now and I'm doing OK. So although it hurt at the time I guess I don't mind any more.' He helped himself to the kleftiko.

'So is that why you were looking up my family? To write a piece for the *Citadel* about my wonderful father, Dr David Ghillyand?' He caught the note of sarcasm in her voice but again felt that thrill of excitement as she confirmed her relationship to the man.

Easy does it, Westbury, don't get over-excited and blow it just when you've got her on your side, he warned himself.

'Not exactly.' Childishly he crossed his fingers under the table against the half-lie. 'I was actually trying to trace *you*, to see if you might have any information about the financial side of the Rouget Corporation,' he explained quickly. He poured them both another glass of wine. 'As you probably know, there was a flurry of trading in the shares just after your father died – enough to rock the market. And then nothing. I thought I smelt a story, and needed to get some info. You'd be surprised how useful St Catherine's House can be to a struggling journalist.' It sounded feeble even to him.

Again Alex looked at him as she contemplated what he had said. She had to confess she was enjoying the evening enormously: Dan Westbury was good company, and not unattractive as he sat gazing back at her. *Why is it always the men who have such long eyelashes?* she wondered. Then again, she knew she could be of use to him, and maybe he could help her. As a journalist he would have a better idea of what to look for and how to find it, as well as having the time to dig it all out. The trouble was, if she agreed to assist him and he discovered some shameful secret, could he be trusted not to publish it?

Oh, what have I got to lose? She made her decision. 'Dan . . . Those certificates you got for me were a bit odd. One of them was mine, but the other belongs to someone with the same name as me, born in the same place but a few weeks earlier. I've never heard of her. I think she might be my cousin – my father's brother's daughter – but I don't know. We weren't a close family. But I would like to track her down. Maybe we could do a deal . . . I help you and you help me?'

Before Dan could answer Ari reappeared with the dessert menu. Alex had to confess the *meze* had beaten her and Dan also admitted defeat. He asked Ari to bring them a plate of fresh fruit and some Greek coffee, preoccupied with Alex's offer – and as he ordered he willed Ari to stop fussing over them so he could resume the conversation.

He knew it was important not to seem too keen. Instead he pretended to mull over her proposition as he picked at the fruit and sipped the thick sweet coffee. When finally he accepted, Alex didn't know whether to be relieved or not. Not wishing to overplay his hand, Dan suggested that if they were going to work together he should really see the certificates. Despite her now placid mood, Dan had witnessed Alex's temper and knew she would not take kindly to discovering not only that Dan had already seen the certificates but that he actually owned his own copies.

For some reason, inexplicable even to Alex, she had brought the envelope with her. She fished it out of her bag, spread the papers across the table and used the salt and pepper pots to hold them flat so that Dan could study them.

He made a pretence of looking at the familiar words. 'Who are Robert and Sally?' he asked, thinking to himself: *Christ, I wish I dared use my notebook. Better not. Concentrate man, concentrate!*

'I'm almost positive Robert was my uncle – that is, David's brother,' Alex began. 'I know he had a brother but if you'd known how offhand my father was you'd understand. No one ever talked about them . . . My paternal grandfather died from the flu epidemic in 1919 and my grandmother when I was only four – so there wasn't anyone else I could ask. I didn't even live with my father, though occasionally I was summoned to Elstree, mainly for a ticking off. Anyway I wasn't really interested in my family. Why should I be? They didn't ask about me.' She knew she was sounding childish but she wanted Dan to understand how lonely her childhood had been, how isolated she had felt. 'I always thought Robert had died long before I was born, but looking at these he was apparently alive a few weeks before I appeared on the scene. So maybe he and Sally and this other Alexandra Marie are still around somewhere. They could be anywhere. This isn't helping, is it?' Alex stopped and looked at Dan.

'I'm not sure, but it shouldn't be too difficult to find out. Surely there must be someone at the Rouget Corporation who might remember them? After all, this other Alexandra Marie was born there; you must have been connected somehow.'

Alex thought for a moment and shook her head. 'Not that I know of, but I could ask around.'

Dan reminded her that, since they now had a deal, any information she could turn up on the money side would be welcome, and he would go back to the Crypt. Alex laughed and asked him where the Crypt was, and Dan explained. As Alex folded up the certificates and put them back in her bag, they returned to inconsequential chat.

Ari approached their table carrying a small tray with two glasses. 'Ah, my friends. I watch you deep in talk and I think: Ari, they 'ave love in their eyes. So I bring you a drink from Ari. Metaxa seven star to add fire to your love.'

Alex stared in surprise at Dan, who opened his mouth to explain, but Alex put a restraining hand on his sleeve. She took the proffered glass and thanked Ari for his sweet thought. 'Why embarrass him?' she asked as he walked away. 'It's easier just to accept, isn't it?' Clinking her glass with Dan's, she took a sip.

The rest of the evening passed comfortably. Dan spoke warmly of his own love of the Greek islands, and Alex became passionate about her work, until they suddenly noticed that they were the last in the restaurant; and despite his genuine friendliness Ari was obviously keen to lock up for the night.

They stood on the pavement watching their breath in the chilly night air. A fine fog was beginning to settle; the dampness made Alex shiver a little.

'Give me a buzz if you get hold of anything, and I promise I'll do likewise.' Dan was busy doing up his coat. 'Sure you'll get home OK?' Alex nodded. 'Watch how you go.' And he bent his head and kissed her lightly on the cheek.

It was an unexpected gesture, and all Alex could utter in response was 'You too.' Then Dan turned and walked briskly up the road, his hands in his pockets and his shoulders hunched against the cold. Alex watched him as he moved in and out of the pools of light created by the street lamps; until, with a slight shake of her head, she also turned and headed for home.

Alex had enjoyed her evening with Dan more than she had expected, but the next day she was not so sure that agreeing to work with him was such a good idea. On the one hand she desperately needed to know about the names on the certificates; on the other, she felt wary, fearful of what she might discover, aware that sharing it with a stranger, particularly a journalist, might not be so clever.

She reran the previous night's conversation in her head, trying to find a reason to cancel the arrangement, but knowing, deep down, that she wanted a pretext to see him again. The question was: where, and how, should she begin trying to find out about Robert and Sally and their daughter Alexandra? If Sally Ghillyand was still alive, maybe there was a good reason why no one ever referred to her and why she had never met her. And what about the other Alexandra? Would she be making trouble if she began digging about? On the other hand, why shouldn't she search for two women who were, after all, her aunt and cousin? Eventually, when Alex stopped making excuses to herself, it became obvious where she should start – and that was back at Elstree, with Malcolm Bratby.

In fact it took Alex a few days to reach this conclusion, she was so busy bringing home files to be studied and reports to be prepared for her clinics and patients the next day. She was also working on a research paper she was due to present at a symposium on the new findings about genes and their links with breast cancer. Nevertheless she found time to phone Dan to thank him for the dinner.

Dan was surprised how pleased he was to hear from her. He too had enjoyed the evening, not just because Alex was willing to help him with the story, but also because he had discovered that under her prickly exterior was a warm and funny lady. She had made him laugh with her tales of life at Vickie's; her dry sense of humour appealed to him. Of course Dan knew that getting involved with one of his sources would be a huge mistake, but the prospect was still intriguing and he caught himself wondering what it would be like in bed with her.

Thoughts of Alex were still floating around in his mind a few days later when he made his weekly visit to the features room at the *Citadel*. He had managed to corner the financial editor to question him about the Rouget Corporation and all its subsidiaries – and had extracted a promise that he would be sent the full financial breakdown of the company and its structure. It was all Dan could get out of him. Now he sat at his desk pondering whether he should look at the Rouget organisation from some other angle. He was toying with the idea of calling Alex when a colleague walked past his desk and bashed him on the shoulder.

'Billington wants you. Looks as if he's rumbled your dodgy exes, mate!'

'Oh, shit!' Dan pushed his chair back and headed towards the features editor's corner.

The subject of expenses was raised as a matter of course every three months and the discussion always followed the same predictable lines. Today proved no exception: the usual reprimands over expensive restaurants, lost receipts and backdated claims. One of the items on his expenses form that month was for his dinner at Ari's. He had correctly recorded the reason for the meal as 'Research re Rouget story', which turned out to be a mistake, since this drew questions from Billington that Dan could not yet answer.

'Peterson told me what you're working on. How's it going?'

'Fine.' Dan knew he was being cagey; but he didn't want to admit he was still hunting around for a firm fix that would give him both the story and the angle he needed. He had thought he was getting close when a contact in one of the big brokerage firms in the City unearthed some information about a lawsuit in the States against the Rouget Corporation, but that had proved to be a dead end. Another dead end had been an inquiry into privately held trusts; without suitable authorisation Dan had got so far and then come unstuck. That Billington was now cross-examining him about his expenses was like having salt rubbed into the wound.

'This claim for dinner at Ari's. Bit steep, isn't it? Who'd you wine and dine this time? And what did you get out of 'em?'

'Oh, come on!' Dan protested. 'You know better than to expect me to tell you the name of a source and what they've given me.'

'You don't tell me, I don't sign it off. Simple, really. Look, Westbury, apart from balancing this bloody section, I've also got to balance the sodding books. How can I do that if I don't know where the legitimate costs are coming from?'

Dan sighed. The old row about hampering a journalist's creativity and right to the privacy of sources was about to blow up yet again when he was yelled at from the other side of the room. Rick was standing, waving the phone at him.

'Westbury! Call for you. Dr Ghillyand. Says it's urgent.'

'Ghillyand, eh?' queried Billington. 'OK, Westbury, you win – but it had better be bloody good!'

Dan was halfway back to the desk before Billington had finished speaking. As Rick passed the receiver over, he grinned and winked at Dan. 'Hope it's nothing contagious!' he said, and turned back to his screen.

'Alex, hi! What's news? Found anything yet?' There was a long pause, and Dan could hear Alex breathing heavily at the other end. 'Alex. Is something wrong?'

'I don't know.' Alex sounded uncertain and panicky. Then the words came out in a rush. 'Dan, I think I'm dead!'

'What are you talking about? You sound very much alive to me, if a bit rough. Look, tell me where you are so I can come over and hear what the hell you're going on about.'

'I'm sorry – there I go apologising again – but I had this odd letter this morning and . . . Oh, Dan, I'm OK really but I'm at Vickie's. Just get here as soon as you can, will you?'

The tone in her voice stopped Dan asking more questions and he had already packed his briefcase by the time she rang off. 'I'm off, but I'll call in for messages later.'

Rick looked up from his screen and swung his chair round to face Dan. 'Who's this Dr Ghillyand, then? V-e-r-r-y sexy voice,' he drawled as he leaned back and put his feet up on the desk.

Dan would not have described Alex as sexy, nor even beautiful or pretty for that matter; but there was something distinctly attractive about her. There was a mask of self-assurance which controlled all she did, from the way she walked to the way she dressed; yet there was also an air of vulnerability, and as he considered this Dan realised he had an urge to protect her. From what and whom he did not know – other than this jerk Rick.

'Dr Ghillyand is a lead on a story and none of your bloody business.'

'OK, OK . . . I only asked,' said Rick, throwing his hands up in mock surrender. 'It's just not every day a sexy woman calls you up, Westbury, asking for "Dan". I reckon she's more than just a lead – but you know best.'

'Oh, fuck off!' Dan replied, resorting to the basic language of the features room, and left the office.

He managed to hail a passing cab and with a promise of an extra tip if the driver could get him to Queen Victoria Hospital quickly he sank back in his seat and wondered what could have upset Alex so much. Dan was paying his fare, including the promised tip, when Alex came out of the building.

'I was watching out for you from my window,' she explained, pointing over her shoulder. 'Thanks for coming down here. I feel such a fool but I didn't know who else to call, and it was the very last thing I expected.'

'Alex, slow down. You're not making much sense – which doesn't seem like you. It's probably because you've still not told me what's up. Now, where can we get a coffee so you can tell me what's going on?'

Defensively she bunched her hands in her pockets and apologised for being flustered. She led the way back into Vickie's, stopping at the main office to collect a visitor's pass for Dan. They walked in silence through the maze of corridors and passages. Dan trailed behind, noting the various people and their uniforms: doctors like Alex in white coats; nurses, radiographers and other hospital staff whose roles he could only guess; porters wheeling patients in chairs and on trolleys; cleaners with large V-shaped brooms sweeping slowly across the scuffed linoleum collecting rubbish; visitors with bags of fruit and bunches of flowers; and the patients themselves. Some sat waiting, their faces expressionless; others walked around holding pieces of paper, trying to find out where they were going. To Dan it all seemed a bustling disorganised confusion, especially when they cut through the casualty department and a group of paramedics suddenly shot past him pushing a trolley and yelling, 'RTA – get him to crash *now*!' Yet he knew that the features room at the *Citadel* would be just as alien to Alex. Here she was clearly at home, and Dan felt slightly in awe of her as he followed in her wake, all her softness vanished beneath the businesslike exterior of Alex Ghillyand the doctor.

It was just an illusion, though, because as soon as they reached the staff canteen the familiar Alex resurfaced. 'Not brilliant, but the best Vickie's can offer.' They got their coffee and Alex led them to a corner table.

'Now then, Alex, what's all this about?' Dan said, unintentionally sounding like the doctor.

Alex took a deep breath. 'I had a letter this morning from the Rouget Corporation – from Malcolm Bratby. He used to work with my father . . . It's not so much Malcolm's letter that upset me but what was with it. I feel . . . Oh, here it is – see what you make of it.'

She fumbled in her pocket and brought out a brown envelope. Inside it was a sheet of notepaper and another, smaller envelope. She gave them both to Dan, who read the note first:

Dear Alex,
    The enclosed envelope was sent to the Rouget Corporation by Mrs MacKay. She was your grandfather's housekeeper many years ago and still draws a pension from the Corporation. She wrote to ask us if we would forward the enclosed as she felt you should have it.
    Don't know what it is but you know where I am if you need me.
    All best wishes,
                    Malcolm

Dan turned to the envelope. It was made of good-quality paper, and Alex's name, care of the Rouget Corporation, was inscribed on it in neat handwriting. In one corner were the words 'Strictly private and confidential' and 'Please forward'. Dan opened it to discover two pieces of paper inside. One bearing a Brighton address was a short note in the same script as the envelope:

I was sent this from Greece to do with as I think best. It is my con-sidered opinion you should have it.

The note was signed 'Jane MacKay (Mrs)'.

The other piece of paper looked vaguely familiar. It was a long sheet and for a moment Dan thought it was another birth certificate, but when he looked again he realised it was a death certificate. The details recorded were precise:

1952 DEATH IN THE SUB-DISTRICT OF: Watford. IN THE: County of Hertfordshire. WHEN AND WHERE DIED: Fourteenth November 1952. The Rouget Clinic. NAME AND SURNAME: Alexandra Marie Ghillyand. SEX: Female. AGE: 0. OCCUPATION: N/A. CAUSE OF DEATH: Aortic Atresia. SIGNATURE, DESCRIPTION AND RESIDENCE OF INFORMANT: Edith Jones. Midwife. The Rouget Clinic, Elstree. WHEN REGISTERED: Seventeenth November 1952.

Dan put the papers on the table. 'You think this is you, don't you? Why? I mean, what makes you so sure it's not the other Alexandra Marie Ghillyand?'

'Of course . . . there's no reason why you should know. It's the cause of death – aortic atresia.' She stabbed a finger at the relevant column on the certificate. 'In layman's terms what it means is that the aorta, the big artery coming out of the heart, is underdeveloped and severely constricted at the time of birth. The foetus is kept alive in the womb by the mother's circulatory system which is doing all the work and maintaining the baby. Once the baby is born the heart can't do the work it's meant to and the baby dies.'

'Sorry, Alex, I'm still not getting the point,' Dan interrupted.

'The point is, Dan, in 1952 there was no way a baby with this problem could have survived more than a few hours. And it's clear from the death certificate anyway – the age is given as "0". You see, this certificate has to relate to a new-born baby. This Alexandra Marie died on November the fourteenth 1952, and that was the day *I* was born. The other one was born three weeks before. And if you look at the details you'll see this death was registered on the same date and by the same person who registered the birth – this Edith Jones, the midwife.'

Alex had been scanning Dan's face as her words sank in. When she finished speaking he let out a slow whistle. 'Jesus Christ, no wonder you were so upset . . . But Alex, let's get one thing absolutely clear right here and now. Whoever you are, *you* are not dead.'

Dan reached across the table and grabbed her hands, giving them a tight squeeze. It was a clumsy gesture but Alex appreciated it and clutched his hands in return.

'The thing is, Dan, if I'm not Alexandra Marie Ghillyand, who the hell am I?'

Dan pondered a while before answering. 'I think you *are* Alexandra Marie Ghillyand, but not the one you thought you were. I think you're Robert and Sally's daughter, not David and Elizabeth's.'

'You mean I'm my own cousin?' Alex asked incredulously.

'Something like that.' Dan let go of her hands. 'May I make a suggestion? I think you – or, if you'd like my company, we – should go and see Malcolm Bratby ... Let's find out what we can from him. Then, when we're armed with whatever it is, we take a trip to Brighton and visit this housekeeper woman ... Mrs Jane MacKay. How about it?'

Alex nodded her head, not trusting herself to speak. Since opening the letter she had been in a flat spin, not knowing which way to turn. Her immediate reaction had been to call Jen. She had actually gone as far as picking up the phone to dial her number before she remembered Jen was away in the States, finalising a big licensing deal for the Beauty Spot.

Not having shared her recent finds with any of her other friends, she had called Dan. She had got the answering machine and had been about to hang up when it gave the number where he could be reached at the *Citadel*. Alex wondered why she had announced herself as '*Dr* Ghillyand'. Probably it was to give her a grip on reality. Recalling her melodramatic statement about being dead, she thought: *Stupid bitch!* However, now that Dan was with her she was sure she had done the right thing.

Any thoughts of carrying on by herself had finally gone once she had involved someone else. Whether she liked it or not, Daniel Westbury was obviously going to be around until the mystery had finally been untangled. It was a prospect that Alex realised she found appealing.

When Alex phoned Malcolm Bratby the next day she did not tell him what was in the envelope he had sent her, although it was clear he wanted to know. Ensuring he remained inquisitive, she asked if she might take him up on his offer of help and, with a friend, come and see him. Although she knew she was resorting to emotional blackmail, it was important that he did not say no. Her ploy was effective: Malcolm assured her he would look forward to seeing them both on Saturday.

'I'll tell security to expect you. The kettle will be ready and boiling at three o'clock.'

Sure enough the security guard at the gate had passes for two. The tension had been growing since leaving Notting Hill. In an attempt to lighten this Alex asked, 'What do you think that old boy would do if there was a serious security threat? Or if I decided not to stop and drove straight through the barrier?'

'Have a heart attack, I expect. Hey, Alex, aren't you meant to park round the side in the visitors' car park?'

'Yes, but parking in front of the house makes me feel more in control. Besides, they wouldn't dare chase me away, would they!' She grinned, enjoying the sound of gravel under her tyres as she turned the car round to park in front of the main door.

'However,' she added, 'from here I play it by the book.'

This meant stopping at reception so that the guard there (who was much younger and fitter than the one at the barrier) could let Bratby know she had arrived. Unsurprisingly he had given instructions for her to go straight up to his office. Officially this was against the rules, since all members of staff were supposed to collect visitors from the front hall, but the guard said, 'I think in your case, Miss, we can make an exception.' Alex smiled at the guard, hissing at Dan, 'I feel such an impostor', as they went up the stairs.

Alex knocked on the door. It was opened immediately by Malcolm, who was holding a steaming kettle aloft.

'I promised to have the kettle ready, so here it is. Welcome to my home from home. Do please come in . . . Oh!' This last remark was prompted by the sight of Dan.

'This is Daniel Westbury. He's the friend I said I'd be bringing. Dan, meet Dr Malcolm Bratby.'

Dan held out his hand, and Malcolm juggled the kettle from his right to his left hand so he could reciprocate.

'Delighted to meet you. I didn't mean to sound inhospitable . . . it's just that I rather expected you to be female – though why, I don't know. Now do come in.' He opened the door wide and stepped aside to let them into the room.

Although she had spent some time at the Rouget Corporation as a child, it had been in the family wing of the Manor House rather than the various offices. Of course she knew her father's rooms, particularly as she had spent so many hours there during the last few weeks, but this was the first time she had been into any other office. She had expected all the offices to be the same, following the grand style of her father's, so Bratby's took her by surprise.

His office had been converted from one of the old butler's rooms, halfway between the maids' quarters and the old kitchen. It was much smaller than her father's, with a lower ceiling and a bit of fancy plasterwork, but nothing ornate, and certainly no chandelier. In fact the old light fitting had been removed, leaving the bare ceiling rose in situ, and fluorescent strips had been added either side. Covered by diffusers, both boasted large collections of dead flies and moths. The desk, with an old-fashioned lamp and sheaves of papers, had been pushed into one corner. Behind it was an ancient executive chair; in front were two comfortable arm-chairs, piled high with precariously balanced folders and lever-arch files. More papers were stacked on the floor. The books on the mismatched shelves were placed haphazardly, some lying on their sides, others standing up. Tucked behind the door was a small table with the makings of tea and coffee, including a variety of mugs. It was here that Malcolm was busying himself, talking to Alex and Dan over his shoulder.

'It *is* nice to see you. Make yourselves at home. You're looking a bit better than the last couple of times I've seen you, my dear. You know, she really has been a bit off colour.' This comment was aimed at Dan. 'But that's only to be expected . . . Oh, don't worry about those – just move the files. Anywhere will do – there.'

Malcolm brought a tray close to the desk. He had clearly made an effort for Alex: next to the cosy-covered teapot were three matching cups and saucers and a plate with an assortment of bis-cuits. He fussily poured the tea for them, checking first how they liked it, before he sat down with his own cup.

'Now,' he said, getting straight to the point, 'I'm sure this isn't just a social call, although you're welcome any time, you know. So, what can I do to help you . . . both?' he added as an afterthought.

This direct approach caught Alex by surprise, but Dan was ready and answered the question. 'Dr Bratby, it's about that letter from Mrs MacKay that you sent on to Alex. Its contents were a bit . . . unusual . . . so Alex wanted to know more about her – and a few other things as well. Didn't you, Alex?' Dan turned to her, egging her on.

Alex carefully replaced her cup in her saucer and began.

'Malcolm . . . you did say that if I needed anything I was to ask you. Well, I wonder . . . could you tell me what you know about Robert and Sally Ghillyand? I came across their names in my father's papers' (*funny how I still think of him as my father*, she thought) 'and I never heard much about them. I assume Robert was his younger brother . . . ?' She tailed off, unsure what else to say.

Malcolm cleared his throat uncomfortably. 'Well, as far as I'm aware . . . yes, Robert was David's brother . . . and I always understood that he died a long time ago. But that's all I know. Remember, I didn't join the Corporation until '67, so of course I never met Robert . . . I'm afraid I don't think I can help you there.'

'What about his wife, Sally, and their daughter?'

'Again, I don't know. I have the impression that Sally's dead, too, but I couldn't tell you about the daughter. Of course, Jane MacKay would definitely know. When I first arrived, your grandfather was still living here, and she was his housekeeper. She was quite formidable. We all called her "Mackers" behind her back – no one would have dared call her that to her face! She was called "housekeeper", but by then there was really nothing for her to look after except Old Man Rouget – sorry, I mean your grandfather.'

Alex ignored his remark and urged him to continue.

'As far as I can recall, she'd been here, with your grandfather, since the early thirties – and she retired a few months after I joined. So, you see, I didn't know her . . . Well, I wouldn't, would I, not being house staff . . . I saw her a couple of times and she terrified me. Very much one of the old school – you know, black dress, white collar and cuffs, keys hanging at her waist. She had the most wonderful posture . . . When I first met her she made me think of Mrs Danvers – you know, from *Rebecca*?'

Alex and Dan acknowledged the reference to Daphne du Maurier's novel, and could envisage the imposing lady standing at the foot of the staircase, her hands held lightly in front of her. The image made Dan smile.

'You can smile, but this was the Swinging Sixties, and here was some faithful old retainer looking like a relic from a bygone age – which I suppose she was – intimidating me just by being there. But never mind that. She would certainly know about Robert and his wife.'

And that was all Malcolm could tell them. Having fulfilled the purpose of their visit, they were both keen to get away, but stayed chatting for another half-hour before making their excuses.

As they walked downstairs Dan waited until Alex was digging through her bag for her car keys. Then he said, 'You know he's got the hots for you, don't you?'

'What?' Alex stopped in her tracks, forcing Dan to do likewise a few steps below her.

He looked up at her. 'I said, you know he fancies you?'

'Don't be silly – he's old enough to be my father.' She did a few sums. 'Actually, he's not, is he? Thinking about it, if he came here in 1967 he's probably only about ten years older than me. But as to fancying me . . . that's ridiculous!'

'No, it's not. You're a very attractive woman. Why shouldn't he fancy you? You've got similar backgrounds – science in some form – and you both know this place. No, I think it would be a good match.'

Dan carried on down the stairs and out to the car, where a surprised Alex caught up with him. The idea of a relationship with Malcolm had not even crossed her mind, and to hear Dan suggest it was upsetting. She began to protest; but then saw the twinkle in his eye.

'Dan, it's not funny! Me and Bratby, indeed. Now, get in the car unless you want to walk back to town.'

Dan did as he was told, pleased that his comments had riled her and that she obviously had no romantic interest in Bratby.

After an afternoon together it seemed only natural that they would spend the evening in each other's company too. Dan noticed that there was a special showing of a film that he wanted to see at the Coronet in Notting Hill and when he put the idea to Alex was pleased to discover she too had intended to see it. Between their arrival back in town and the start of the film they went to a local wine bar for an early supper. It had crossed Alex's mind that she could rustle up a meal in her flat; but, although Dan had met her there earlier that day, she was not yet ready to invite him into her space; so she left the suggestion unmade.

Over a bottle of Chardonnay and a plate of pasta they discussed what Malcolm had told them. Both agreed the next move would be a visit to Jane MacKay in Brighton.

'She sounds awful, Dan. As Malcolm was talking about her, I could see her perfectly. In fact, he made me think of Matron at my boarding-school. She was such an old bat that you never dared be ill. We all had a theory that if you did go down with some bug or other you'd be cured immediately – the bug would take one look at her and leg it in the opposite direction!'

Dan laughed. 'Maybe old age will have mellowed her, but from what Bratby says I doubt it. That sort never mellow – they just get crabbier. It's funny what you said about school, though. Bratby's room made me think of my university days . . . tutorials discussing deep and meaningful topics – none of which proved to be of any use in the real world.' He looked at his watch. 'Come on, we'll miss the start of the film if we're not careful. Let's get the bill.'

They settled into their seats just as the lights were going down. Alex found herself uneasy and was aware of how stiffly she was sitting, very conscious of Dan next to her. She could feel the warmth of his arm against hers on their shared armrest, and willed him to put it round her. Almost as if he could read her mind Dan shifted his arm to rest it along the back of the seat, his hand gently across her shoulder. Alex relaxed, and moved slightly closer to him, noticing as she did so that his casually placed arm now held her a little tighter. It was a good feeling, one she had not enjoyed for a long time. Not since Peter had left her fourteen months before.

Watching the film, she thought about Peter and was pleased to notice that for the first time she could do so without any bitterness or regret for what might have been. Maybe Jen was right. Maybe it was time to move on. Heaven knows, it had taken her long enough. Those first months after the split had been hell. Wanting him back; inventing excuses to call him; despising herself for not being able to let go. Hours spent each night crying herself to sleep. Making mental notes to tell Peter about this or that before remembering he was no longer there to be told. And then, after all the pain, the physical loneliness that seemed to be with her for ever before it was replaced by a numb emptiness. Alex was not sure when the depression had lifted and she had forgiven Peter for leaving; but obviously she had.

Am I mad to think about getting involved again? Especially now when I'm so confused? I've got enough problems trying to work out who I am at the moment without having to worry about someone else. In the darkness she glanced up at Dan, who sensed the movement and gave her shoulder an extra squeeze.

Dan too was not paying enough attention to the film, his mind constantly wandering. He had not been joking when he told her that Malcolm fancied her. It was quite obvious – from the trouble he had taken over the tea to the fleeting disappointment when he discovered her friend was male. Dan had liked being introduced to him as Alex's friend, but had also been surprised at his own reactions to Malcolm's evident attachment. As much as he hated to admit it, he had felt more than a tinge of jealousy – which was one reason why he had suggested the film that evening. There was no way he was going to let Bratby get his hands on Alex.

It seemed odd, sitting in the dark with this woman. Although he had had a couple of serious girlfriends, there was no one at the moment. Having lived with one partner or another for several years, he had made the decision to be on his own for a while. That was not to say he inhabited a sex-free zone, but he had made it clear that he did not want to become heavily involved with anyone. Now, unexpectedly, he discovered he was once again ready for a relationship. Dan carefully moved his arm and put it round her in the dark, expecting her to flinch as he did so. He was pleased when Alex did not appear bothered, but settled herself closer to him.

But would it be fair to start something with Alex when she was obviously feeling so lost? After all, it couldn't be easy to discover suddenly that technically you were dead, and that the man you had regarded as your father was someone else. On the other hand, maybe his support would help her through it. Again the warnings about getting involved with sources went through his head, but he pushed them to one side. A relationship with Alex would not be easy, that much he knew; but he was certain he should stop worrying about it and follow his instinct. He felt her move and gave her a hug. She felt so right tucked under his arm. He would be crazy to allow some sort of vague journalist's moral code to stand in his way.

By the time they left the cinema, both knew they would be spending more time together. They walked down Portobello Road hand in hand, talking lightly about the film. This time Alex had no qualms about inviting Dan in for coffee. Nevertheless she hoped it was clear she was not inviting him to stay the night.

Inevitably their conversation returned to their meeting with Malcolm Bratby.

'I know it's not much to go on. But you can see why I've got to find out who I am, and what this is all about, can't you?' asked Alex as they sat together on the settee.

'Yes, of course I can, but who are you trying to persuade? Me or you?' Dan said softly.

'Oh, I don't know.' She ran her fingers through her hair. 'Did you mean it when you said you'd come with me to Brighton?'

'Yes, of course I did.' He got up. 'It's time I made a move.'

Alex felt disappointed. Although she did not want him to stay the night, she was not yet ready for him to go. Reluctantly she followed him to the front door, where he turned and looked at her.

'This afternoon was useful, but this evening was great. You're good company, you know?'

He bent down and, taking her face in his hands, he kissed her. Alex hesitated for a split second before responding, wrapping her arms round his neck to return his kiss; enjoying being held and the early stirrings of sensations she had thought she would never feel again. Slowly they pulled apart and, without saying another word, Dan left.

Alex was tempted to phone Jane MacKay to arrange a meeting but in the end she decided to write. She received a prompt response, with an invitation to Brighton.

During the few weeks between her first letter and the visit to Brighton, Alex and Dan were in touch almost every day. They either spoke on the phone or met for supper. Neither of them talked about their impending trip until the day before, when Dan offered to drive.

Alex accepted his offer and fell silent. Since hearing from Jane MacKay she had again begun asking herself questions that ranged from the practical to the irrational. Should she cancel and forget the whole thing? Why couldn't she just relax and enjoy her fledgling relationship with Dan? His presence added to her turmoil. On the one hand she wanted him, almost needed him there. Yet her doubts about getting involved again had resurfaced. Once again her thoughts had come full circle.

'I'm scared, Dan.'

'Of course you are. God knows what you're going to be told tomorrow. But if you don't find out now you'll spend the rest of your life wondering "what if", by which time it will be too late, because all the people who can answer that will be dead. Anyway, you won't be by yourself, will you?'

As Dan reassured Alex he was also asking himself questions. Was he really encouraging Alex for her own well-being? Or was he more concerned with following up his story? Alex was still his only lead. Beginning to care for someone who was the linchpin in that story was proving to be as difficult as he had feared.

As they drove down to Brighton the next day, wrapped in their own thoughts, the conversation was somewhat strained. It was only when they parked outside the old Victorian house that the tension eased a little.

'OK?' queried Dan.

'I'm fine. In fact, I've just been remembering that I met Mrs MacKay a few times when I was small. She was a shadowy sort of person who used to usher in the tea-trolley when I went to visit my grandfather. I wonder if she remembers me.'

They made their way up the tiled path and rang the bell labelled with Mrs MacKay's name. After a short wait a gentle, elderly voice with a slight Scottish accent came over the intercom, directing them down the hallway to the last door on the left. Then with a buzz the latch was released to let them into the building.

As they reached the door to Jane MacKay's flat it was opened by a small neat woman with white hair severely scraped back into a bun at the nape of her neck. She was dressed in a blue wool skirt with a matching sweater and wore a hand-knitted shawl over her shoulders. There was a walking stick in her right hand, but she stood ramrod straight as she held the door open for them. Her stance immediately reminded Alex of Malcolm's comment about her 'most wonderful posture'; although she was a mite slighter and smaller than Malcolm's description had conjured up, Alex could understand why he had found her so imposing.

They were shown into a large sitting-room. The furniture was heavy and old-fashioned, with bookcases and glass-fronted cabinets against the walls. The sofa and armchairs were upholstered in a fabric with a cabbage rose design that matched neither the worn carpets and rugs nor the embossed wallpaper. Everything was spotlessly clean, and the ornaments on display, mainly china animals and a few framed photographs, gave the room a homely feel.

Alex and Dan sat down in the two armchairs that had been

placed to one side of the cast-iron fireplace. A tea-tray, a plate of sandwiches and a home-made cake were arranged on a low table in front of them, with another armchair opposite. Dan found himself thinking that, if nothing else, he would always remember this story as the one that was punctuated by tea in china cups and comfortable armchairs.

Jane MacKay excused herself to go and make the tea, giving Dan very short shrift when he offered a helping hand. 'I may be old, but I'm not incapable.'

Chastened, Dan sat down again. Alex smiled at him and soothed the back of his hand as it lay next to hers on the abutting arms of their chairs. With this gesture the last vestiges of tension evaporated while they waited for their hostess to return. As with their visit to Malcolm a few weeks earlier the conversation did not really begin until they had all settled with their tea and had sandwiches on their plates. Jane MacKay faced them and they could not help noticing that her seat was higher and firmer than theirs, making them feel like naughty children about to be scolded for some minor misdemeanour. Alex shrugged the feeling aside and cleared her throat a little before she spoke.

'Mrs MacKay, I wanted to see you about the certificate you so kindly sent on to the Rouget Corporation for me. As you know from my letter, I did receive it. But as you can appreciate it has left me somewhat curious.'

My God, thought Alex, *I sound as if I'm about to give a Sunday School lecture. Just relax and ask what you want to know.*

'I need to know . . .' She paused for a moment. 'I wonder if you could tell me who this death certificate came from, and what it has to do with me?'

'Why, it came from Edith and Rose. You know they stayed in Greece after your poor mother died?'

'I'm sorry, but apart from seeing their names on various certificates I don't know anything about Edith and Rose. Who are they?' Alex said in a puzzled voice.

'You really don't know?' Mrs MacKay shook her head in disbelief. 'They were the midwives at the Clinic who tended both your mother and your aunt when you and your cousin were born. They also went with you as nannies when you all went to Greece. Why they chose to stay there on that heathen island of Kalymnos I'll never know.'

Dan's chin came up suddenly. 'Did you say Kalymnos?'

'What's so special about Kalymnos?' queried Alex.

'It's just that I know it very well. I've been going there since '84. It's how I know Ari.'

Alex stared at Jane MacKay and frowned. 'But that still doesn't explain why they had a death certificate with my name on it when we all went to Greece.'

'No, lass, you misunderstand me. When I say you all went to Greece, I mean just Dr David, Miss Elizabeth and you. And the certificate . . . it can't be about you. Like as not it's about Dr Robert and Mrs Sally's wee one, not yourself.'

Alex swallowed hard, feeling as she had done when she had first seen the double entry in the register at St Catherine's House. Quietly she had agreed with Dan when he had surmised that Robert and Sally's child was still alive, and in so doing had convinced herself that she was that child. Dan, understanding that Alex was rapidly having to reassess her theories, took over the questioning.

'Mrs MacKay, are you stating categorically that Robert and Sally's daughter is dead?'

'That I am.'

Alex tried to quash the rising panic that was threatening to engulf her. She turned to Dan, eyes wide in a white face, and he reached over the chairs' arms and took her hand. It felt cold and clammy in his.

'Alex, it's OK. There's some logical reason for all of this – and between us we'll find out what it is . . . I promise we will.'

Jane MacKay was full of regret when she saw Alex's reaction. 'I'm sorry . . . I was so sure you would have known about the baby. I mean, I wouldn't have been so careless with my words if I'd thought otherwise. I'll make a fresh pot of tea.'

Tactfully she stood up and took the teapot into the kitchen, leaving Alex and Dan alone in the cluttered room.

'I'm going mad!' Alex whispered. 'Did you know my mother was meant to be a bit insane? But she's *not* my mother, is she?'

'You're *not* going mad,' Dan said softly. He took her firmly by the shoulders. 'It's not much fun, I grant you, but you're as sane now as when we walked in here an hour ago. And what do you mean about Elizabeth Rouget being mad?'

Before Alex could answer they heard the tap of Mrs MacKay's

walking-stick as she made her way back into the room. Straight-backed, she sat down again. Then she leaned forward to pick up her cup and saucer and, without looking at Alex, said, 'Your mother was not mad, just a rather spoilt woman who never heard the word "No" in her short life. I know they say it was madness that made her go out again that night when she fell to her death, but I believe it was drink and not madness that killed her! I know I shouldn't speak ill of the dead, but she was a right madam, your mother, and no mistake!'

Now it was Dan's turn to look puzzled. 'How exactly did Elizabeth Rouget die?' he asked, careful not to call the woman Alex's mother. He had come across references in the press cuttings to her death in Greece and the fact that the body had been flown home, but in the few paragraphs about 'The sad accident and death of socialite Elizabeth Ghillyand (née Rouget)' and a brief description of the private family funeral there had been hardly any details. At the time it had not bothered him; he had been more concerned in finding out about David. Now, belatedly, his curiosity was aroused; especially as Alex appeared to accept Jane MacKay's scathing comment about Elizabeth.

'You're quite right, Mrs MacKay.' Alex gave her a rather weak smile. 'I'm being a bit melodramatic.' Then she turned to Dan and spoke to him in a flat, matter-of-fact voice.

'You have to understand that I was barely eight months old when she died, so I don't remember her at all. However, my father' (*I must stop calling him that*, she thought) 'told me that the night she died in Greece they had been out for dinner. Elizabeth had had some kind of emotional problems after my birth, but apparently they had a pleasant evening and Elizabeth had finally seemed to be settling down. I suppose the problems would have been recognised today as post-natal depression . . . or maybe it was post-partum psychosis? Not much they could do about that in the early fifties,' Alex mumbled, the habit of making a diagnosis too entrenched to be broken.

'Anyway, she'd been drinking and my father had difficulties in persuading her to leave – apparently she made a fuss about wanting to stay because there was dancing at the restaurant. When they got back he had to put her to bed . . . she was too drunk to do it herself . . . and that was the last time he saw her alive. The next morning she had gone and the staff – I suppose that would have included

58

Edith and Rose?' She looked at Jane, who nodded. 'They all said they hadn't seen her since they had both got back from dinner the night before. Her body was found halfway down the mountain later that day. The assumption was that she'd decided to find her way back to the restaurant and she'd fallen because she was drunk. End of story. And then my father brought me home to England, where I was farmed out to various people, brought up by assorted nannies and dumped in boarding-school.' Alex shrugged as she finished speaking, as if to indicate she was not really interested in what she had been saying.

Dan knew this wasn't the case; that Alex cared dreadfully, not so much about David and Elizabeth but about her own seeming lack of any emotional roots. He could sense she was terribly adrift, and knew the time had come for them to leave, but before they went there was something he wanted to know.

'Mrs MacKay.' His voice broke through the silence that had settled over them after Alex had finished speaking and it made the old woman start. 'What about Robert and Sally, Mrs MacKay? What happened to them?'

'I'm sorry, I can't tell you.' She seemed to tense in her seat and sounded crisp and formal again.

'You mean you don't know?' Dan pursued the question.

'I mean, young man, that it's not up to me to say. It was bad enough living through it all when I worked for Mr Rouget . . . I don't see why I should have to revive it all now. No, Mr Westbury, it's not another word you'll get out of me! Edith and Rose started this, not me, and I think they should finish it. Now, if you don't mind, it's been a long afternoon and I'm tired.'

'But Mrs MacKay, surely . . .' Dan tried again, but Jane MacKay was having none of it and rose to her feet.

Alex automatically stood up too. Dan, making a mental note to try to come back and see the old woman without Alex, followed them out into the hall. Mrs MacKay held open her front door and as they left gave a small bow of her upright head.

'Good afternoon, Miss Alexandra.'

Alex stopped halfway out of the door and turned back to face Jane MacKay. Now she could clearly remember her as she had been on those occasions when she had visited Elstree as a child.

'You know, you were the only person who ever called me that. It made me feel like someone important.' And very quickly she leaned towards the old woman and planted a gentle kiss on her wrinkled cheek before turning again into the hallway and almost running down the path, embarrassed at her own show of sentiment and the tears that were suddenly pouring down her face.

Dan completed the farewells as quickly as he could and caught up with her by the car. Not saying a word, he put his arms round her and held her as she buried her face in his jacket. Then with a jerk she pulled her head up and drew away from him, rubbing her eyes and nose in an attempt to tidy herself up. For a moment Dan could see her as the solemn child she must have been when she paid those enforced visits to Elstree.

'To hell with tea,' said Dan. 'What you need is a drink.'

They got back into the car and Dan drove down to the seafront, stopping at the Metropole. Alex found a tissue and finished mopping herself before repairing her make-up. It was not until they were sitting in the bar with a drink and bowl of nuts between them that they spoke to each other again.

'Alex, if you really want to discover what all this is about, you're going to have to track down these midwives, Edith and Rose, and talk to them. I asked Mrs MacKay if she had their address in Greece, but all she gets is a Christmas card from them. I could see if the *City* can trace them if you want . . .'

'No, Dan. You're probably right – but I need to think it through, get to grips with it all and work it out for myself. You know, for the first time in my life I think I can empathise with my patients when I have to give them bad news. I hate doing it, but it goes with the job. Now I've some idea of how they feel – out of control, as if someone or something else had become part of me. It's like a huge physical lump I just want to push away.' To illustrate her point she held up her hands and shoved at an imaginary mass, grimacing as she did so.

Undeterred, Dan continued his theme. 'Why don't we *both* go and look for them? I've already told you I know Kalymnos quite well. I need a holiday . . . and I'm sure you could do with getting away as well. Why don't we both take a break and go to Kalymnos? What do you think? I couldn't go immediately – I'm in Manchester over the next few weeks, on a story that goes into court soon, and I still need to do some research. There's a couple of other things I'm doing as fillers – but maybe after that?' Dan tried to make it sound unimportant.

Alex considered it for a moment, then shook her head. 'No, Dan, I've already said I have to sort this out by myself and I mean it . . . Christ!' she exploded. 'How can people be so cruel to each other? That bastard of a man who called himself my father must have known the misery he made of my childhood – he must have realised that one day I'd find out about all this crap!'

'Oh Alex,' Dan sighed, appreciating her anguish but not sure how to comfort her.

'Don't "Oh Alex" me! The only reason you wanted in on this was to get another bloody byline. The moment the trail cools down a bit you tell me you're off to Manchester. It's cheap, Dan, shoddy and cheap, to offer help and support and then pull it away from me. You want a story? I'll give you a great one if you want. People come to Brighton for dirty weekends, don't they? So you go and book us into a nice room and then you can write up what it's like being in the sack with the wonderful Dr David Ghillyand's daughter. I know that's all I am to you, so why not use it?'

It was Dan's turn to hold his hands up in front of him. 'Whoa! Hold it right there! Yes, I admit when we first met my interest in you was purely as a journalist. But in case you haven't noticed it over the past few weeks I've got to know you much better and I now fancy you – you, Alexandra Ghillyand – something rotten. I'd much rather stay here and help you work this whole bloody mess out than go off to Manchester on a story, but I have to earn a living, and I do it as a journalist. For that I go where the news is and over the next few weeks that's Manchester. As to booking a room here – there's nothing I'd like more than to go to bed with you, but not like this. When you and I go to bed – and we will – we're going to make love. Which may sound quaint and old-fashioned, but it's why I'm not going to book a room. I refuse to be on the receiving end of some weird sort of grudge fuck. I'll be in the car when you're ready to go home.'

Alex watched him go. She knew she had been totally unreasonable; her vicious remarks were deliberately intended to make Dan feel the pain that was tormenting her. Of course she accepted that Dan genuinely cared about her. In truth she believed that over the weeks they had known each other the research for the story had become secondary to helping and supporting her. Wearily she got up and followed him out of the hotel.

They drove home in silence, Alex aware she had hurt Dan, but not yet ready to let go of the anger that had prompted the outburst. Right then she needed to nurture the rage; she found it easier to deal with than the other complicated emotions that were tumbling through her.

When they got back to her flat she did not ask him in. She did not even kiss him goodbye when she said, 'Good night'. Dan roared off up the road as she let herself into the flat.

Alex slept heavily and woke that morning feeling as if she had been hit by a bus.

Dan tried to sleep but after two hours of tossing and turning he gave up and spent the night in the kitchen alternating between orange juice and coffee. He finally fell asleep with his head resting on his arms at the kitchen table, and woke with a start when the phone rang. Bleary-eyed he answered it, automatically checking the time. It was nine-thirty.

'Dan, it's Alex. Please don't say anything . . . Just listen. I want to say I'm sorry. I was wrong to take it out on you. You don't deserve what I chucked at you yesterday and if I could unsay it I would because I know I hit below the belt. If you never want to see me again I'll understand. However, if you'd let me, I'd like to take you out to dinner to say sorry properly. How about Ari's?'

At his end of the phone Dan gathered his thoughts.

'Apology accepted,' he said, 'and if I have at least made you realise how fond I am of you then maybe it was worth it. And although you really don't have to buy me dinner I'm going to accept that too. It appeals to the gigolo in me to have a feisty woman buy my food!'

Alex laughed with relief that no lasting damage had been done. They agreed to meet at Ari's at seven that evening; although neither of them said it, they both felt they still needed the space that the rest of the day offered them.

Dan also needed some real sleep. As he crawled under his duvet he was aware that while he had told Alex he was fond of her, and she had accepted this, she had said nothing about her feelings for him. He fell asleep wondering what it would take to get Alex to tell him how she felt.

That evening it was Dan who reached the restaurant first. When Alex arrived it was clear he had been there long enough to order a bottle of wine, which was waiting on the table with two glasses and a plate of olives.

Alex was not sure whether she should simply sit down or give Dan the usual friendly peck on the cheek. Dan solved the problem for her by standing up and going to meet her halfway across the room, giving her a hug and a kiss.

As they chatted about this and that over their meal, neither referred to the previous day's row. Finally Alex could bear it no longer.

'I know it's yet another apology from me . . . But, Dan, I really am sorry about yesterday.' She put her fork down on her plate. 'You're quite right, I was being totally unfair, and I knew it – I just wanted you to understand how traumatic this is.'

'I think I understand more than you give me credit for. What I can't figure out is that, while you know about how Elizabeth died, and in quite a bit of detail it seems, you know nothing about Robert and his family. If you ask me, it's a bit odd it's so patchy.'

Alex fiddled with the stem of her wineglass, twirling it between her fingers. 'To my father I was a nuisance – something to be acknowledged when necessary but otherwise ignored in case I got in his way. There were occasional visits to the Manor House, but they were usually prompted by Cecil Rouget. My father would be around for five minutes before making some excuse and leaving. Birthdays were spent at school, Christmases with friends . . . and although cards and presents arrived I knew he hadn't chosen them himself. I also knew he hadn't even bothered writing on the cards – the handwriting was always different, depending on which secretary had been given the job of sorting it out.'

Dan quietly poured the rest of the wine, trying hard not to distract her. Alex carried on speaking without glancing in his direction.

'It was so difficult for me at school. The other girls' parents and other relatives would visit and take them out . . . They'd come back full of stories of where they'd been and what they'd done, and show everyone the presents they'd been given. I can't tell you how left out I felt. Girls can be so mean to each other. At least my father's name kept appearing in the papers – I could show that off to the others. But as far as my mother was concerned I had nothing except a photograph, which I kept by my bed. She was a truly beautiful woman. I'd always known about her death . . . I mean the basic facts – you know, that she'd had an accident in Greece – but I never knew the details.'

Alex looked at Dan for the first time since she had begun speaking, but as he made no comment she continued.

'Anyway, I began to make up stories about her. I told myself she'd been kidnapped by bandits and died trying to escape, to get back to me and my father . . . That she was a sweet, generous woman who'd climbed down the mountainside to rescue a stray lamb and in saving the animal had forfeited her own life. You get the picture?'

Dan silently nodded.

She went on, 'I'd also woven into all this a single fact that stayed the same with each story, no matter how far-fetched it got; and that was the total, undying and desperate love my parents had for each other. This, I told myself, was why my father didn't want me around. I was a constant, painful reminder of what he'd lost, and therefore he couldn't bear to have me near him.' She turned to Dan and said mockingly, 'There's nothing quite like the female adolescent mind for creating drama and tragedy.' He nodded again but still said nothing, not daring to interrupt.

'Then, finally, it happened! It was a week before my twelfth birthday and at last my name was read out in house assembly – I'd been given an extended curfew because my father was visiting. Dan, I couldn't believe it! I remember going to my house mother to check, and when she confirmed it I was in seventh heaven. It was the best birthday present I could ever have wanted. And I knew exactly why he was coming – it was to tell me he'd made a dreadful mistake; that he wanted me with him, even though I made him think of my mother. He wanted to beg forgiveness for all the years he'd been keeping me at arms' length. Boy, was I wrong!'

Alex shook her head as the memories flooded back. She took a sip of the coffee Ari had brought while she was talking, then resumed her story.

'My father had come to tell me he'd decided I was old enough to hear the truth about my mother. I was certainly ready to listen. After all, hadn't I already gone through every imaginable scenario imaginable? But within a few minutes that carefully constructed image lay in tatters around me. He gave me chapter and verse about the night she'd died. Believe me, Dan, the stuff I came out with yesterday in Brighton was the bare bones. According to my father, Elizabeth was a manipulative bitch, a lush and a sex-mad whore – his words, not mine. He also said my mother was neurotic and mentally unstable, and that basically she had it coming to her.'

She stared at Dan and when she spoke again her voice was unsteady. 'I don't know how I got through the rest of that meal. By the time I got back to school I hated my mother. It didn't occur to me at that point that my father had let me down. As far as I was concerned, my mother had done that. I shot upstairs to that precious photo and tore it to pieces. Of course, the next morning I carefully picked them all up and taped them together again. After all, no matter what she was and what she had done, she was still my mother – and the photo was all I had of her.'

Alex let out a deep sigh. 'Looking back on it, I think that was almost the moment I stopped trying to like my father. Maybe he thought he was doing me a favour, telling me his version of the truth . . . But he was so vitriolic in his condemnation. I mean, what right did he have to destroy the illusions of a kid? After that I always made sure I could stay with a friend during the holidays, so I could avoid him. That was also why I never asked more about the family. He'd reduced one load of dreams to dirt. I wanted to keep what few I had left intact.'

'I'm not surprised.' In his mind's eye Dan could see the lonely child that must have been Alex when she was twelve; he could guess at the misery she had felt. He also began to understand the confused emotions she displayed as each new piece of information had come to light. How must she feel having spent forty-odd years loathing a man who it now appeared was not her father?

Alex made an effort to lighten the tone and declared, 'This is my shout, so let's get the bill so I can pay up like an honourable lady.'

Ari raised his eyebrows when Dan refused to accept the bill, indicating it belonged to Alex. It was while she was waiting for Ari to return with her cheque card that she casually asked Dan if he would like to accompany her to a supper party a friend was holding.

'That would be lovely, thank you. But on one condition.' Alex looked uncertainly at Dan as he continued. 'There's an industry awards thing coming up. It's one of those nights when everyone pats themselves on the back and says how wonderful they are, while patting each other on the back to stick the knives in. God help me, I've drawn the short straw this year, and the *City* have sent an invitation for me and a guest. It's more a royal command than an invitation, but I wonder if you'd accept my invitation and be my partner for the evening?'

'After a build-up like that, who could resist? You've got yourself a deal.'

'It was then, after I'd said yes and put it in the diary, that he told me it was black tie. I ask you, Jen, what on earth am I going to wear? There will be all those glam women from the papers – and yours truly. Oh, shit!'

Jen had phoned Alex on the Monday to find out how her week-end had gone and Alex had barely started telling her when her bleeper had gone off. So Alex had invited her friend round for the evening.

Once they got talking, Jen was more interested in the fact that Alex and Dan had had a row and that Dan had done the honourable thing by not staying in Brighton. 'Listen, hon, I know I'm the one who's been nagging at you to get a fella, but I was just wondering . . . Your Dan's not gay, is he?'

Alex roared with laughter. 'Oh, no. He's straight – it's just possible he's a man with principles.'

'You really care for him, don't you?'

Alex nodded miserably. 'Why do they always come along at the wrong time? One way and another I've been pretty rotten to him. I'm amazed he's still around.'

'Maybe he's still around because of what he says – maybe he genuinely fancies you. And why not? Look, hon, what counts is when they do stick around in the bad times. You know, when you've got a stinking cold, with a red nose and runny eyes, and you look and feel like the wreck of the *Hesperus*, and you're snivel-ling into his hanky. If he's still there making hot drinks, you know you've got a good 'un. I think Dan sounds sweet, perfect for you. You're mad not to give in. I'm looking forward to meeting him at my party – so you'd better make your mind up, because if you don't want him I'll have him!'

'Oh no, you don't! It's just . . . I'm afraid he realises I threw out that stupid invitation to bed purely out of spite. I really lost control. That's what scares me.'

'For crying out loud!' exclaimed Jen, slapping the flat of her hand against her forehead. 'Just for once in your life will you stop being so bloody analytical? You care for Dan? So tell him. If you want to do it, then do it. Now, let's get back to what you're going to wear to this "do". You can borrow something of mine, but I doubt I've got anything that's right for you. If you want I'll come shopping with you and help pick something out. It'd be fun tarting you up, hon!'

Apprehensively Alex looked Jen up and down. She was wearing a bright pink leotard and orange leggings, over which was a voluminous green shirt. On her feet were red ankle boots with orange socks rolled down over their tops, and her spiky hair was streaked with pink and green.

Seeing her glance, Jen laughed. 'Don't worry, I'll save the psychedelia for me. Anyway, this is because I did an interview with a woman's mag this afternoon and came straight on from the studio.'

They began talking about work and it was not until Jen was leaving that she returned to the subject of Dan.

'Another thing, go to Greece with him. A holiday will do you good. A holiday with *him* will be even better. If that doesn't persuade you then look at it in your usual practical way. If you do unearth something really ghastly, at least you'll have someone around to lend you a shoulder to cry on when your Auntie Jen ain't around.' Without waiting for a response, she disappeared out of the door and up the steps in a whirl of colour.

Despite Jen's offer, Alex decided to shop by herself. It was not that she doubted Jen's ability to make her look stunning, simply that she thought the outfit might end up wearing her instead of the other way round. She did not want to hurt her feelings, however, and explained that the only time she could go was the day of Jen's party, when her friend would be busy preparing for that. With grim determination she set off for the West End.

Alex had never enjoyed going shopping for clothes. She would usually spot something in a window, dive into the shop, try it on and buy it after mentally assessing what it would go with in her wardrobe. The idea of going out to buy a specific outfit felt odd.

By lunchtime she was flagging; by three o'clock desperation had set in. So far she had tried on long and short and everything in between. Straight skirts, full skirts, swirly skirts. Bright colours, dark colours. Dresses, suits; plain, patterned and downright glitzy. None of the clothes felt right. She had returned to the evening-wear department of Dickens and Jones, trying to remember if it was in there or in Selfridges she had seen a blue dress that might do, when she caught sight of a iridescent green tucked at the back of a rail.

It was a straight shift with a deep V back that came to just above the knee when she held it against her. Over this was an exquisite beaded jacket made of a heavy organza. It looked extravagant but classic, and the colour was perfect for her. The dress was made of emerald shot silk that shimmered with a gold thread; the jacket matched the green of the dress, whilst the beading picked out the gold. Almost not daring to look, she checked both its size and price. She did not want to let herself down, nor embarrass Dan in front of his colleagues; but she had to be realistic. Although she had inherited a large amount of money from her father's estate, she had not actually received it yet, since there was some dispute over the precise sum. The outfit was hardly suitable for wearing on her ward rounds. To her delight the dress was not only the right size but also marked down from £699.00 to just £99.00 as a July sale special. Alex could not believe her eyes. What if they had made a mistake? With a nonchalant air she approached an assistant.

'Would Madam care to try it on?'

'Y-e-s, but could you confirm that this is the correct price please?'

'Yes, it is. One of last season's that we found lurking in the stock-room.'

Once again Alex returned to the now familiar changing-room. The moment she looked at her reflection she knew her hunch had been correct. At last she had found what she had spent all day looking for.

The assistant came in and when she caught sight of her customer, all her artifice evaporated, 'Oh, don't you look smashing!'

Alex was thrilled; the assistant must have seen hundreds of women a week, in hundreds of pounds' worth of clothes. Her remark had been so spontaneous that Alex grinned at her. 'It's not bad, is it?'

The woman grinned back. 'I'll meet you by the till, shall I?' Alex nodded happily.

An hour later, with the dress and jacket packed in tissue paper in a glossy carrier bag, Alex had bought a pair of dark green high-heeled shoes and was wandering through the jewellery department when she remembered the suite of gold and emerald jewellery wrapped in velvet at the back of a drawer in her bedroom. It had belonged to her mother; her father had sent it to Alex when she was twenty-one with a note saying, 'You might as well have these. I gave them to Elizabeth in Greece. Pity to waste them.' There had been no reference to her twenty-first birthday. She had seldom worn the jewellery but knew it would complement the dress perfectly.

Back in her flat that evening, Alex was thoughtful as she got ready for Jen's party. She was not looking forward to introducing Dan to Jen; it was the formality of being seen to have a partner, of being part of a couple again, that made her nervous.

Almost immediately after they had arrived, Jen grabbed Alex's arm to hiss at her, 'Well done, hon, he's adorable!' which had made her blush.

Jen's home was a spacious mansion flat in Victoria. Even though she often gave huge parties, this was a cosy gathering of a dozen people who sat round the large glass-topped table, elbows propped on its surface as they ate the copious quantities of food that Jen had prepared. It was as they were dipping amaretti biscuits into sweet dessert wine and helping themselves to fruit that Dan became aware of the conversation Alex was having with the man on her other side.

'. . . for the hospital to lay down a general policy on what I can and can't tell my patients. I mean, by all means give guidelines, but who the hell does the board think it is? People are all different and need to be treated differently. One blanket rule doesn't work.'

'So you think everyone should be told all the details, no matter what?'

'No, Charles, that's not what I said. I think doctors should be allowed to tell their patients as much or as little as they want to know. Every case is individual. For example, two of my patients had to have lumpectomies. One was an intelligent woman with a very positive outlook – which I'm sure even you appreciate is important – and her attitude was: Get this thing out of me so I can get on with my life. She didn't want to know the details, so we didn't tell her any more than was necessary. But the other, an equally intelligent and positive woman, could only face up to her op after we'd spent ages beforehand discussing it in great detail so she had even the smallest fact. That was her way of coping. If I'd been forced to tell one more, or the other less, than they wanted to know, it would have been morally wrong.'

'OK, so you're saying you approve of open files and reports on everything?'

Alex frowned, and through a set jaw answered Charles slowly. 'No, I'm saying there should be choice – options – so people can have the right to find out what they want to know if they want to know it, that's all.'

'In that case, consider a child who has been adopted.' Charles leaned towards her, eyes shining as he got into the swing of the debate. 'For argument's sake, we'll call him John.'

Dan began to listen closely, sensing Charles was about to tread on dangerous ground.

'Let's say John knows he's been adopted, that he adores his adoptive parents, yet at the age of eighteen decides he wants to find out about his natural parents. But, for whatever reason, his biological mother doesn't want him to know. Who's got the right there? Suppose his mother is a respectable married woman who never told her husband about John. Has his mother got the "right" to retain her privacy, or has John got the "right" to dig around, find out what he can, and maybe present himself on the doorstep to upset his mother's new life?'

Alex faltered as she related Charles's words to her own situation. 'I . . . er . . . I don't know.'

'See?' he said triumphantly. 'It's not a question of right or wrong, is it? There's all that greyness in between.'

Under the table Dan squeezed her knee. 'Ignore him. He's pissed!' he muttered, hoping Charles would shut up and stop upsetting Alex. Jen too had picked up the end of the conversation and, sensing Alex's disquiet, skilfully changed the subject by telling a scurrilous story about a soap star who used the Beauty Spot, which caused much hilarity round the table.

Yet Alex could not ignore what Charles had said, and on the way home asked Dan if he thought she was doing the right thing.

'If you're still worrying about what Charles said, then I think you're being silly. It's not the same situation at all. What you've found out so far has affected only you, hasn't it?'

'What about those two midwives – Edith and Rose? Won't it affect them, when I start asking questions?'

'It might do, but if they don't want you to ask them, why send that death certificate in the first place? It was as clear a signal as any that they want to tell you something.' He negotiated his way up Kensington Church Street. 'Do I take it you've decided to come with me to Greece, then?'

'No, not yet. I'm still not sure if I'd be doing the right thing. Look, do you mind if you don't come in this evening? I'm absolutely bushed.'

'No, of course not. I'll call you tomorrow and let you know the details about the dinner on Tuesday.'

Dan kissed her on the cheek and watched her go down the steps to her front door, checking she was safely inside before driving off.

It was one of the rare occasions when Alex had pulled rank to get Sam to do an extra shift so she could leave early and spend a leisurely hour having a hot bath and getting ready for Dan's dinner. Her plans had gone awry mid-morning: her bleep had gone off and when she called the extension Sam had asked her to come to Princess Alice Ward, where one of her patients had died. No matter how many times she witnessed death, Alex could never get used to it. As a cancer specialist she knew she had to contend with possibly more deaths than some of her associates, but that did not stop her feeling she had personally failed every time she signed a death certificate. Ironically she regarded cases that went into remission as her patients' successes, not hers; instances that merely proved she was doing her job properly.

After spending the rest of the morning giving sympathy and support to Jean Stellar's family, and reassuring them that in the end Jean felt no pain, she then frantically set about rearranging her schedule so she could get to the Royal Lancaster Hotel on time to meet Dan. Her lazy bath became a quick shower and as the time she had hoped to spend on her hair and make-up had disappeared she just threw it all together and hoped for the best. She did not know it, but her rush meant that her hair looked natural, healthy and bouncy and her face had a freshness and sparkle.

When she arrived at the Royal Lancaster, Alex was relieved that, despite the July drizzle, Dan was waiting for her under the canopy outside. He escorted her in and directed her to the ladies' cloakroom where she could leave her wrap, while he went off to deposit his mac. As she climbed the stairs to the foyer, Dan was standing

71

with his back to her, chatting to a group of people. The men were all in dinner jackets, and the women were wearing outfits whose predominant colour was black. Alex anxiously smoothed the silk of her dress over her thighs, fearing her look was completely wrong. Taking a deep breath, she lifted her chin, walked towards Dan and tapped him on the shoulder. He turned round; then his eyes opened wide in amazement and he gave a long slow whistle.

'Wow! You look fabulous!'

At the same moment Alex had her first sight of Dan in his dinner jacket. Astonished, she realised he was one of the sexiest-looking men she had ever seen. *Oh, boy*, she found herself thinking. *This is it!*

She had not really been listening while Dan was making the introductions and he was now finishing, 'This is our illustrious editor, Russ Peterson. And this, everybody, is . . .' Dan hesitated for a split second. '. . . is Alex,' he concluded.

Alex realised why he had not given her surname, nor her title of 'Dr', and was grateful; yet she still felt out of place, and uneasy at the presence of so many journalists.

'How's that story of yours going then, Westbury?' a man whose name she had missed was asking Dan.

'I flatly refuse to discuss on-going stories with half of bloody Fleet Street in earshot.' Dan neatly sidestepped the issue.

Russell Peterson reached for a glass of champagne from a waiter with a laden tray and handed it to Alex. 'So what do you do, then? In the same crazy world of media' (he pronounced it 'meejah') 'like the rest of us poor misbegotten fools, or have you got more sense?'

Alex shot Dan a murderous glance. *Christ!* she thought. *Now what? Why on earth didn't we think this through and realise people would ask who I am and what I do – and journalists ask even more questions than most people! I shouldn't have agreed to come.* Rapidly she thought through her day as she sipped her drink, playing for time, hoping a suitable answer would come to mind.

'I'm a bereavement counsellor.'

After all, on days like today it wasn't so far from the truth; and she certainly knew enough about the subject to handle any questions. But wait until she and Dan were alone. How dare he put her on the spot like this!

At that moment the toastmaster called dinner and everyone

72

began shuffling towards the main ballroom. Dinner was accompanied by a lot of chat and in-jokes which Alex did not understand, despite Dan's attempts to illuminate her. By the time the coffee and *petits fours* were being served the room had acquired an atmosphere of contained expectation, as the main ceremony arrived: the awards themselves. Alex did her best to appear interested, but the categories meant little to her; she recognised only a few of the names and faces that flashed up on the large screens on either side of the podium.

'The nominations for Feature Writer of the Year are . . .' The list dragged on. 'Daniel Westbury for his work on the *Citadel*.'

Dan sat up straight amid the polite applause from around the room. 'Peterson, you didn't tell me,' he hissed.

'I didn't know if you'd get through to the shortlist – but now you know why I wanted you here,' Peterson hissed in reply.

In the dimmed lights Dan grasped Alex's hand under the table. Although a few minutes ago he had not even known he had been nominated, now it had suddenly become terribly important to him. Alex too was now fully attentive as the statutory envelope was opened.

'And the winner is . . . Daniel Westbury for his work on the *Citadel*.'

Dan let go of Alex's hand to thump the table in delight. He kissed Alex as he rose from his seat to go and collect his award. Everyone at the *Citadel*'s table was whooping noisily, and Alex couldn't help joining in.

'You must be very proud of him,' said Julia Peterson, Russell's wife, above the clapping and cheering. It was obviously a popular win.

Alex nodded: not only was she proud of him, but she liked the fact that the others regarded her as someone Dan would naturally want to share in his success. Even her place card linked her with Dan. 'Daniel Westbury – Partner', it read. For once she did not mind being seen as an adjunct to someone else.

Dan had reached the stage and was holding the award – which was designed out of glass and marble to look like an iceberg with only a third showing. He stepped to the microphone and grinned at the audience, looking totally unlike the serious, heavily lit photographs of him that dwarfed him from the screens on his left and right.

'I'll keep it short – just three thank-yous. First, to Russ Peterson. The last time I won one of these, the bugger fired me, saying I'd hate his guts but it would make a writer of me. Well, it looks as if he was right. Just don't say "I told you so!"' This was directed straight at Russ amid much laughter from around the room; Peterson's methods were well known. 'Second, to the rest of the *City* team for giving me my head. As a result of that attitude I've covered some interesting – and unusual – stories. And, third, I want to say my biggest thank-you to those who have enabled me to be an investigative journalist – they are the people who have let me interview them and dig around in their lives. Without them none of us, and especially me, would be here. Thank you . . .'

Alex was sure that his last thank-you was partly intended for her; and Dan could not have said it more publicly if he had tried.

'. . . I know I'm intruding but I'm being as gentle as I can while doing my job.'

Alex felt choked. When Dan rejoined their table he was greeted with further congratulations and yet more champagne. There was no opportunity for Alex to tell Dan that she understood what he had meant; but there would be plenty of time later, when they got home.

The emotion and champagne hit her. All her doubts about her feelings for Dan had crystallised in those few moments when she had been sitting next to him, waiting to hear if he had won. Now she knew the attraction was much stronger than she had first thought. A great wave of affection had swamped her when Dan looked at her from the stage. It was a feeling she had not experienced for a long time – not since Peter – and, although she would not go so far as to say she loved Dan, she knew that at last she had to let go and move on. It was now Dan's turn.

Once the final awards had been announced and the lights were blazing brightly again, Alex excused herself and followed a number of women out of the ballroom and downstairs to the ladies'. As before, the chatter around her was all about the infighting and politics and reshuffles that seemed to make up the newspaper business.

Alex stood in front of one of the floor-to-ceiling-length mirrors that lined the walls, reapplying her lipstick. Behind her in the reflection were several huddles of gossiping women. Suddenly she felt completely isolated in their midst. Against their subdued sophisticated colours, her bright emerald and gold stuck out like a sore thumb. She was sure they were talking about her.

How could I ever have thought this was a classy outfit? she asked herself incredulously. *I look gaudy and cheap.* She compared her shimmer and glitter with the cool elegance of the other women; all, in her eyes, wearing understated clothes and jewellery, not like her excessive necklace, making her feel gauche, not a highly competent woman with a solid medical career.

I just don't belong with these people, she told herself as she replaced her lipstick in her bag. *So where do you belong, then?* asked another small voice in her mind. *You don't belong anywhere, do you?* Alex stared at her reflection again as she considered the dialogue running through her head. She contemplated the reflected women behind her. Suddenly she knew what to do.

Purposefully she made her way upstairs and back to the table. As she sat down, Dan turned to her. 'Everything OK?'

'Yes, fine. Dan . . . you suggested we should go to Kalymnos together to find Edith and Rose. Is your offer still open? If it is, then I'm game.'

Dan looked at her in surprise. He had more or less resigned himself to the idea that nothing would induce Alex to make the trip. None the less he was sure that by finding the two old women – and he had no doubt that he would – they would at last dig up all the facts.

'Are you sure? What made you change your mind?'

'Don't you know, mate?' Rick, who had also been sitting at the *Citadel's* table that evening, had been openly listening to their conversation. 'It's a woman's prerogative to change her mind!'

Dan scowled at Rick but said to Alex, 'Tell me later.'

Soon afterwards they left, and took a cab back to Alex's flat. Alex was barely through the door before she kicked off her shoes and headed for the kitchen, offering Dan a cup of coffee, or something stronger, as a nightcap. Dan grabbed her by the wrist as she passed and led her to the sofa, where they sat down.

'I don't want anything else. I just want to know why the change of heart. What's made you decide to go to Greece?'

Alex sighed, looking down at her lap as she tried to explain how she had felt earlier that evening. The sense of not belonging, not just in Dan's crowd but generally; the feeling of drifting, of having no roots. After the revelations about her mother all those years ago, she did not want any more illusions that could be shattered. She was too old to live in a world of 'what ifs'; she had decided she would rather learn the truth, no matter what it was, than carry on living in a permanent mental no man's land.

Dan was sitting facing her, holding her wrists as she talked. As she finished speaking he gently lifted a hand and tenderly stroked her cheek. Alex just looked at him. Then, without saying a word, she stood up, pulling him with her. Still holding on to him she led the way to her bedroom, where she put her arms round his neck and kissed him, pressing herself against him. Dan felt the beads on her jacket as they rubbed against the cotton of his shirt. He drew her towards him as their tongues met, eager and searching. Her eyes were closed and he kissed each eyelid delicately and then her cheeks. Alex lifted up her chin, wanting him to kiss her mouth again, but he ignored it; instead, with the tip of his tongue he traced a line down her nose and round her lips before moving down her neck.

He pushed a corner of the shiny jacket off her shoulders and kissed the bare skin as he removed it inch by inch. Alex watched him, letting him undress her, but replacing her arms round his neck. She ran her fingertips round the edge of his collar, and made curls in his hair as she wrapped the strands round her fingers. Raising his hands, Dan untangled her fingers and turned her round. Starting at the nape of her neck with a kiss, he traced a sensuous line down her spine as it was revealed by the V back of her dress. When he reached the top of the zip he carried on, taking the metal fastener with him. Alex curved her back, enjoying the sensations he was creating in her.

She wanted him. Turning back, she began to undress him, first his jacket and then his bow-tie. When that was hanging round his neck she began undoing his buttons, pausing only to nuzzle his chest as gradually she uncovered it and continuing after she got to the top of his trousers. Dan reached behind her to undo her bra and bent down to kiss her full breasts, catching each taut nipple between his teeth.

Running their hands down each other's bodies, they quickly removed the rest of their clothes. The last item Dan removed from Alex was the heavy gold and emerald necklace that lay gleaming against her otherwise bare skin. When they were standing completely naked in front of each other they finally moved towards the bed. Alex lay down and Dan again began to shower kisses around her shoulders and her whole body, while Alex caressed his back and solid flanks. He had reached her hips and automatically she spread her legs, feeling his tongue stroke the inside of her thighs then flick inside her. He gave her a loving smile as he slid one leg across her waiting body. Alex reached down and began running her fingers along his glistening skin. Dan hovered over her, delighting in her arousal.

At last he could bear it no longer and as Alex let him go he guided himself into the warmth that was awaiting him. Alex gripped his back and they found their rhythm, enjoying the build-up of tension in their own and each other's bodies. Alex felt the almost forgotten wave beginning to rise like a ripple in her lower belly as it spread through her and she came to a shuddering climax. Involuntarily she gripped Dan, who let out a great gasp before collapsing, breathless, on top of her.

Alex wrapped her legs round him and gently squeezed her muscles, holding him inside her, wanting him to stay there and relishing the weight of his body on top of hers. Dan sighed and attempted to move. 'No, don't. Stay there a little longer.' He was happy to do as he'd been told. Alex ran a hand down his back and across his buttocks, taking pleasure in their firm fullness. With her other arm she flicked the duvet over them both.

It was several hours later that they eventually stirred. Dan had rolled off Alex, but only so he could lie next to her, pulling her into the crook of his arm as he held on to her, legs still entwined.

Dan moved first; as he carefully extracted his arm from beneath her she also shifted.

'You were right,' she said sleepily. 'That's how it should be.'

He knew she was referring to their Brighton quarrel, but rather than say, 'I told you so', Dan had the good grace to say nothing. Instead he planted a kiss on her dishevelled head, gave her a hug and whispered, 'Go back to sleep.' Which she did.

When Alex finally woke up at seven o'clock she felt a momentary rush of embarrassment, particularly when she caught sight of their clothing strewn around the room. At some point in the night they had disentangled themselves and Dan was sleeping curled up beside her. She eased herself out of bed, endeavouring not to disturb him. Putting on a dressing-gown, she padded into the kitchen where she made a pot of real coffee. She was staring out of the window, feeling oddly smug and listening to the gentle plop and hiss of the coffee machine, when an arm came round her middle, making her jump.

'I'm sorry – I didn't mean to startle you. But I woke up and missed you.'

Alex turned in the circle of his arms. He had tucked a bathroom towel round his waist. 'I was going to bring you a cup of coffee,' she explained.

'What, then kick me out?'

Alex was about to protest, then realised he was teasing her. 'No, not exactly. But I do have to get to work.'

'Now I know I've died and gone to heaven.' Dan raised his eyes to the ceiling.

'Why? Because I've got to go to work?'

'Yes. It means I can become a toy boy.'

Alex looked at him quizzically before unwrapping his arms from around her. 'Dan, how old are you?' she asked uncertainly.

'I was born six years after you. Why? Surely you're not bothered that I'm younger than you?'

'No, not really,' she said a bit too quickly. 'I just somehow thought you were older,' she finished feebly. It had not occurred to her that she was the elder of the two. As much as she hated to admit it, it did seem odd that she had come to depend upon someone younger than herself.

'Well, I'm not. And to keep up the cliché I thoroughly enjoyed the "Older Bolder Woman" approach last night.'

Dan was amused to see Alex blush. 'I was a bit of a hussy, wasn't I?' she said.

'Totally. Now, what about that coffee?'

Once again Dan had removed the tension between them and Alex mentally kicked herself for having put it there, however momentarily, in the first place.

By eight o'clock they had both showered and were ready to leave. Dan felt a bit conspicuous in his dinner jacket from the night before, and they both made a great play of checking whether the neighbours would spot him leaving her flat, which of course they did not. Having already verified that Alex had not changed her mind about the trip to Greece, Dan promised to call her later that day to discuss the arrangements.

When Alex got to the hospital she scanned her diary, trying to identify a convenient time for her to take some leave during the next few weeks. It was while she was turning the pages that she came across her imminent appointment with the solicitors.

She had forgotten all about it.

Having been brought up by a wealthy family, Alex had always been aware that if she had financial problems she could turn to the Rouget Corporation for help. Yet her own pride had made her determined to be financially independent; and in this she had succeeded.

Alex had always known that most of her father's personal wealth, and his interest and holdings in the Rouget Corporation, would be hers when he died, but she still refused to squander money. Being honest with herself, she had to admit that the money would not go amiss; she still had to pay her share of the £30,000 needed by the Tenants' Association to cover the underpinning work on the block that housed her flat; and a more reliable car would also be useful. But she had not bothered to query the delay in settling probate on the will in order that the funds could be transferred to her.

As she was shown into the waiting-room at the firm's City office she wished she had the strength of mind to tell Oliver Widnes that, because of her hostility towards David Ghillyand, and her doubts about his actual relationship to her, she did not want the money, but she knew that she would sit there meekly and accept it.

'My dear, so sorry to keep you waiting. Do come through.'

Alex looked up to see Oliver Widnes standing in front of her. The firm of Widnes, Newport & Bray had offices around the world and therefore suited the needs of the Rouget Corporation. They had handled the family's affairs ever since Cecil Rouget extended his fledgling company from Austria to England in 1925. It was a foregone conclusion that they would look after the legal matters of the Ghillyand family as well.

Alex sat down in the leather-upholstered director's chair opposite Oliver, watching him across his imposing desk. His secretary appeared with two cups of tea. As Alex sipped hers, Oliver flicked through the papers in a file on his desk. At last he looked at her. Taking his glasses off, he dangled them between his fingers. His elbows rested on the arms of his chair. He cleared his throat before speaking.

That's what I do when I have bad news for patients, Alex thought. She put her tea down and waited to hear the worst.

'My dear, there is no easy way for me to tell you this, so I'll get straight to the point. I know sorting out your father's will has taken an unconscionably long time . . . but, you see, just after he died a large amount – a very large amount – of stock in the Rouget Corporation was suddenly released on to the open market. The board of directors were most concerned, as under the Articles of Memorandum and Association they are not allowed to buy their own shares. It was a serious threat, and could have given another company a major controlling power. No one knew where this holding had originated, so it was investigated very closely by both the Corporation itself and the Department of Trade and Industry.'

This was the first Alex had heard of a DTI inquiry, and her anxiety increased.

Oliver continued, 'I'm not going to bore you with all the ins and outs of the investigation – but what I can tell you is this. It appears your father established a trust, signing over half of his interest in the Rouget Corporation. His original holding of thirty per cent was given to him by your grandfather, Cecil Rouget, when you were born. We have looked most carefully into this situation, and it seems that the documentation prepared at the time of his assigning his shares was legal and properly registered. The reason we were unaware of this during his lifetime is that, under the terms of the trust, he maintained the voting rights. Also, it would appear, he had all dividends paid to himself. Then, as far as we can ascertain, funds were transferred on a regular basis to the trust's beneficiaries.'

Alex frowned, trying to understand what Oliver was saying. 'Are you telling me my father was a crook?'

'No, no, indeed not. What he did was legal – a document had been properly drawn up and signed by people empowered to do so. But the action was somewhat irregular and it does mean that your inheritance has been considerably reduced. Oh, don't get me wrong. As the owner of fifteen per cent of Rouget Corporation stock you are still a wealthy woman. A very wealthy woman indeed. It's just not as much as we all thought it would be.'

Oliver Widnes paused, expecting Alex to ask how much she had inherited. Instead she asked, 'Who were the beneficiaries – I believe that's the right term' – Oliver nodded – 'of this hidden trust?'

'I can't tell you that, particularly as they are now *ex*-beneficiaries, having dissolved the trust on David's death. I'm sorry, my dear . . . Although it is your inheritance we are discussing, the rest of the holding details come under matters to which only the board of the Rouget Corporation are privy. I am not at liberty to divulge that information. Client confidentiality and all that.'

Alex stared at him as she tried to piece together the information she had been given. Why had her father, who was not known for his generosity, signed away so much of his control of the company, and in such a way as to conceal the fact during his lifetime? Like everything else, it did not make sense.

'What now?' was all she eventually asked.

'Now we can go ahead and transfer all David's interests to yourself. You do know that there is no property involved? I mean, because he was living in rented accommodation in the village for the last years?'

Alex nodded, wearily. She had always thought it odd her father hadn't bought a house once Cecil Rouget's death and subsequent bequest of the Manor House to the Corporation had obliged him to move out. Now she was glad: one less thing to worry about.

Oliver was still droning on, pompously explaining the situation. 'The board have approved the transfer but have asked me to point out that your position as a fifteen per cent shareholder does not entitle you to a position on the board.'

'Good.' said Alex. 'I didn't think it would. And anyway it's not a position I'd want.'

She stood up and leaned across the desk to shake hands with Oliver, who had also risen to his feet. He came round from behind his desk and escorted her to the door.

'By the way . . .' Alex enquired as an afterthought. 'How much is fifteen per cent of the Rouget Corporation worth?'

Olive Widnes smiled. At last she was asking the sort of questions he expected from his clients. He felt on firmer ground. Returning to his desk, he pulled out a sheet from the bottom of the file.

'I had the department draw up some figures for you . . . just in case, you know. This figure here is what, at current prices, you could expect as an annual dividend. This one is the estimate against the lowest prices recorded and that one's the highest.' He pointed at the columns of figures as he spoke. 'Whichever set of figures you look at, you really should be comfortable for the rest of your life.'

Alex stared at the paper in her hands. 'How much?' She gave a nervous laugh as she looked at the numbers. They certainly did make her a very wealthy woman. 'And here was I hoping it might cover underpinning the flat and a new car!'

Once again, Oliver reckoned he had successfully handled a potentially difficult situation. He mentally ticked off another client file he could finally close and put back into the system. The DTI investigation had been intense and very thorough. The sale of the shares had caused grave concern among members of the board, who believed a rival company had been quietly buying them up in small blocks to launch them on to the market at a time when they could do the most damage to the Rouget Corporation.

Their release had coincided with the announcement that the Rouget Corporation was being sued by farmers in the wheat belt of America, who were taking action against Rouget Agricultural Inc over changes in the formulation of fertiliser. Oliver knew this was potentially sensitive litigation; and the sudden flood of stock on the market did little to allay investors' fears. However, the shares had quickly stabilised and recovered. The investigation had ascertained that the shares sale had definitely not been part of any conspiracy or insider dealing, but had been instigated by a private stockholder in Greece who had no links with any other company. Once these facts had been established, the board instructed Widnes, Newport & Bray to conclude probate proceedings.

Alex was still debating the ethics of keeping the money three weeks later. She and Dan were in her flat getting ready to leave for Kalymnos the following morning.

'No, Alex. You're not going to talk both of us round in circles again.' Dan was determined not to repeat the conversations they had been having ever since Alex had discovered how much she was inheriting from David Ghillyand.

'David . . . your father . . . Dr Ghillyand . . . call him what you like, but one fact remains. He named you in his will as the person who was to receive the shares. It doesn't matter what his relationship is, or was, to you – Alexandra Marie Ghillyand was to inherit, and that's what you've done. Has it occurred to you that it might be his way of saying sorry for giving you such a miserable time of it?' he added as an afterthought.

Alex looked up from the holdall she was packing on the bed. 'The only reason he would have done that was because he thought he could replace affection and love with a few thousand pounds!'

'Honestly, the way you're talking about the money, you'd think it was a couple of quid. Not closer to half a million a year. And that's another thing . . . OK, so you're not interested in the money, but aren't you even the tiniest bit curious as to who owned this trust that held the other fifteen per cent of the shares – the fifteen per cent that should have been yours?'

'No, I'm not. I'm quite satisfied with what I've got.'

'Well, let's put it another way . . . *I'm* curious about it – no, let me finish,' he said, seeing Alex take a breath as if she were about to argue with him. 'It was that flurry of shares that got me interested in your family in the first place. It would be odd if I wasn't still interested, wouldn't it?'

'I suppose so.'

'Right, so are you sure – one hundred per cent certain – that there's no other member of the Ghillyand family who might be tucked away somewhere holding the money from this magical, confidential trust that no one is allowed to know about?'

'Dan, I've told you till I'm blue in the face. There isn't anyone at all, unless . . .' Alex sat down on the bed, the dress she was packing half folded in her lap.

'Unless what?'

'Well, there is the obvious, isn't there? Robert and Sally. I know everyone seems sure that Robert is dead, but what about Sally? I mean, Mrs MacKay said their baby died but she wouldn't say anything about Robert and Sally. Who knows where they are. Maybe they held the trust?'

'It's possible, I suppose,' Dan said thoughtfully as he sat down beside her. 'But it would be a bit odd – I'd have thought that David's death got enough coverage and obits, here and abroad . . . By the way, did you know CNN picked it up?' Alex shook her head. 'Well, they did. So if Robert and Sally were around don't you think they'd have tried to get in touch with you? Or at least send something to the funeral?'

Alex got up and began folding a sun-dress to shove it into her bag. 'Why should they? They hadn't seen David for years. As a family we simply didn't operate like that. I wish we had. It would've made things easier for me – I wouldn't be in this bloody state now, and you wouldn't be firing your bloody journalist's questions at me. Can't you just accept I don't feel right about the money?'

'It's the way you're coolly writing off half a million pounds' income a year that gets me. On the other hand, maybe it *is* easier for you to worry about the cash instead of what we might find in Greece. But Alex . . . I hope you haven't built up your hopes too high. I can promise you, if there's anything to find, including your aunt and uncle, we'll find it. But it might be a blank – and end up being just a cracking good holiday.'

Alex sighed and sat on the bed. 'I know, I know . . . but I don't want to think like that. After all these months I've got to start getting some answers instead of speculating all the time. I want to know where Robert and Sally are and who I am. Dan . . . I just want to get it over and done with so I can get on with other things –'

The phone rang, interrupting her.

'Hello, Alex. It's Malcolm Bratby. From the Corporation, you know.' Alex smiled as he identified himself.

'Yes, Malcolm. How are you?'

'Fine, thank you . . . Yes, fine. Alex, I'm phoning because I understand you're off on holiday tomorrow. I . . . um . . . thought you . . . er . . . might need a lift to the airport . . . Of course, I'd pick you up after your holiday as well.'

'Oh, Malcolm, it's very kind of you but . . .' Alex paused as she realised that Dan had been right about Malcolm Bratby and that he did fancy her. She did not want to hurt his feelings; nor did she want to lie to him. '. . . I'm actually going on holiday with a friend and we've got it all sorted between us. It's sweet of you to offer and I do appreciate the thought.'

'Ah well, that's all it was, just a thought. Have a lovely time. A September holiday will set you up nicely for the winter. Where are you going, by the way?'

Alex could hear the disappointment in his voice. 'Kalymnos. It's one of the Greek islands.'

'Kalymnos!' Malcolm sounded surprised.

'Yes, Malcolm . . . I know my parents lived there just after I was born. That's one of the reasons I'm going. I'll let you know what it's like when I get back in a couple of weeks.' Alex did not want to get involved in a discussion with Malcolm about Kalymnos; thanking him again for his offer, she ended the conversation.

'I couldn't help overhearing some of that,' Dan said as she went back into the bedroom. 'Am I really just a friend, Alex? I hoped by now I was a bit more than that.' There was a note of genuine hurt in his voice.

'Dan! You know you're more than that. At least I think so. That's the trouble.' Alex dragged her fingers through her hair. 'While I'm tangled up in this puzzle I can't think straight about anything. Yes, I care about you. Yes, you matter to me. But I have to be honest and ask myself is that because you're a wonderful man? Or because you're a wonderful man who's helping me out of a mess?' She looked at him unhappily.

Dan had more sense than to push his point. He knew she cared but he wanted to hear her say it. 'Hey, I'm sorry. It was an unfair thing to ask. Particularly tonight. Forgive me?'

Alex nodded. 'I'm sorry, Dan. I can't lie to you, and you wouldn't want me to, would you? I probably do care – really care – about you. It's just all such a muddle at the moment. Hell, I'm so wound up about this trip I doubt if I'll get any sleep tonight.'

'At the rate you're doing your packing, it won't be worth going to bed. Remember we've got to get up at four.' Dan gave her an affectionate slap on her bottom as once again she turned her attention to the holdall.

Next morning the alarm woke them and in the half-light they dressed and stumbled out of the door and into the car. As Dan pulled away from the kerb, Alex could not help looking back over her shoulder at her flat, thinking to herself: *Will I have all the answers when I come home?*

At Gatwick Dan embarrassed Alex by showing his press card at the check-in desk to ensure they got good seats. (He assured her it was standard practice, and certainly the check-in woman was not surprised.) On the plane, Alex, suffering from lack of sleep, curled up in her seat and dozed off. She slept for most of the four-hour flight, only stirring when Dan gently woke her up.

'Hey, sleepyhead, we're going to be landing at Kos in about twenty minutes. I want you to see the islands as we come in.'

Alex blinked at him and stretched, before turning to look out of the window beside her. Down below through the wispy clouds was the turquoise and aquamarine of the Aegean, broken up by small islands. As the plane began to bank, a larger land mass came into view. Dan pointed across her. 'Look . . . over there . . . the large island – that's Kalymnos.'

She followed his pointing finger and squinted into the shimmering heat. Then she swallowed hard: suddenly she was afraid; the trip that had seemed a good idea in London was taking on different proportions now she was almost there. If she could have turned the plane round she would probably have done so.

Alex sat back in her seat and shut her eyes. Dan took her hand and was about to speak when the stewardess leaned over him.

'Oh dear. Feeling a bit sick? Here, suck a sweet. You'll find it helps.'

Alex opened her eyes and glared at the woman with the carefully made-up face, neat hair and mechanical smile. She was about to make a sarcastic remark when a quick squeeze of her hand by Dan stopped her. Instead she took the proffered sweet and said, 'Thank you.'

The plane came slowly to a halt and the door swung open. As Alex and Dan gathered their hand baggage, a wave of heat enveloped them. Alex hesitated for a moment at the top of the stairs, smelling the mixture of diesel, dry grass and sea, and heat before she followed Dan and the other passengers to the crowded terminal building. Everyone crowded round the one luggage reclaim belt, but no one seemed to be particularly rushed. Once they had reclaimed their luggage, Dan led the way past the customs desk and out on to the tarmac.

'Dan!' A young man was heading towards them, a huge grin on his face. Dan dropped his bags and the two men hugged each other, amid much back slapping.

'Alex, come and say hello to Yani. He's an utter rogue but a good taxi driver if ever you need one on Kos. So, you old crook, what are you going to sting me to get us down to Mastihari?'

'Dan, it's been a bad season. Everyone else pays five thousand drachs, but for you I do it for four.'

'Two thousand, or I go and chat up Christine to sneak us on to the coach.'

It was obviously a routine played out by the two men many times before. Then a pretty blonde woman came up, and she and

Dan hugged each other. Dan introduced her as Christine; her uniform bore a 'Small World' logo above the pocket. She joined in the banter before excusing herself as more people came through from arrivals.

'That looks like my lot. Spot them a mile off. Nice to meet you,' she said to Alex. 'No doubt I'll see you at Manolis's at some point. Have a good holiday.'

'You really do know your way around, don't you?' Alex was impressed.

'Yup, and this is Kos. Wait till we get to Kalymnos.'

There was a note of suppressed pride in his voice. Alex found that suddenly her doubts and fears had vanished: she had been wondering whether Dan's claims about his knowledge of Kalymnos had been exaggerated, but now it was evident that, if anything, he had underplayed it. Watching him standing there talking happily to Yani, she thought she had never seen him so alive, or looking so boyish. Clearly he felt very much at home.

Yani took them down to Mastihari and refused to accept a penny for the cab fare (obviously another part of their routine), preferring to join them for a drink as they ordered lunch at the harbour taverna. Dan explained that the ferry to Kalymnos would leave in a few hours' time.

To Alex the thought of sitting for three hours waiting for a ferry, listening to Dan and Yani chatter about people and places she did not know, did not appeal. However the calming sound of the sea, the gentle breeze and the good food and wine made the time go quickly. When, at about five o'clock, Dan told her it was time to make a move she was surprised.

'Ah!' said Dan knowingly. 'That's the magic of Greece. Come on, or we'll be stuck inside.'

He grabbed the luggage, hurried round the small harbour to the waiting ferry and legged it up the stairs to the top deck, where he was sitting reserving a seat for Alex when she finally caught up with him.

The ferry began to roll as her engines sputtered into life. Twelve hours after they had left Notting Hill, they began the final leg of their journey. As they headed out across the water Alex could see Kalymnos ahead of them; every time she checked it was getting bigger on the horizon.

From a distance the land looked bare and rocky, but as they got closer she could see that it was in fact green. The harbour grew in front of her eyes and the town of Pothia, nestling in the valley between the mountains, began to take shape. The late afternoon sun glimmered off the windows of the softly painted buildings, and the purity of the light flooded the place. Alex had assumed they would go straight ahead into the harbour but the ferry began to change course, veering to the left and round the headland.

Dan let out a sigh. 'Oh, good! We're coming into Myrties.'

Alex raised a questioning eyebrow, bemused at his evident pleasure.

'It's just that it's prettier than Pothia and I want your first proper glimpse of the island to be the best possible, that's all.'

He spoke defensively, the smugness he had been displaying all day dropping for the first time, to be replaced with a silent entreaty to Alex to like Kalymnos as much as he did.

It was only when they finally moored that Alex could understand why Dan loved it so much. Unlike the town they had seen, Myrties did not have a harbour, just a stone jetty. Tied to this were several small-cabined boats, which were taking it in turns to ferry people across a narrow strait of water to another island. A path led from the jetty, between squat bars and square white buildings with blue-painted shutters, to a small road overhung with trees. Everything seemed relaxed, with a mixture of people hanging around at the top of the jetty. There was a priest in his black robes chatting to a group of men in old jeans and shirts. Bare-footed toddlers played around their mothers' feet and the bags of groceries held there, while the older children leaped with great agility from one small boat to another, helping them to moor and cast off. Over it all swelled the sound of voices chattering and calling to each other.

'Dan, it's lovely. It's so . . . so Greek,' she finished lamely, smiling at him.

His face lifted with relief. He helped her off the boat and together they walked up the jetty to the road. At the top they turned right to what Dan told her was the square. This in fact proved to be little more than a tree growing in a built-up concrete tub outside a couple of bars where the road widened. A few taxis were waiting, and Dan quickly got himself and Alex into one. He explained that they would have a cab to themselves for their first journey, but usually the taxis operated a sharing system whereby they crammed in as many people as possible who were heading the same way and charged them a flat fare each.

'The taxi-bus service can be crowded, but like a lot of things here it's cheap and efficient,' Dan continued as the taxi swung round a steep hairpin bend and began to climb up the mountain. After a few more bends Dan asked the driver to pull over. 'Look at that view!'

Alex did as she was told and looked out of the back of the taxi. They were right on the edge of the road, which was unfenced, lined only with occasional large white-painted stones. It fell away into a steep drop down the mountainside, which was prickly with greenery, undergrowth and olive trees curling their way skywards. Beyond that Alex could see the road they had just driven up as it disappeared under the trees. To the right spread the village of Myrties; further on, Dan told her, it ran into the village of Massouri. But what made Alex gasp was the view; to the left was the sea, glinting and turning gold in the now setting September sun. She could see the little boats bobbing across to the other island. This was Telendos, Dan told her, and if she looked carefully she would see the Old Man of Telendos. Dan drew his extended finger along the outline of the rugged mountain-top, showing Alex the profile of a bearded man, sleeping with his mouth open.

'There's an Old Woman as well,' he said as they continued their journey over the top of the mountain and down the more gentle descent to Panormos, where they were staying for the fortnight. The taxi turned right at the square (another tree in a concrete tub) and right again before it came to a stop outside a three-storey terraced building.

They had barely got out of the taxi when a little round, stooped woman, dressed in black and wearing an apron over her skirt, flung herself at Dan, squeezing the breath out of him in a huge bear-hug.

As soon as he could untangle himself Dan made the introductions. 'Alex, meet Sylvie, Ari's sister. Sylvie, this is Alex, who is a very good friend.' He emphasised the last two words, but that did not prevent Sylvie from chuckling to herself and giving Dan a knowing wink.

Alex did not mind. They had arrived; now she was here, she felt it was right to have come. Sylvie led her up the stairs at the side of the building and into a small apartment. The first thing she noticed was how cool it was. It was a simple square room with a double bed in the middle, two small tables on either side and a curtained alcove which served as a wardrobe. To the left was a little bathroom and in the corner a tiny kitchenette.

Dan eventually persuaded Sylvie that, as always, everything was perfect and that what they needed now was a shower. With one last chuckle at Dan, Sylvie left.

'Come on,' said Dan. 'Let's get sorted . . . have a quick shower . . . and then I think we'll stroll along to Kantouni for supper. How does that sound?'

'Fine' was all Alex could say.

An hour later they set off for Kantouni. It was a gentle ten-minute walk along a road scented with frangipani and honeysuckle, and down on to the beach. The path on the beach was a wooden walkway that suddenly ran out. Alex kicked her shoes off and walked with Dan further along the sand until they came to steep steps leading into a place called 'Sun and Surf'. Dusting the sand off their feet they went inside. It was a pretty, open-air taverna with coloured lights and a bar down the right-hand side.

As before, Dan was greeted like a long-lost son by the owners, whom he introduced as Manolis and Diane. Alex warmed to them immediately. Manolis was a big jovial man with a twinkle in his eye; Diane was a tall, vivacious Australian. Seated at the bar with drinks, Alex and Dan began to discuss the menu but Manolis announced he would choose for them. Alex was not bothered: she was tired after the journey and was content to let others take control.

As they moved from the bar to a table for their meal, Alex asked Dan, 'Do you think Manolis and Diane might know anything?'

Dan looked blank for a second, having momentarily forgotten why Alex had agreed to come with him to Kalymnos. Then he replied, 'They might, but I don't think we should ask them tonight. Look, I know you're keen to start digging around, but to get the best out of people here they need to feel they can trust you. They love visitors, but they love their home first and foremost. Let them get to know you first – it won't take long, I promise. Get used to being here . . . give yourself a chance to relax and find your way around before you start cross-examining people.'

'Dan, you might be on holiday but I'm not!' said Alex sharply. She knew she was being unreasonable by raising the subject so soon, but had suddenly wanted to get started.

'Please, Alex. Trust me?' Dan was beginning to sound as tired as Alex felt.

She looked across the bar and the beach to the sea, where the waves were rolling in to the shore. 'I'm sorry, Dan. I guess I'm just tired.'

'You're allowed to be. Don't forget, we've been up since four . . . and it feels like eleven-thirty. Now, eat your dinner . . . We'll talk this through properly tomorrow morning. OK?'

Alex smiled at him. 'OK.'

Part Two

David Ghillyand swung his chair round to face the window. Now he was leaning back, staring across the view, not seeing the fields and countryside as he mulled over the news he had heard that morning. Of course he had known that Robert had applied for and been granted an interview for the position of Research Director, but he had assumed Cecil had agreed to see him out of respect for David. It had never occurred to him that the interview was genuine, nor that Robert would get the post.

'Damn and blast!' he swore to himself as he turned back to his desk. Having Robert around could make things complicated.

'Language! There's a lady present!'

David jumped at the voice. 'I didn't hear you come in.'

'No, I know. Whatever you were thinking about, you were deeply engrossed. You look particularly handsome when you're being serious. Aren't you going to offer me a seat?'

David sighed. 'Elizabeth, I wish you wouldn't keep doing this. I *have* got work to do. Why don't you go and play with your friends instead of interrupting me the whole time?'

Elizabeth Rouget stopped leaning against the door, where she had been standing watching David since she had silently crept into the room. She walked across the thick carpet to loll on his desk. Her chestnut hair rested in neat curls on her cashmere-clad shoulders.

'May I remind you, Dr Ghillyand, the war ended four years ago and I've just returned from finishing school in Switzerland, not an evacuee billet. I am now eighteen and no longer a child. I do not "play with my friends".' She made the expression sound like a sneer. 'I'm very much an adult and you'd better remember it.'

With unhurried dignity she then turned, sauntered back across the office, and with a charming smile opened the door and went out. David watched it shut quietly behind her.

He had to admit that since she had been away she had certainly grown up: the Elizabeth of old would have slammed the door. Besides, Elizabeth's childhood prettiness had not faded; indeed, she had grown into a real beauty. Her figure had lost what little puppy fat it had possessed and there was no doubt it was a woman's hips that had swung away from him. Across the desk he had noticed that her large, almond-shaped eyes had been deftly lined in black and the mascara carefully applied to her lashes. Her cheeks had been slightly rouged and her lips painted into a crimson pout. Elizabeth knew exactly the effect she wanted to create; and she had succeeded brilliantly.

David thought it precocious for a girl of her age to be so self-possessed but at the same time admired her for it. With a shake of his head he put Elizabeth – and Robert – out of his mind and returned to his work.

A couple of hours later he received a telephone call from Miss Wilmot, Cecil Rouget's secretary.

'Dr Ghillyand, Mr Rouget is extending an invitation to yourself to dine with him and his daughter this evening. He has a small dinner party for ten, here at the house, and would like you to escort Miss Elizabeth. It is formal, and you are expected at seven-thirty for eight o'clock in the library.'

David murmured his thanks. The word 'invitation' was a polite way of saying he had been commanded to attend. As usual, Elizabeth had proved her point.

Like the rest of the top personnel at the Rouget Corporation, David had a small cottage in the grounds, for which he paid a peppercorn rent. It did not take him long to return home that evening to change, before walking back to the Manor House. As he lit a cigarette, blowing the smoke into the warm evening, he considered the reports he had been reading earlier that day. Given the choice, David would far rather have been at his desk rereading them than having dinner with his boss and escorting his spoilt daughter. He took a final drag on his cigarette before throwing it to the ground and stamping it out in the gravel in front of the house. David rang the bell marked 'Private' and greeted Simmons as he let him in.

The Manor House was divided into two, with the business offices of the Rouget Corporation in the west wing and the family apartments through a double-door in the east. As David made his way through the second door he could hear voices drifting from the library. When Simmons announced him, Cecil Rouget came bowling towards him, his face wreathed in smiles.

'So glad you could come, David. Scotch?'

David accepted. The small, round but nevertheless imposing man put his arm across David's shoulders and steered him towards a group of people at the far end of the library.

Cecil lowered his voice confidentially. 'Very glad you could come. As you know, I usually rely on Elizabeth to be my partner on these occasions, but Lockton has brought both his wife and his sister . . . What could I do? Poor girl, it's so boring for her. I hope you don't mind looking after her for me this evening?'

'No, no, of course not. Only too glad I was able to oblige.' What else could he say? That spending the evening with someone fifteen years his junior would bore him rigid? As they reached the group in the corner there was a flurry at the door.

'Oh dear, I'm so sorry I'm late down. Do forgive me.'

David couldn't help giving a wry smile. Elizabeth had timed her entrance perfectly. She was wearing a sleeveless purple dress in crêpe de chine with an embroidered bodice; her waist was nipped in and the skirt fell to the ground in a swirl of fabric. Elegantly draped around her neck and hanging down her back was a long chiffon scarf. Amethyst and diamond jewellery sparkled at her ears and wrist.

'My love, you look charming,' beamed her proud father. 'Doesn't she, David?'

'Absolutely glorious.'

Elizabeth dimpled prettily. Then, as if realising she was forgetting her manners, she insisted on acting as hostess and getting David's drink herself, by way of a penance for being late to greet her father's guests.

She led him to the tray and shooed Simmons out of the way.

As she poured David a Scotch and water, without looking at him she said, 'I told you I'd ensure you don't forget I've grown up. And this, Dr Ghillyand, is just the beginning.'

Elizabeth handed David his glass as she finished speaking, again bestowing on him her most charming smile. Picking up a sherry for herself, she tucked her arm into his and guided him back to the other guests.

'Do let me introduce you. Mr and Mrs Lockton . . . Mr Lockton's sister Miss Priscilla Lockton – Dr Ghillyand, Development

Director here at the Corporation. Mr Lockton is employed by the Rouget Foundation . . . May I introduce you to Mr William Smythe and his guest Miss Maria Eropolos. Dear William looks after the legal side of our Greek concerns and is here on business for just a few weeks. In fact, William is the reason for our little party this evening. We do like to look after our own people when they visit us. And I believe you know George and Jennifer?'

Elizabeth carried out her duties as hostess with aplomb, as she had done on many other occasions since her mother's death when she was ten.

David shook hands and smiled as necessary at the rest of the group, noting with amusement that it was obvious from the tone in her voice that Elizabeth did not approve of Maria Eropolos. But it was the description of William Smythe's position within the work of the Rouget Corporation that made David pay attention. Something he had read had caught his imagination. He wanted to talk with this man, but unless he could sit near him at dinner he might not be able to do so easily.

Thinking quickly, he began to pat his jacket pockets. 'Oh dear. I seem to have left my cigarette case in my coat pocket. Do excuse me.' And before Elizabeth could stop him he slipped out of the door. Checking that none of the servants was around, he stepped silently into the dining-room.

The table was laden with crystal and silver; the candelabra gleamed and the flowers in the centre of the table gave off a fragrant aroma. David walked round the table, looking at the place cards. As he had expected, Elizabeth had placed him on her right but to her left were Mr and Mrs Lockton. On David's right was Lockton's sister. At the other end of the table, to Cecil's right, she had positioned Maria Eropolos and William Smythe. Quickly David picked up Mr and Mrs Lockton's cards and swapped them with those of William and Maria, thus placing William directly opposite himself. Then he slipped out of the room as quietly as he had entered it.

'Got it,' he said as he walked back into the room, remembering to remove his cigarette case from his inside jacket pocket. He was about to open the case when Simmons announced that dinner was served.

David offered his arm to Elizabeth and they followed her father into the dining-room. They all settled around the table, identifying their places from the cards. David assisted Elizabeth into her seat at the head of the table.

'Oh!' Elizabeth let out a soft exclamation of surprise as William Smythe and Maria Eropolos sat down to her left.

'Is anything wrong?' William asked her.

'No, no. I just stubbed my toe. Silly of me.'

David's expression gave nothing away as he too sat down, but he could not help noticing the puzzled sideways glance Elizabeth gave him.

The dinner went well. The rationing that the rest of the country was still experiencing obviously did not affect the Rouget house-hold. Cecil boasted that he had caught the trout himself in their own lake, Tykes Water; as ever he tried to cultivate the image of the perfect English gentleman, despite traces of the Austrian accent he had never been able to lose, although he had been a British subject since 1926.

The conversation drifted from topic to topic in the usual way until, over the cheese, David was at last able to talk to William Smythe.

'How are things in Greece?' he asked casually.

'Mainland Greece is not good – still trying to rebuild. Coming out of Athens was dreadful. The ports are in even a worse state than they were before '39, which is saying a lot. Those Greeks get themselves so tangled in red tape over the small things that they can't see the bloody huge ones going on under their noses.'

'Such as?'

'Well, for example, it took us seven and a half hours to get through the port authorities and on to our boat. They thought Maria was going to run away and not come back. It's ludicrous, I mean, I know she's a very wealthy woman . . . But if we'd wanted to get her belongings out of the country I'd have married her. And she would have travelled on my British passport – not her own Greek one. In fact the reason we haven't married is because she wants to keep her independence. I can't say I blame her. She owns land and other holdings – including oil – that make her enormously rich. Why should she give that up, and become a refugee in my care here in England? I ask you. No sense, those bureaucrats. And while we were arguing about that I saw, with my own eyes, two lorry-loads of cigarettes being driven round the back of the docks and straight on to the boat – no questions asked.'

David looked across the table at the handsome woman on William's left. Everything about her, from her immaculate dark hair to her soft hands and manicured nails, spoke of wealth and class. Despite what he said, it was obvious that William Smythe was living very nicely off Maria Eropolos. The term gigolo sprang to his mind. Maria in turn got to travel with him and had the benefits of male company without the encumbrance of a husband. David reflected on the way in which the very rich not only could flout convention but were applauded for it.

'Double standards, as usual. Are all the authorities there so corrupt?' David made the question sound light as he quartered an apple.

'The word "corrupt" has nasty connotations, don't you think?' William had sat up in his chair a little and was taking more interest in the seemingly casual remarks. 'Let us just say, someone who knows his way around can always tell you how to work the system.'

Elizabeth had been listening to the conversation, one elbow on the table with her chin resting in her hand. 'This is beginning to sound like some awful cops and robbers story. Maria and I won't have you two brutes lowering the tone of the evening. If you want to talk like that I think it's time the ladies and I withdrew. Ladies . . .'

Elizabeth stood up and everyone followed her lead, the men settling back into their seats after the women had gone into the drawing-room.

David once again turned to William. 'I'm aware of some of the work the Corporation is undertaking in Greece. In fact I was reading a report only today.' David poured himself a glass of port and passed the decanter on. 'I think I might have to go out to pay the plant a visit. As you say, someone who knows his way around could be useful. May I let you know when I'm coming?'

William smiled. 'But of course. I'm sure Maria will insist you stay with us, and I'll be only too happy to act as your guide, both official and unofficial.'

David gave a slight nod of his head and lifted the glass of port to his lips. William had turned to answer a question put to him by Cecil. David made few comments as the conversation about the newly prepared antibiotic, Chloromycetin, flowed around him, preferring to watch the men as they talked, drank and pulled on their cigars. He covertly studied William, noticing how he in turn

100

seemed acutely aware of every movement and word of Cecil's. He also wondered how much of Maria's attraction was her money.

'Well, gentlemen,' said Cecil, getting up from the table, 'I think it's time we joined the ladies.'

The others followed him across the hallway and into the drawing-room. Elizabeth rose from her armchair and drifted elegantly across towards David, tucking her arm in his.

'I hope you had a jolly time talking politics and money – all those things we women don't understand . . .'

David looked down at her and gave a snort of laughter. 'My dear Miss Rouget, don't spoil the image by going all coy on me. It doesn't become you.'

Elizabeth frowned and pulled her arm away from the crook of his elbow. With a flounce she turned and walked towards the doors that opened on to the terrace. David watched for a moment before following her, only to be stopped halfway across the room by Lockton, who wanted to discuss a project he was handling. By the time he had caught up with Elizabeth she was leaning on the wall looking at the lake shimmering distantly in the moonlight. She appeared wrapped in her own thoughts, but David knew she had positioned herself carefully to achieve the maximum impact.

'I'm sorry,' he said as he stood by her side. 'I did not mean to offend my hostess.' There was a slightly mocking tone in his voice.

Elizabeth glanced at him. 'Then why did you rearrange the place cards at dinner? Don't deny it – I know you did it.'

'I'm not going to deny it. *Mea culpa*. I admit it. But when I discovered that William Smythe was here this evening, I wanted to talk with him. And if he had sat at the other end of the table it would not have been possible, would it?'

Elizabeth gazed back at the view before answering smoothly, 'You only had to ask. I'm not so unreasonable, David. In fact, I could be most helpful if you'd let me.' It was her turn to mock him. 'I know you want more than you're currently getting from the Corporation. If you look after me properly, I can make sure you get it. As you once told me, I'm not stupid when it comes to power and money. And I know just how to nurture Papa, to ensure that the people I hold in special regard are fairly rewarded. I think you understand my meaning?'

She turned to look up at him from under her eyelashes. David grabbed the top of her bare arm and pulled her round to face him.

101

Elizabeth began to struggle, but David tightened his grip, while with his other hand he lifted her chin and very firmly, and not too gently, kissed her.

The sound of her slap echoed round the terrace. David laughed, and rubbed his cheek.

'Sometimes getting what you want can hold surprises,' he said. 'In business dealings you should always make sure you know exactly what you're getting before entering negotiations.'

Elizabeth tossed her head; the light sparkled on her earrings and there was a glint in her eyes as she walked back into the drawing-room to join the other guests.

By midnight everyone had left. As David passed Elizabeth on the way out he thanked her for a pleasant evening and added, 'Remember what I said about business dealings.'

After he had gone, Cecil Rouget put an arm round his daughter's shoulders. 'And what business advice did Dr Ghillyand have for you, my love?'

'Oh . . . nothing. It was a bit of a joke that began over dinner, that's all.' She kissed her father's cheek and said good night.

Upstairs in her bedroom, Elizabeth kicked off her shoes and discarded her dress, letting it fall to the floor. Then she sat down at her dressing-table and removed her bracelet. As she inclined her head to take off her earrings she caught sight of herself reflected three times in the mirror and its wings on either side. She stopped fiddling and scrutinised her face, biting her lower lip as she turned this way and that. While she stared at her reflection, she released her lower lip, touched her mouth and finally let her fingers drift down her chin and throat and across her shoulder to the top of her arm where David had gripped her so tightly.

It was not the first time she had been kissed, but the others had been boys from local schools who had been drafted in for end-of-term dances. They had been snatched by slobbering lips and sweaty palms when Mademoiselle was not looking – in truth not enjoyable, but Elizabeth thought she should allow them their fun, even though she could not understand the fuss.

But tonight had been different.

David had not slobbered; his mouth was dry and solid against hers. His grip had been firm and determined. In response, Elizabeth had felt a small tremor go through her, like the butterflies she felt when she had to give a recital, but much more exciting.

She closed her eyes and tried to relive the moment. For a moment she pictured him on the terrace, his tall figure against the moonlight. Then, with a shrug of her shoulders, she opened her eyes and began fiddling with her earrings again.

Never mind, she told herself. *It was the first of many. Whether you like it or not, David Ghillyand, I intend to marry you!* Dropping her earrings into the silver bowl on her dressing-table, she slipped into her silk nightgown, climbed into bed and fell instantly asleep.

Robert Ghillyand stood inside the doorway and surveyed the well-equipped laboratory. When he had heard that the position of Research Director at the Rouget Foundation was about to become vacant, he had wanted the job immediately.

Over the years the Rouget Foundation had gained a solid reputation, augmented by the government contracts they had gained during the war. This in turn meant that the equipment and materials they needed had always been available. Increasingly frustrated by the shortages and restrictions under which he'd been working for the last few years, Robert had pursued the appointment with a zeal that his brother David would not have recognised. The interview board, however, had appreciated what Robert could offer, and gave him the post.

The door behind Robert opened and he glanced round quickly.

''Morning, Robert. I thought it would be friendly to greet you on your first day.'

Robert looked at his brother. 'Hello, David. I wondered if we'd bump into each other.'

The two brothers had not seen each other for six years, when they were still in their twenties. Both of them had been approached by the Ministry of Defence in 1943 and invited to join the research teams working on germ warfare. David had accepted the offer, since he regarded it as a secure position that would also fulfil his personal ambitions. Robert had refused, explaining in his usual quiet but firm way that his interest lay in curing, not harming mankind. When David heard of Robert's decision, he had gone to his flat to try to persuade Robert to join him. They had failed to agree; and while Robert had grown calmer, and more emphatic that he would not change his mind, David had become more and more enraged.

103

'You must be mad!' David had shouted. 'You and your bloody principles! They'll leave you high and dry – and on the breadline. To hell with curing the common cold – the future is *this* way, whether you like it or not. Just think what mustard gas did in the last war . . . what a powerful weapon it was. My God, think how much our knowledge has grown since then. Think of what we could do today with the right information. It's mind-boggling just to imagine it!'

Robert had looked up coldly from his armchair. 'Yes, I remember mustard gas. And I remember what it did in the last war. It killed thousands and thousands of men and ruined more lives and families than bear thinking about. It was mustard gas and shell shock that killed Father. Oh, I know they said it was the flu. But if he hadn't been so weak from four years at the front it wouldn't have touched him. And what about Mother? Look what mustard gas is doing to her. By killing her husband it's indirectly killing her.'

He stood up to face his brother. 'It was all right for you, tucked away at school. I was the one who had to be her "little man" . . . I was the one who'd go and hold her hand when the loneliness was too much for her . . . And even years after he died I'd listen to her night after night as she cried herself to sleep. So don't tell *me* what mustard gas can do. I was the one who was there.'

Robert had walked to the door to show his brother out, but before he got there David had grabbed him and spun him round.

'Don't you dare tell me how you suffered being at home! You had it easy. No, it was because of you and your so-called "delicate" chest that I wasn't there . . . that I was bundled off to that dreadful school.'

Robert brushed David's hands away. 'Look, we both know there was nothing wrong with my chest – never has been. But how else do you expect a new mother to act? Her husband's just died and then her baby – the last thing they shared together – gets the same illness. Of course she was worried – and frightened. Can't you see it was nothing to do with her feelings about you, or me? It was because of *Father* I was kept home till I was thirteen. It was because she wanted to hold on to *him* that I was held back, and you were shoved forward. You were the bright one, and two years older. So she sent you to school as soon as she could afford it. And eventually I caught up . . . But how can you be so angry with her? She worked all the hours God gave, to give us an education, and all you want to do is abuse it. You make me sick.'

David picked up his hat. 'I make *you* sick? You really are a mummy's boy, aren't you? No guts, that's your trouble. And who the hell do you think you are to tell me what Mother did or didn't do for us? I know too well what she did, and what it cost her – what it's still costing her – which is why I thought you'd want to take up this offer. It's a chance, a chance for both of us to pay her back, to say "thank you". But you're so bloody high and mighty, you'd let your own selfish misguided principles stand in the way of helping your own mother!'

'That's below the belt, David. You know I do what I can – just like you – but I won't stoop to germ warfare. Do you know, I actually pity you? Getting on is one thing, but this . . .' Robert gave a sneer of disdain. 'I hope you and your money will be very happy together.' He moved back to the door and opened it for David.

'Oh, don't bother to show me out. I just hope you don't change your mind, because by then you'll be too late. I won't be back. In the future, if you need any help, don't come to me, baby brother.'

David had pulled his hat firmly on to his head and stormed past him, leaving him shaking with rage.

Since that occasion, the two men hadn't seen each other. Now they observed one another warily across the lab. It was David who made the first move, holding out his right hand to his younger brother. 'Funny how things turn out, isn't it?'

'Yes, I suppose it is.' Robert shook David's hand. 'And you should say that ultimately we both got what we wanted – you the position and money, me the chance to work with a research foundation whose work, in my mind at least, is totally ethical.'

David nodded his agreement at Robert. Nevertheless he wondered if Robert was really so naïve as to believe that none of the various divisions that made up the Rouget Corporation was involved in other, less high-minded, types of research. Well, David wasn't going to be the one to tell him; from his point of view, he would rather they were, if not exactly friends, at least on speaking terms.

Smiling, he said, 'We all make mistakes, Robert. At least we're finally working together, although how much our paths will cross I don't know. After all, you're with the Foundation and I'm with

105

the Corporation. However, if I know Cecil Rouget and his feelings about "family ties", I'm sure we'll meet socially at least.'

Suddenly the door behind the two men swung open and a blonde, plumpish young woman burst through the door, stopping abruptly as she saw David and Robert.

'Oh, dear! I knew I was going to be late! I'm Sally Chambers, your assistant and general lab technician. I double up, as we're still short-staffed. But I meant to be here and welcome you on your first day, and show you round. I'm sorry.'

'I'll leave you to get acquainted with Miss Chambers and your new lab. If you need anything, let me know.' David walked away through the preparation room.

Sally had taken off her jacket and was slipping on her white lab coat. 'Fancy a cuppa while I tell you what's what?'

Robert began to put on his own lab coat, which he had slung over his shoulder. 'Well, as I want to get started, I don't think we've got time to go over to the canteen –'

'Who said anything about the canteen?' Sally interrupted him with a wink and turned back into the preparation room. She went to the far end of the room and from a cupboard brought out a tin kettle, two mugs, tea and powdered milk as well as a packet of biscuits. 'I know we're not meant to do this in here. But it takes so long to go over to the canteen, I do sneak the occasional mug now and again.' She grinned at him as she lit the Bunsen burner and set the kettle over the flame.

'I should tell you off for taking liberties, shouldn't I?' said Robert with a smile.

Sally nodded her head. 'But you won't.'

Robert laughed. 'No, I won't, because I like the occasional cup of tea, too. Just don't get caught, or get me in trouble and thrown out before I've even started.'

Sally gave a chuckle, and busied herself making the tea. Once they had steaming mugs in their hands she began to show him round the lab that he could now call his. First there was the prep room itself. Here, carefully labelled, were the chemicals and apparatus. The poisons and more valuable items were stored in a locked cabinet. Sally had one key and she gave Robert the other, explaining that these were the only two in existence.

Then she led him out into the lab itself. Sinks, refrigerators, heating units and shelves lined the walls. In one corner was something that looked like an oversized cupboard. 'That's the dark-room,' Sally explained, lifting the heavy cloth covering the door to show him the small developing and printing area. In the middle of the lab was a wide, scrubbed wooden bench with a few stools tucked underneath it. The room was light and airy but the windows still had their blackout blinds rolled up above them, ready to be pulled down to darken the room if necessary. The smell of the acids and chemicals lingered and as Robert looked around he felt a lift of excitement to think that all of this would now be his to work with.

'You can't wait to get started, can you?' observed Sally, sensing his eagerness.

'No, I can't. Do you know how difficult it's been, undertaking the type of research I do? To come from a set-up like Corsmith – which was good, but lacked resources – to a place like the Rouget Foundation is . . . Well, it's like a dream come true. Especially as I've been given an open brief. Sally, it's what I've always wanted. I don't just want to find out about cures – I want to find out what causes disease in the first place.'

'But that's what I want to know,' said Sally excitedly. 'I mean, diseases like TB and polio. What causes them? How are they passed on? If we can discover patterns, we can start finding out how to prevent them, can't we? That's why I fought to be allowed to do this kind of work. I was going to train as a nurse – but, like you, I want to go that one step further . . . What do you think of Hench's findings about cortisone? I mean, do you think it might have any real effect?'

They began to talk about papers recently published in the *Lancet*, and anyone entering the lab on Robert Ghillyand's first morning would have thought that he and Sally Chambers had been working together as a team for many years.

Over the next months they developed a comfortable rapport. Not only did Robert discuss his ideas with Sally; she, in turn, began to put forward some of her own theories. Robert would listen intently, a contemplative frown on his face, and when she had finished would discuss the points raised, treating her as an equal, not merely as his assistant technician.

The lab that had been so empty when Robert had first arrived

107

began to take on a cluttered appearance as more and more experiments were set up. When these required precise monitoring, Robert quickly learned to rely on Sally's attention to detail and meticulous record-keeping. Often she stayed late to finish writing up her notes, or arrived early in order to set up the equipment for the day's work.

One morning they had stopped for an illicit cup of tea in the preparation room to discuss the results of a series of experiments with mould spores and natural sponges. The rows of Petri dishes and agar jelly had, after promising beginnings, showed no changes for several days.

'The question is: why? I was so sure that this time we'd got the calculations correct. And they were doing so well up until a few days ago,' said Robert, more to himself than to Sally.

Sally was equally puzzled. 'I don't think we've gone that wrong. Whatever it is, I feel we're almost there. I'm sure it's something really obvious but I couldn't tell you what. Have another look at my notes. Here . . . this is where we started this batch . . . See if you can spot what I've missed.'

She leaned across and gave him her notebook. As he took it from her, his hand brushed against her. Sally pulled it away suddenly, as if it had been burnt. Robert did not notice; he was once again scanning her neat records to see if he could identify what was eluding them.

Sally swallowed hard and turned to the sink to wash out her mug, hoping that Robert would not notice her flushed face. When Robert touched the side of her hand it was as if an electric current had passed through her. She was not a stupid woman and had known for the last few months that she felt more for Robert Ghillyand than she ought; yet she could not help it.

Are you aware of it too, I wonder? She stole a furtive sideways glance at Robert as she swilled the cloth round her mug, but he was engrossed in her notes. As always she dried the mug properly and spread the teacloth on the radiator; they had enough trouble with damp and mould in this outside corner of the prep room, especially now during the winter. As she smoothed the cloth, she again looked at Robert, resisting the urge to go and stand next to him, to put her arms round his shoulders or run her fingers through his auburn hair. She picked up her mug and bent to put it away in the cupboard; then a slow smile spread across her face.

'Give me those notes a minute.' She snatched the book from Robert.

'Hey, I was reading that!'

'I know . . . but I think I've got it. We've been going about this the wrong way. Look in the cupboard.'

'But there's nothing in there except the tea things.'

'And what else? Think about the cupboard itself.' Sally's eyes sparkled and her voice had risen.

'It's barely a cupboard – just doors built round an alcove. It hasn't even got sides or a back, just the original wall full of damp, mould, insects and . . . My God!'

Robert jumped off his stool and flung open the cupboard doors, tossing the tea things out behind him. Sally crouched next to him while he reached his hand into the back of the space. As he had remarked, the cupboard had no back, just the plastered bricks of the old building. Slowly he ran his fingers down the clammy plaster, then pulled them out and inspected the black mould smeared on his fingertips.

'You're right. Christ, I feel such a fool! It's so bloody obvious. Here we are, spending weeks trying to develop moulds on natural sponges so we can start refining them. And all the time we've been heading in totally the wrong direction. I can't believe we didn't see it before. Trying to grow fruit and milk moulds in bright, dry conditions is one thing – but mildew . . . common or garden mildew! How often have we stood here and remarked on the smell of the damp cupboard. Damp doesn't smell, but what it produces does. It's literally been under our noses all the time!'

'Well, we worked it out eventually,' said Sally, still squatting next to him on the floor.

'Sally, you're wonderful!' He turned to look at her, grabbed her suddenly by the shoulders and planted a kiss on her forehead. She was so surprised that when he let go she toppled over. Robert laughed as he helped her up. 'Are you game to start again? Right now?'

'Of course,' she replied, cursing herself for feeling that same tingle.

Sal, this has got to stop! she told herself severely as she busied herself round the prep room and lab, clearing away dishes with bits of decaying fruit, week-old milk and samples of natural, untreated sponges.

No sooner had she thrown out the old tests than she began setting up the new ones in the cupboard. As always Sally carefully watched and recorded the changes in each dish, observing how quickly the mildew attached itself to each sample of sponge and noting down the catalyst, the other substance in each dish. As the tea things made way for more and more Petri dishes, the musty smell of mildew increased and this time they could almost see the samples growing before their eyes.

For the next week Sally left her bedroom at her parents' home in Radlett at seven o'clock to catch the bus at ten past. Each day Robert was already there. As they continued to get the desired results, the sense of companionship between them grew stronger. It was prompted by their mutual expectant hope that they would succeed in their goal. Yet for Sally it was a bitter-sweet feeling; maybe they had only known each other for six months, but she was head over heels in love with the man who was her boss. And Robert was concerned with nothing but his work.

'Sally, I can't ask you to give up the Christmas party.' Robert was gazing at her with his usual thoughtful frown.

'You're not asking. I'm volunteering,' she said firmly, thinking to herself: *You fool, Robert. Can't you see I'd rather be anywhere with you than at a Christmas party?* Carefully she touched her lab coat pocket, where she had placed a lone sprig of mistletoe. It had been growing on the oak tree by the bus stop and she had snapped a piece off as she waited for the bus. *It's the best excuse yet for a proper kiss*, she had told herself determinedly as she handed over the fare.

It was mid-afternoon when Sally began to set out the necessary tubes, funnels, evaporating dishes and jars. The Christmas party that Cecil Rouget held each year for his staff's children was just beginning, supervised by the housekeeper Jane MacKay. Mrs MacKay was assisted by staff from the Rouget Clinic, the twenty-bed private hospital and nursing home which was connected to the Rouget Foundation. Cecil none the less supported Aneurin Bevan's National Health Service because it would create a demand for more drugs and boost the output and therefore the profits of the Rouget Corporation.

Sally could hear the local orchestra (which would later perform at the adults' party that evening) playing 'Oranges and Lemons' and the squeals of the children as they were caught by the 'chopper'. She hummed along with the familiar tune as she pulled down the blinds against the late afternoon dusk, shutting out the lights from festivities over in the Manor House.

As she secured the last blind, Robert pushed his way backwards through the door from the prep room, carrying a tray with jars full of sponges and mould.

'These are all number one jars,' he said as he carefully lowered it on to the bench. 'Ah, good. All ready. You know what I want to do. Extract the moisture from this' – he indicated a jar – 'to start isolating the active enzymes.'

He picked up one of the jars and deposited its contents evenly in the evaporation jar. This he suspended in a water bath on the stand over the Bunsen burner; into the top of the jar he placed a bung with a glass tube projecting from it. Slowly he turned up the heat under the water, watching as it began to bubble.

Sally watched closely, noting down the degrees by which the heat was increased. The sponge began to shrivel in the heat and the mould floated in the jar. Steam drifted out of the glass funnel, leaving behind a greasy, sooty residue. Neither of them spoke; the only sounds were the hissing of the burner, the bubbling of the water, the scratch of Sally's pen and faintly, from the other side of the blinds, the noise of the Christmas parties as the children's ended and the adults' began.

Painstakingly they set up jar after jar. In some cases they collected the steam being emitted from contents; in others they bubbled it through water or acids, distilling it into other jars. Each time Sally kept a record of what they had done and ensured that the same twelve sets of experiments and methods were used for all fifteen different sets of sponge and mould cultures. It was close to ten o'clock when they finished.

Robert turned off the burner and Sally stretched as she put down her pen. 'I'll open the blinds,' she said as she jumped off her stool. She swayed a little as she walked to the windows. 'Wheee!' she exclaimed as she unwound the cord and released the blind. It rattled upwards with a clatter and she giggled.

'What's the matter with you?' asked Robert, laughing at her.

'It went whoosh!' she explained. She waved at the blind and

111

moved on to the next one. 'See?' she said as she let that go too. 'It's fun!' She was unsteady on her feet.

'Let me try,' said Robert, walking towards the window.

Sally handed him the cord. With great glee he followed her example and let it roll itself up. As it did so, it took the cord with it, and this wrapped itself around the roll of cloth at the top of the window above their heads. Sally began to laugh, and Robert joined in.

'We'll be in terrible trouble if we don't get it down.' Sally held her fingers across her mouth.

'I'll get it down.' Robert heaved himself up on to the shelves under the window and, wobbling, slowly stood upright. He grinned down at Sally, forgetting why he had climbed up there in the first place. 'I bet I can get all the way round the room without stepping on the floor.'

He set off, edging his way from the shelves to the sinks and heating units. Where necessary he dropped to his hands and knees and when he came to the dark-room he paused for a moment before gripping the top edge of the curtain rail and swinging round it, his feet dangling near, but not touching, the floor. When he returned to his starting-point, Sally jumped up and down, clapping her hands.

'Me too! Me too!' she cried, and scrambled up on to the shelves beside him.

Once again Robert set off, showing Sally the footholds as they made their way round the room. They reached the dark-room and, as before, Robert swung round it successfully but when Sally tried she didn't push hard enough. She missed her footing and fell in a heap on the floor.

'I win! I win!' Robert crowed from on top of the bench.

Sally had been examining the palm of her hand and now looked up at him, her eyes filling with tears. 'Look,' she said, holding her hand up to show him. 'I cut myself.'

Sure enough there was a deep gash in the palm of her hand and because she was lifting it up to Robert the blood was running down her wrist and on to the sleeve of her white lab coat where it began to make a red stain. Robert jumped down, obviously worried.

'We should do something about that.' He seemed a little scared at the sight of so much blood.

'It doesn't hurt.'

She shook her head widely from side to side, leaped to her feet and wiped her hand childishly against her hip, smearing the blood further across her coat. They glanced at each other for a moment; then Sally gave a giggle and sprang up on to the bench again.

'Come on, last one to the window's a sissy!'

'That's not fair! You started before me!' yelled Robert as he jumped up beside her.

As they caught up with each other, they stood in a basin under the window. Sally's hand was still bleeding badly but she didn't notice it. Instead she was gazing out of the window across to the Manor House.

'Oooh, look! It's a party!'

She pressed her nose to the window and Robert did the same, putting his arm round her waist.

'You'll squash it, you'll squash it!' she cried, feeling upset at the harm Robert might do, and she plunged her hand into her pocket to rescue the sprig of mistletoe.

It looked bedraggled as she dangled it between her fingers. Still standing in the sink, she held it over their heads and lifted her face, eyes closed and mouth puckered, towards Robert. Robert put his arms around her and gave her a smacking kiss on her waiting lips.

'No. Kiss me properly.'

Robert did as he was told. Sally dropped the mistletoe and her arm came down to join the other one she had already wrapped round his neck.

'What the hell are you two doing?'

David had entered the lab without either of them hearing him. Sally looked at him over her shoulder and she tightened her hold on Robert, suddenly feeling afraid of David. Robert had pulled Sally closer, as if trying to protect her.

'We can go all round the lab without standing on the floor,' Robert announced proudly.

David stared in amazement at the two white-coated figures standing in the sink with their arms around each other.

'Cecil told me to come and find out why you weren't at the party. Now I think I know. What on earth is that odd smell in here? It's making me feel ill.'

He gazed round the room, trying to identify its source. Noticing the apparatus on the benches, he walked across the lab and peered at the various labelled solutions and residues that Sally had set out on the trays ready to put away. As Robert crawled out of the sink and helped Sally down, David eyed them both.

'What exactly have you been extracting in here?'

Robert slapped a hand over Sally's mouth. 'Sssh! It's a secret.'

David glanced at the notebook lying open on the desk. Seeing him look down, Sally pulled away from Robert and shot across the room. She grabbed the notebook and held it behind her back. Her lower lip trembled and she looked as if she were going to cry.

'It's mine!' she almost shouted. 'Robert, tell him he can't look!'

Her pulse had increased; she could feel her heart beating against her ribs. Beads of sweat had broken out on her top lip and she was beginning to shake.

David was observing both of them closely, fascinated. Then he glimpsed Sally's lab coat.

'Good God! What on earth have you done?'

He involuntarily moved forward, startled by the sight of the blood, even though his experience told him that the size of the stain was probably out of all proportion to the injury.

Sally let out a small mewing sound of terror and darted behind Robert.

'I only want to help.' David tried to sound reassuring. What had they been up to? 'Let me have a look.'

After glancing at Robert for his approval, Sally slowly walked towards him, holding her hand out in front of her. David cast an eye over the gash in her hand and then studied Sally's face. Whatever she had done should have hurt, and hurt badly, but all she seemed to be feeling was fear of him. The hand didn't seem to be bothering her at all.

As if to confirm his observations she said, 'It doesn't hurt, not at all.'

'I still think it should be looked at. As for whatever else you've been up to . . . Well, I don't know what it is . . . But something's had a very odd effect on you. You're both as high as kites! It's quite a party trick.'

'The party!' Sally pointed over her shoulder out of the window to the festivities taking place opposite. 'Come on, let's go!'

Her fear had totally evaporated as quickly as it had come; it was as if her emotions had changed just because she'd seen something cheerful. David was interested to note that before Sally dragged

Robert out of the room, she was not so befuddled that she didn't secure her notebook; nor did she leave the lab or prep rooms unlocked. After one last look round the lab, David sniffed the air warily before he too was hauled out to the party.

Cautiously Sally pushed at the lab door with her shoulder. It was unlocked, so she wasn't surprised to see Robert sitting at the bench holding one of the jars from the night before. Even though it was a cold December day, the windows were open, but a strange pungent smell still lingered in the lab.

'Tell me we didn't do what I think we did,' Sally greeted Robert.

'Which bit?'

'Did we really make everyone play "Oranges and Lemons"?'

'Oh yes. And we tried to make them walk round the room without touching the floor.' Robert glanced up at her. 'What have you done to your arm?' he asked, worried by the sight of the sling she was wearing.

'It's that cut I got yesterday. You know, it was fine last night – didn't hurt at all. But now it's got a dozen stitches in it and it hurts like hell.' She shuddered as she recalled their antics of the previous night. 'God, Robert. What on earth did we inhale yesterday?'

'That's what I intend to find out. It was powerful stuff. We must have been breathing it in for at least six hours, if not longer. There's one thing I want to ask. Tell me what you remember – about how you felt and how you feel now. Including what you remember about that injury.' He put out his hand to gently touch her bandaged one. Instinctively she lifted her free hand to protect the hurt one, then apologised.

'Sorry, but it really is very sore.'

'Will you be able to work?' Robert sounded genuinely concerned.

'Of course. I might be a bit slower than usual, but at least it's not my right hand. Look, I'll get my notebook and we'll write all this down.'

By the time Sally returned to the bench with her book, Robert had a cup of coffee ready for her and they began to compare notes. Both admitted to feeling horrible that morning, with headaches, stomach cramps, nausea and a peculiar tingling sensation in their limbs, which felt heavy and leaden.

115

'What about last night?' asked Robert. 'Can you remember any-thing of how you felt then?'

'Yes, unfortunately I can. Most of the time I felt really good, even when I did this.' She nodded at her hand. 'Quite euphoric, in fact. But there were moments when I felt exactly the opposite, absolutely terrified. Like when we were walking round the room. I was really scared I was going to touch the floor and when I fell off . . . You know, it's odd . . . but I was more "hurt", if you like, by the fact that I'd fallen – rather than because I'd physically injured myself . . . if you see what I mean.'

'Go on.'

'I mean any pain I felt wasn't a physiological reaction transmitted across synapses to the central nervous system. It was different – more an emotional pain and a fear of the pain itself. For a split second I'd have done anything – and I mean anything – to have avoided that. Then I spotted the party . . . and it was as if that was the only thing that mattered. As if I was responding to whatever the immediate stimulus was. Like when David came into the room.'

Sally groaned as she remembered their conversation with him, shaking her head as if she were trying to wipe it out.

'When he came in,' she continued, 'I felt really scared again, really threatened. Not that he knew it. But when he was trying to read this' – she indicated the notebook – 'I was absolutely petrified. It wouldn't have taken much to get it away from me. Anyway, Robert, how about you?'

'Much the same. I know exactly what you mean about feeling threatened. When David wanted to look at your hand – and like you I was afraid he might hurt you – well . . .' Realising he was about to say something he might regret, Robert changed tack. 'You know how people say you can taste fear?' Sally nodded. 'Well, I could. I really could taste it. Hell, I was scared of my own brother, just because he asked me a few, not unreasonable, questions!'

'And what about the other end of the scale?' Sally asked softly, keeping her eyes on her notes. Although she dared not look at him, she wanted him to tell her how he had felt when he thought she was in danger.

Robert glanced at the sink, remembering their kiss and the sen-sations it had aroused. Then he saw Sally's face and chuckled. 'We must have looked ridiculous!' He ran his fingers through his hair, turning away from her, embarrassed. 'Of course, the good bits

116

made me feel very good indeed.' He paused before continuing quickly, 'Sally, would you like to go out with me?'

Inwardly Sally felt a surge of delight. Outwardly she smiled shyly at Robert. 'Yes, please.'

Robert let out a sigh of relief and smiled back. 'Good, because I've been trying to pluck up the courage to ask you for ages, and didn't know how. After last night it would've been silly *not* to ask.'

Before Sally could speak there was a knock. Without waiting to be told to come in, one of the office runners poked his head round the door of the laboratory.

'Mr Rouget wants to see you both in his office immediately, with any notes on what you was brewin' last night. Boy, am I glad I ain't in your shoes!' He disappeared as abruptly as he had arrived.

'You do realise', said Robert, straightening his tie, 'that the entire staff of the Corporation, Foundation and Clinic saw our performance.'

'Don't remind me.' Sally picked up her notes. 'Let's go and face the music!'

On their way to Cecil Rouget's office on the first floor of the Manor House, they passed a number of people. Some made ribald remarks; some grinned and winked at them; others stared after them, saying nothing until they had gone by, then whispered in huddles. Miss Wilmot greeted them in her usual impassive manner, giving away nothing about their likely reception from Cecil.

She buzzed on her intercom. 'Dr Ghillyand and Miss Chambers are here for you now, Mr Rouget.' They heard the distant voice tell her to 'Send them straight in.'

They knocked on the door and were surprised when it was opened by David. Cecil was sitting behind his large desk. The light from the ornate chandelier gave the room a warm glow. In front of the desk were three seats.

David settled himself comfortably in a winged chair. He crossed one elegant leg over the other, smoothing the creases in his trousers, and indicated that Robert and Sally should take the other two chairs by the desk. As they sat down, Miss Wilmot brought in a tray with coffee. Cecil waited until they all had a cup and saucer in their hands. Once Miss Wilmot had left the room, he sat back and looked at Robert and Sally across the expanse of his desk.

'Please relax. I'm not planning to punish you for your behaviour last night. I think you have punished yourselves enough. Everyone

117

saw you, so reprimands are unnecessary. How's that hand, by the way?' Sally mumbled that it was fine, and Cecil continued, the niceties out of the way. 'No, what I want to know is precisely what you were working on. What made you act as you did?'

Robert thought carefully before he answered. 'Mr Rouget, whatever happened last night was not intentional. But I do think the work will prove to be very useful. We've been developing basic material to try and extract residues. Last night we were starting to produce those residues.'

'But what exactly for?' Cecil leaned forward a little.

Robert took a deep breath. Explaining research projects to Cecil was always difficult. His staff knew that, despite his basic training as a pharmacist in Austria before the First World War, his understanding of modern pharmaceutical matters was not good; it was his business acumen that mattered. Robert knew the next five minutes would prove crucial to him. If he could persuade Cecil that his project would lead to sound financial profits in the future, he would be allowed to carry on. If not, Cecil Rouget could stop his work and push him in another direction.

'Enzymes,' he began. 'I want to look at enzymes and pain control. Look, when you hurt yourself, various chemical processes occur in the body to help protect it. Some of those chemical reactions assist with pain control; others tell you where and why you're hurting in the first place. What I want to do is identify the chemicals that help to control the pain and re-create them synthetically in the lab, so they can be used as painkillers. When you have an operation, it's often not the invasive surgery that's so tiring – it's the way the body peaks and troughs as it tries to cope with the pain. Pain is exhausting. Control the pain and you have better results. Hospitals become more efficient, and operations take less time, so more people can be treated.'

Cecil nodded his head. 'Yes, that makes sound economic sense. And the first company to market such a chemical – such a drug – could . . .' He left unsaid the rest of the sentence, about making a lot of money, but everyone guessed what he was thinking. 'So what happened last night to make you think you're succeeding?'

Sally raised her bandaged hand. 'This did. I cut myself quite badly and didn't feel any pain.'

'Hmm. How soon can I have a report on my desk about your experiments?'

'Well, it'll take a bit of time. You see we obviously inhaled something last night, but whatever it was had some nasty side-effects. I'm rather nervous of releasing anything too soon. I mean, we've yet to backtrack through the notes and find out exactly which experiment gave these results. The trouble is, with fifteen variants in cultures as base material, and the twelve extraction tests we've been running on each, we can't yet tell you which combination caused that effect.'

David, who had been listening to his brother, suddenly asked, 'So did you keep notes?'

'Of course we did, Dr Ghillyand,' Sally replied indignantly. 'Just because you saw me acting like a six-year-old doesn't mean I'm not professional in all laboratory ethics and procedures.'

'I'm not saying it does. You have the notes with you?'

David held out his hand for her book, and Sally stretched over to pass it to him. He began to study it, quickly scanning the early pages which detailed the methods they were intending to use. He flipped through the notebook, checking the information. Towards the end he paused, and began to read Sally's notes more closely.

'What have you found, David?' asked Cecil quietly.

'Nothing to tell us what caused the effects, but I can tell you roughly when it happened. Look.'

He offered the book first to Cecil, then to Robert and Sally, pointing from one page to the next as he did so. On the left-hand page Sally's handwriting neatly recorded the specific features of their experiments. On the right-hand page the account continued with the same attention to detail, but the handwriting had changed. It was obviously Sally's, but it looked younger, as if it had been written by a child.

'Let me see that.' Robert grabbed the book back and read Sally's notes. 'It would appear to be the batches done with the Kalymnian sponges rather than the Cuban ones, and the amylase with the sulphuric acid.'

Cecil rubbed his chin thoughtfully. 'I want that report. I want to know all that you did and all of the results. I also want notes on what you remember about last night – your symptoms, your reactions. You will also have a full medical examination at the Clinic. Finally I want you to carry on working on this until I say stop. Anything else you are doing must cease immediately. Redo the experiments. But this time you will work with the equipment in an isolation tank. And you will use rats.'

Robert opened his mouth as if to speak, but Cecil waved him down.

'Now, Robert, don't argue. When you joined the Corporation I gave you *carte blanche*, to work as you saw fit. You shall be allowed that freedom again when you have completed this extra task.' He emphasised the word 'extra'. 'Now go. I expect your reports before we close on Christmas Eve.'

'But that only gives us two days!' said Sally, incredulously.

'Well, off you go and get on with it, then.' Cecil buzzed Miss Wilmot, who opened the door; it was clear the interview was over. As they all started to leave, Cecil called out, 'One moment, David. Please stay. I wish to discuss something else with you.'

Once the door had shut behind Robert and Sally, David settled back into his seat.

'You do realise the commercial implications of this, don't you?' Cecil asked him. David nodded. 'It is probably a long way off, but I want you to watch those two and keep me informed. I want to know about any chemicals, materials or equipment they request; and I want them to have it. In the New Year I will need you to go out to Kalymnos. I want reports on sponge supplies – and I also think it's a good idea to remind those lazy bastards that they work for me. Please ask Miss Wilmot to make the arrangements.'

The intercom buzzed on Cecil's desk again and the door opened.

'You don't have to worry about announcing me,' said Elizabeth as she entered the room. 'Papa's always pleased to see me, aren't you?' She walked round the desk and kissed her father's cheek, then sat on the arm of his chair and leaned on his shoulder.

'You know exactly how happy I am to see you.' The cold demeanour of the businessman had been instantly replaced by the smiles of a loving father.

'Now, Papa, I bet you haven't asked David yet, have you?' She was gently teasing him, and David raised an eyebrow in wry bemusement at the total adoration on the older man's face as he looked at his daughter.

'It's your invitation. You ask him, my love.'

'Papa and I would be delighted if you would be our guest at Christmas lunch on Sunday.'

It was more a statement than a question. Although David was

120

not doing anything to celebrate Christmas, he had hoped to let the day pass quietly. Yet he could not refuse.

'Good, that's all agreed, then. Now off you go and let me earn a few pence so I can buy you a lovely present.' Cecil kissed his daughter, who slid off the arm of his chair and walked back round the desk to wait for David as he rose from his seat. Opening the door for her, he indicated that she should lead the way.

'I am glad we're spending Christmas together. It'll be so cosy. Bring a pair of walking shoes. We might go out after lunch to the lake. Papa likes a sleep after a big meal, and Mrs MacKay will certainly ensure we have loads to eat. I'll see you at about midday on Sunday, then.'

As Elizabeth was going down the stairs ahead of him, she suddenly sat sideways on the smooth wooden banister and slid down it, laughing, to the ground floor. Then she turned and blew him a kiss before she disappeared into the private wing of the Manor House.

'I can't breathe! You shut the window so I wouldn't get any air! Let me out of here! I'll tell Papa what you're doing to me!'

Elizabeth pushed the blankets off the bed and tried to walk across to the door, but her legs gave way underneath her.

'What is going on in here?'

Sister Browning had been talking to Matron at the other end of the corridor and had heard the noise from there. Other members of staff scuttled past Elizabeth's door, not wanting to be drawn into the situation, grateful that Elizabeth Rouget was not their patient. After making her excuses to Matron, Sister Browning had bustled into Elizabeth's room to investigate. Sobbing uncontrollably on the floor in front of her in a crumpled heap was Elizabeth. Nurses Edith Jones and Rose Haggerty were trying to help her to her feet.

'She was hyperventilating . . . getting herself all worked up,' explained Rose as they successfully got Elizabeth back into bed.

'They're trying to kill me, Sister.'

Elizabeth raised a tear-stained face to the stocky middle-aged woman standing at the foot of the bed, and for a moment Sister Browning actually felt sorry for her. She was pale, and her skin had the translucent appearance of someone who had been gravely ill.

121

Trying to push home her advantage, Elizabeth gave another little sob, but she had overplayed her hand and Sister Browning's resolve toughened again.

'Nonsense! I think it's time you realised, young lady, that as far as you are concerned I am in charge and no amount of posturing and performing from you is going to change that. Now, I'm sorry you're still not well enough to go to *The Third Man* première on Friday night. It's all we've heard about. But you're not going, and accusations against my staff won't change that either. You're almost better, and the sooner you learn to do as you're told the sooner you'll be out of here.'

Sister Browning turned to Edith. 'Nurse Jones, tidy that bed and then join Nurse Haggerty in my office. And if I hear so much as a peep out of you, my girl . . .'

She left the threat hanging in the air and swept out of the room, the two staff nurses following in her wake.

'Jones, Haggerty . . . I've told you before. Just because Miss Elizabeth is Mr Rouget's daughter, she thinks she can get her own way. Her hyperventilation is the equivalent of a child's tantrum. So I'd ask you both to remember that and respond accordingly. Elizabeth has had a nasty attack of influenza but that is all. Now go and get on with your work, both of you.'

Edith and Rose gratefully left Sister Browning and went back to join Ruby, with whom they had been making swabs in the store cupboard when Elizabeth had started yelling.

'The old bag!' said Edith with feeling as she packed the cotton wool into another swab. A shortish, thin, fair-haired woman in her mid-thirties, Edith Jones had been friends with Rose Haggerty ever since they trained together. 'Honestly, Rosie, I'd like to see her cope with that, that –'

'Cat?' Rose was even shorter than her friend, with a rounded figure and dark hair piled up under her starched butterfly cap. She counted the swabs and began packing drums.

Edith laughed. 'Yes, Elizabeth's just like a cat. Stroke and soothe her and she positively purrs at you. But if you so much as go near her when she doesn't want you, then out come the claws.'

'Hello, Edith . . . Rose . . . May I go in and see Elizabeth?'

The two nurses looked at each other, uncertain how much of their conversation Dr David Ghillyand had heard. Rose nodded her head, making her cap rustle, and David set off down the corridor to

Elizabeth's room, where he knocked on the door and waited for her response before going in.

Elizabeth's eyes lit up when she saw her visitor, the dramas of a few minutes ago forgotten. 'David, how nice of you to come and see me! It's the third time this week. People will begin to talk,' she said, teasing him.

'No, they won't. Especially as I've come to say goodbye. I'm off to Greece on Saturday for about six weeks.' David was standing by the window with his back to her as he spoke, his voice unemotional.

'It won't stop me, David,' she cried, her gentleness evaporating. 'I intend to have you. And, since I always get what I want, you haven't a hope in hell!' she finished triumphantly.

David turned to face her. 'Elizabeth, what more do I have to do to make you realise I'm not interested in you? You're a child – you bore me!'

He was leaning over the trolley across her bed, speaking softly but firmly. Despite the way the words hurt her Elizabeth didn't take her eyes off him. Before he could straighten up she had pushed the covers off her bed and knelt up; then she wrapped her arms round his neck and pulled him towards her.

David was taken by surprise and, as she pressed her lips against his, his mouth opened automatically, his tongue meeting hers. With his arms round her back, he could feel her warm skin through her nightgown and was keenly aware she had nothing on underneath it. Suddenly he seemed to realise what he was doing and pushed her away.

Elizabeth lay back on her pillows and laughed at him. 'You say you're not interested in me, but you can't help yourself, can you? Poor David, you tell me I'm a child but you don't think it, do you? I could give you the key to everything you want – but you can't have it without me as well. Think about it while you're in Greece. You know Papa will look after his son-in-law. Now go away, I'm tired.'

She stretched her arms above her head and scrambled back under the bedclothes, allowing David a flash of her thigh before he walked out of the door.

Damn the woman! he swore to himself as he strode purposefully back to his office, not realising that only minutes before he had thought of her as a girl. *She's right, and she knows it. Maybe I should marry her*. He stopped and viewed the buildings and land around him, envisaging himself as their owner, but the image of Elizabeth laughing at him made him shake his head and carry on his way.

Ever since the night of the Christmas party, Robert and Sally had been working hard re-creating their experiments to reproduce the same residues and solutions they had previously extracted. Having already done the work once, they were finding it both boring and frustrating, when they were eager to carry on to the next stage. Therefore they were both keen to get through it as fast as possible, yet knew they must be as thorough as before.

After their meeting with Cecil Rouget, David had made a point of coming to the lab to see them. When he made his visit, Sally was on her own.

David greeted her warmly. 'I just wanted to say that I'm sorry you're having to redo all this.' He indicated their work with a sweep of his hand. 'It can be quite a bore going over old ground sometimes, can't it?'

Sally flushed a little; his words echoed her feelings, but she simply nodded her agreement, willing him to go away so she could get on.

'Look,' David continued, 'I feel slightly responsible. After all, if I hadn't seen you two, Cecil would never have known until you were ready to present him with your full findings.'

'Yes, I know,' Sally said tightly.

'I can't help that now, I'm afraid. But maybe I can help in another way?' Sally tipped her head quizzically as David carried on. 'I know rewriting the notes can be as much of a nuisance as redoing the work.'

'Yes, it certainly can.' Sally spoke with feeling. 'Especially since the research secretaries are trying to get their own work out of the way before Christmas. They just can't cope with this lot as well.'

'I thought that might be the case. So if you like I'll get Miss Grigson, my secretary, to type them up for you. Pop them over to her each day, and she'll push them out in no time – well, it'll certainly be quicker than you writing them up, won't it?'

'Do you mean it?'

It was David's turn to nod.

'That will help no end. You're right, of course – redoing the tests is definitely holding things up. Robert – I mean, Dr Ghillyand – and I are keen to get on to the next stage . . . Oh, but I wonder . . . Could I ask a favour?'

'Go on.'

'Well, it sounds silly . . . but I'd be grateful if you didn't mention to Robert that your secretary was typing the notes for me. He feels it's important to keep the Foundation's work confidential. Don't misunderstand me. I'm sure he wouldn't mind *your* secretary doing this – after all it's really part of the same thing, isn't it? It's just probably better not to bother him with it.'

She and Robert had already had one heated debate about the commercial aspects of the Rouget Corporation's development work, and how it relied upon the Foundation's efforts for its research material.

'Don't worry, Sally . . . I won't say a word. And I'll also make sure that Miss Grigson doesn't either.'

David had returned to his own office to give Clare Grigson firm instructions about the notes that Sally Chambers would be bringing over to her. 'I know you always keep a carbon copy, but this time I want two copies of everything you type up for her. *All* of it, no matter how trivial it may be. And as I've been asked by Miss Chambers to make sure my brother doesn't know that you're helping her out, I've promised her you won't tell a soul.'

The system had worked smoothly. Once the original experiments had been redone and Robert and Sally had been allowed to move on with their work, Clare Grigson continued to type up Sally's notes; on his return from Greece, David had insisted she did so. Clare told Sally that it didn't take her long each evening, and Sally was so grateful that she didn't have to spend time bent over her battered old typewriter that she happily let her continue. Robert accepted the neatly typed notes from Sally, not thinking to question when she had time to prepare them for him, even though she was with him all day in the laboratory, and lately had been spending most evenings with him too.

'Robert, it's six-thirty. Why don't we pretend we're human beings for once? Let's finish now, and go into Watford to see *Mr Blandings Builds his Dream House*? It's the new Cary Grant film at the Odeon.' Sally flexed her fingers and put her pen down.

Robert was still fiddling with the equipment in the isolation chamber, unaware that she had said anything. Sally got off her stool and walked round the other side of the bench, waiting until he had finished what he was doing before tapping him on the shoulder.

'I said, what about breaking off now and going to see a film?'

Robert considered for a moment before agreeing. 'I tell you what, I could even treat you to fish and chips afterwards.'

When they got outside it was drizzling. 'You wait here and I'll go and get the car.' Robert darted off, taking the umbrella with him. While she was waiting under the porch the rain suddenly got heavier and two figures who were walking over from the Clinic began to head for cover. As they ran under the porch, Sally stepped to one side to give them room.

'Thank you. We thought we'd make it to the bus stop before it got worse, but we mistimed it. Isn't it horrible?' said Edith Jones.

Sally peered out at the rain, looking for Robert. 'Yes . . . I hope we don't have to park too far from the cinema.'

'Oh, that's where we're going!' said Rose Haggerty. 'It's our night off, and we both adore Cary Grant, so we thought we'd treat ourselves. Edith, if we don't run for it we'll miss the bus.'

'Hang on a minute,' said Sally. 'Here's Robert. I'm sure we can squeeze you in.'

Robert of course agreed to giving Edith and Rose a lift; they got in the back of the car while Sally climbed in the front. Although they didn't know each other well, they had all seen each other around. Besides, Robert and Sally's performance at the Christmas party had turned them into local celebrities, recognisable to most of the staff employed by the Rouget organisations. As Robert concentrated on his driving Edith and Rose chattered excitedly about the film. Sally joined in whenever a question was directed at her; but most of the time she sat listening to the two women in the back.

When they reached the cinema Robert let all three of them off so they could queue. As Sally got out of the car, he leaned across the seat. 'If you get to the front before I arrive, get the two-and-fourpenny seats . . . Here's the money.' He handed her a ten-shilling note.

'Robert, that's unnecessary. The one-and-nines will do perfectly well.' A car behind was honking its horn.

'Don't argue. I don't want to have to sit with those two! All right, I'm going,' he said to the car behind as Sally slammed the door and joined Edith and Rose under the cover of the canopy.

'He's ever so nice, that Dr Ghillyand. Don't you think so, Edith?'

Edith agreed with Rose and then blushed when Robert ran up to the queue, meeting them at the ticket office.

'Ah, here you are.'

Robert let Edith and Rose go before them in the queue and when he and Sally got inside the women were waiting for them. 'Thank you for the lift, Dr Ghillyand. Enjoy the film,' said Edith.

'You too, girls.' And he steered Sally towards the stairs leading to the circle.

They settled into their seats as the lights were going down. Sally grinned to herself at the thought that Robert was prepared to be so extravagant just to be alone with her. After the film was over, they stood for the national anthem but when the lights came up Robert made Sally sit down again.

'I'm not being mean, but I don't want to bump into Edith and Rose again. Let's give them time to get out before we leave.'

They remained seated while everyone around them scrambled into soggy raincoats and untangled umbrellas from among the debris of ice-cream cartons under the seats.

'It was a good film, wasn't it?' Robert asked hesitantly, as if trying to make conversation.

Sally turned in her seat and gave him a quizzical look. Usually Robert was relaxed, and the tone of his voice surprised her.

'Very. But have you ever seen a bad Cary Grant film?'

He shook his head. 'You know, *I'd* like to do that one day.'

'What?' The conversation was growing even more strained.

'Like Mr Blandings . . . build my dream house. Of course, to do it I'd need to have the right person with me. Someone who could put up with all the mess and chaos. Someone who wouldn't be too worried about things being just so.'

Sally's heart sank. As Robert carried on talking she thought she was going to cry. Earlier she had been so happy when he insisted that they sat upstairs; now she realised it was not because he wanted to be alone with her but because he genuinely did not want to sit with Edith and Rose. Suddenly she knew that he was going to tell her it was over. He had been odd all evening, not once attempting to hold her hand or put an arm round her. It had felt as if there was a greater physical barrier than just the armrest between them.

127

'I'm sorry, sir, madam, but we're closing now.'

They glanced up at the usherette and, trying not to let her feelings show, Sally struggled into her coat, resisting Robert's attempts to help her.

Robert insisted on stopping to buy the promised fish and chips, but they ate them in the car in a silence that continued on the way home, while the rain still beat against the windscreen and the wipers swept it from side to side. Suddenly Robert slammed on the brakes.

'I can't stand this any longer. What do you say?'

Sally gave him a startled look. 'What about?'

'What about?' he queried. 'Sally, weren't you listening back there in the cinema? I was asking you to marry me!'

Sally stared at him. Then she began to giggle before throwing her head back and roaring with laughter. Now it was Robert's turn to look startled.

'What's so funny?'

'Oh, Robert, of course I'll marry you.' Sally did not know whether to laugh or cry. 'I thought you were trying to tell me it was all over!' She reached over and kissed him. As she pulled away, Robert saw the tears streaming down her face.

'You daft h'ap'orth.' He laughed as he used his handkerchief to mop her eyes. 'Do you really think I could imagine life without you?'

'I do love you,' said Sally. She took the handkerchief from him and blew her nose loudly.

Robert gently let out the clutch and released the handbrake. Sally leaned her head on his shoulder, and carefully he drove through the rain back to Elstree.

'Lady Quigland! Papa, how could you? We've already discussed this. I told you I would not have that woman present me at court.' Elizabeth scowled at her father across the dining-table. 'She still treats me as if I were five years old. Every time I see her she pats me on the head like some little lap-dog. Papa, she's ghastly!'

For once Cecil Rouget refused to be deterred by his daughter. He sighed and went over the old argument. 'My love, I know she's a bit of a relic . . . But she does know everyone who is anyone in London. She's highly respected and, most important, she is your guarantee of a successful Season.'

Elizabeth pushed her food round her plate with her fork as she considered what her father said. He was determined that she would come out into society with style, and find herself a suitable husband. Elizabeth knew that her father's notion of a suitable husband was one with a title. She couldn't tell him she planned to marry David Ghillyand – not yet. She must make him believe it was his own idea, or that of somebody he trusted. Elizabeth picked up her water glass and sipped it thoughtfully. *Maybe Lady Quigland isn't such a bad choice after all, she mused. I could use her to influence Papa and also make sure I choose where and when I have my ball.*

Elizabeth suddenly beamed at her father. 'I'm sorry, Papa. You're right. Lady Quigland does know her way around, so we really should take her advice. You said she didn't advise having my Coming-Out Ball here at the Manor House? Well, if she says we're too far outside London, then we should listen to her.' Elizabeth rose from the table and walked to the other end, where her father was sitting. She dropped to her knees, looking up at him from under her lashes. 'Do you think we're too late to book Claridges?'

Cecil looked down at her and stroked her chestnut curls as she rested her chin on her folded arms on his lap. Elizabeth could sense his disappointment at not being able to show off his daughter in his own home to the people he thought mattered, but she was determined to have her own way. Gracefully she stood up and took his hand.

'Come on, Papa. Let me pour you a cognac. We'll have coffee in the living-room, Simmons.'

Elizabeth gave her order as she let her father lead her across the hall and into the other room. As he entered, he stopped and turned his daughter to face him. His eyes were shining.

'I know . . . we'll have two parties! One that is nothing to do with the Season – just a party – and the other will be your ball, Elizabeth. It will be the best ball in London this year, last year and next year! With two parties, you'll be sure to have a wonderful time, my love!'

With a squeal of delight, Elizabeth gave her father a huge hug. 'Oh, Papa, it will be such fun!'

Elizabeth waited a few days before pretending accidentally to bump into David as he came out of his office after work. He was not sure quite when he agreed to take Elizabeth to see how the building work was progressing on the Festival of Britain site on the south bank of the Thames, but at eight o'clock that evening he was pulling up to the door in his MG Midget and helping her into the two-seater.

As they drove towards London, Elizabeth talked happily about the forthcoming Season. Despite her seemingly artless chatter, however, she was keeping a close eye on David, ensuring she asked him questions at the right time, getting him to talk and making him laugh. By the time they arrived and parked the car, David was actually enjoying himself.

They strolled along the walkways with other visitors who had come to view the new buildings that were beginning to rise, phoenix-like, out of the rubble. There was no doubt the construction would be magnificent when it was finished. Like everyone else they had already seen the plans published in *The Times*. Now at last they could see for themselves where London's new concert hall – the Royal Festival Hall – would be – and the Dome of Discovery, and the magical Skylon.

Elizabeth suddenly threw back her head and laughed. 'David, isn't it wonderful to be alive? To be a part of all this?' With an elegant sweep of her arm she indicated the mud, dirt and excavations as well as the walls of the new buildings. As she finished with a flourish, she began to wobble on her high heels and nearly toppled off the walkway. David caught her arm and steadied her, tucking her arm into his elbow.

'Come on, let's see where we can get a cup of coffee.'

Elizabeth smiled to herself, pulled her collar up against the March night and snuggled up against David as they walked along by the Thames. The river moved slowly below them, the lights of the city reflected in its oily water.

'Look. Let's get some coffee here.' David pointed to a van pulled up against the Embankment wall.

'David! We can't! It'll mean drinking it here – in the street.' Elizabeth was genuinely shocked.

'You really have been protected, haven't you?' He was highly amused by her reaction. 'The cups will be clean, and I bet it will be first-rate coffee.'

Ignoring her protests, he walked up to the van; because he was holding her arm tightly, she had no choice but to go with him.

'Two mugs of coffee, both white. One with sugar, one without.' As he passed her a mug, Elizabeth was tempted to throw it at him. How dare he treat her like this? Like some common tart who could be bought for the price of a cup of coffee from a van! What stopped her was partly the warning look in David's eyes, daring her to rebel; and partly the smell of the coffee. Its bitter aroma sliced through the chilly air, and almost against her will she took a sip. She felt its warmth as she swallowed it, and she was glad she had not wasted it after all.

'Good girl.' David smiled at her as he watched her through the steam rising from his own mug into the cold night air. *Christ, but you're gorgeous!* he thought to himself. *Especially now, when you're not trying to be.* He felt a tingle of desire crawl across his belly; quickly he suppressed the feeling.

Despite what he thought, Elizabeth understood exactly what effect she was having on him. The wind was blowing her hair, leaving it in tousled curls; she had pulled the large collar of her coat round her face – having practised in front of the mirror, she knew how vulnerable it made her appear. She also managed to look innocent as she used the tip of her tongue to lick the froth of coffee from her lips.

David had moved towards her, to protect her from the wind, and she was aware of his closeness. She tensed as he moved again. *Kiss me, David. Kiss me, David*, she silently implored him, while cradling the mug between her hands. But the moment passed; abruptly David finished his coffee and handed his mug back, reaching out to take hers as she too drained the mug.

'It's getting late. I've got a busy day tomorrow and, from what you tell me, so have you.'

Elizabeth nodded, briefly disappointed, until David offered her his arm to escort her along the Embankment to the car. Although he hadn't kissed her, she had to admit it had been a splendid evening. He had been in a receptive mood and Elizabeth reckoned that the time was now right. As David steered the car north up the Edgware Road, Elizabeth began to speak again.

'Of course, it's terribly sweet of Papa to let me have two parties. Actually, the first one is really for him, even though he says it's for me – but I don't want to spoil his fun. Oh!' She paused, as if a thought had suddenly occurred to her.

By now they were almost home and had left the street lights

behind them. As they drove up Brockley Hill, David had his head-lamps full on, but it was a clear crisp night and the moon lit their way. 'What's wrong?' he asked.

'I've just realised. Of course, for my Coming-Out Ball I don't need an escort – it would rather defeat the object of it all, wouldn't it? But I will certainly need a partner for Papa's party. David, would you be willing to escort me?' She caught her lower lip between her teeth and lifted a wide-eyed anxious face towards his.

David pulled sharply on the steering wheel before slamming on the brakes as the car mounted the verge. Without a word he switched off the engine and turned to Elizabeth. The expression on his face made her draw back from him slightly, although her gaze did not waver.

He stared back at her for a moment. 'You tease.' He was not being complimentary. 'I've been wanting to do this all evening but I've been holding back because I thought you were a lady!' Then he roughly pulled her into his arms.

This time neither David nor Elizabeth pretended to be indignant as they kissed each other passionately. David held her head in his hands, wrapping the silky curls of her hair round his fingers. He caressed her neck and began to undo the collar of her coat. Elizabeth let him think she didn't notice when he stroked her throat and ran his hands over the swell of her breasts; she was enjoying the sensations that surged through her body. It was only when he tried to move under her sweater that she put her own hand on top of his, gently restraining him. 'David, please. A flirt I may be, a tart I am not!' She managed to sound apologetic, although every fibre of her body was screaming out for him.

No you don't, she thought. She straightened herself, smoothing down her sweater, and patting her hair back into shape while she reminded herself of her plans. *I intend to make you beg for it and for me, David Ghillyand, before this Season is over.*

After David started up the car again, they continued their journey in silence. He stopped at the front entrance and got out to see Elizabeth safely inside the house. She stood on tiptoe to kiss his cheek.

'Thank you for an *interesting* evening.' As she was about to shut the door behind her she turned and opened it a little again. 'I take it you've accepted my invitation, then?'

Without waiting for confirmation, she gave a light giggle and

132

left David standing there feeling as if he had lost a game he didn't even know he'd been playing.

For Elizabeth the next few weeks passed by in a rush. Despite her misgivings about Lady Quigland, Elizabeth began to like the old woman. Cynthia Quigland had been presented at court in 1907. In regaling her protégée with stories of what the Season had been like when she was a débutante, she also, unwittingly, added to her pupil's repertoire of tricks. Admittedly Elizabeth updated some of her sponsor's tips but their basis was the same. Thanks to Lady Quigland, she honed her skills as a flirt, and by the start of the Season she was already being talked about the length and breadth of London.

The whisper started when she and Cynthia made their rounds of the couturiers, who all adored her; she had a perfect figure, sparkling looks and, of course, Cecil Rouget's money. Bond Street and Knightsbridge opened their doors to her and she swept in and out of the establishments, stopping to chat with the other débutantes and their mothers and sponsors, all of whom remarked – against their will – that she was a beautiful and charming girl. These meetings were as important as any other social engagement. By the time the Season was upon them, Elizabeth was both hugely popular and, more important, had a full diary.

Cynthia Quigland had indeed been a good choice as sponsor, and it was with great pride she sat in Cecil's vintage Rolls-Royce as it queued down the Mall with those of the other girls who were coming out that year. Elizabeth perched on the end of her seat, not daring to sit back in case she creased the dress Norman Hartnell had created for her. At first he had left her in the capable hands of his *directrice*, but walking through the showroom one day he caught sight of her, and, without much persuasion from his old client and friend Lady Quigland, had undertaken to design her presentation gown personally. It was the only one he did that Season.

The traditional heavy satin gown was simple and understated, lending Elizabeth an air of cool dignity that her fellow débutantes lacked. The secret lay in its shape. It had been carefully boned and structured to show off Elizabeth's figure to its best. Lady Quigland had taught Elizabeth how to move in it so she appeared to glide rather than walk. The only adornment was rows of tiny seed pearls on the cuffs and down the small of her back, pointing the way towards the requisite train. Against this simplicity the compulsory headdress of tulle and three ostrich feathers did not look out of place or seem an afterthought, as it did with so many of the girls.

Unlike the other débutantes, Elizabeth did not fidget while awaiting her turn. Once it came, she calmly took her place at the head of the queue and gave the footman her invitation. When her name was announced, she paused for a second, then moved elegantly along the red carpet to curtsy twice before her King and Queen.

Outside Buckingham Palace, Cynthia told her she could remove her headdress, but Elizabeth exclaimed, 'Oh, no! I want Papa to see me arrive home exactly as I left. Except now I am officially an adult.' If there was a glint in her eye as she said this Lady Cynthia Quigland did not notice it.

Back at the Manor House, Elizabeth carefully lifted her gown as she walked across the gravel. She had checked her father's diary the day before and knew he would be in a meeting with David. Her fear that day was not that she would bungle her curtsy to her monarch, but that she would arrive home too late to interrupt the meeting. She needn't have worried. Her timing was perfect.

Graciously she swept up the stairs, remembering all that she had been taught about how to hold up her dress and head without looking at her feet. The staff she passed stood back and watched, while she pretended not to notice them. At the very moment she reached the top of the broad staircase, the door to her father's office opened and the sun cut across the dark corridor as he emerged with David. Elizabeth moved slowly into the sunlight and with great dignity curtsied to both men.

David recognised it as a magnificent performance, which he knew was for his benefit. He was about to laugh when he saw Cecil standing next to him. Unashamedly the man had tears running down his face as he looked with pride at his daughter. David glanced at Elizabeth again and what had seemed to him moments ago to be a cheap charade had now become a gesture almost of humility. He suddenly realised what this occasion meant to the man at his side, who had fled his own country to struggle and fight his way to the top and be accepted in a strange one.

The thoughts raced through David's head; instinctively he

stepped across to Elizabeth, who was still in her deep curtsy, and held out his hand. Delicately she placed hers on his and he raised her to her feet. They stood looking at each other in silence. David bent to kiss her hand, then without a word he turned and walked downstairs. Elizabeth let him pass.

All at once the moment shattered as she picked up her skirts in one hand and with the other finally pulled off her feather headdress while she ran across the corridor to her father.

'Oh, Papa, it was wonderful!'

'Honestly, Robert, you should have seen her. Talk about amateur dramatics run wild. I mean, why doesn't she simply throw herself at David and get it over and done with?'

'You mean like you did with me?'

Sally flushed. 'Well, it worked, didn't it? Anyway, you're always so wrapped up in your work you wouldn't notice if the ceiling fell in. Unless it mucked up an experiment,' she retorted. 'Now, come on, help me finish writing out these invitations. It's your wedding too, you know!'

Robert turned back to the pile of white cards in front of him and carried on writing names and ticking them off his list. He finished his pile before Sally. Putting down his pen, he leaned back in his chair to watch her.

'Sal, if you hadn't been high on the sponge residues, do you think you'd have kissed me that night?'

She thought for a moment before answering. 'Well, I did have that mistletoe with me . . . But if you want the truth I'd probably have been too much of a coward to use it. Why?'

'I'm just thinking about the effect it had. Not the painkilling side, but the way it enhanced emotions. Do you realise what it might do if it were given to people in the wrong circumstances? I mean, with us it was great. I doubt if I'd ever have plucked up the courage to ask you out if you hadn't kissed me . . . But just imagine that stuff being wafted over, say, a football stadium, when you've got all those rampant male hormones on the loose. Or if it had been used in the war. You know . . . "We have nothing to fear but fear itself." The results could be devastating!'

It was Sally's turn to put her pen down. 'Honestly, Robert, sometimes your paranoia about the bad side of scientific research

135

gets the better of you. Anyway, we've almost finished the work on the residues. So I can give a simple report to Cecil on the possibilities for pain control. Then we can get on with the next task.'

Robert opened his mouth to respond but Sally ignored him, not wanting to get into another argument about the ethics of their work.

'Like getting these wedding invitations out on time!'

And, dismissing Robert's comments, she goaded him back to his envelopes.

As the Season continued, Elizabeth became increasingly popular, much to the annoyance of the mothers and sponsors of the other débutantes. Since all the men who attended the circuit of teas and balls, Henley and Ascot, were totally enthralled by her, she was never short of an escort or dancing partner. Part of Elizabeth's appeal to these men, these 'Debs' Delights', was her lack of interest in them as potential husbands. The harder they tried to impress her, the more impervious she became. As the Season wore on she began to grow bored with the attention, which in turn made her begin to insult her admirers. Although the men didn't mind, regarding this as one of her amusing foibles, their families did.

Eventually Elizabeth's behaviour became so outrageous that, a few nights before Cecil's own party at the Manor House, Lady Quigland insisted they spend an hour together to review her progress.

Elizabeth flounced into the living-room and sat down inelegantly in Cecil's big armchair. Cynthia opened her mouth to tell her that 'Young ladies do not sit down like that', when she shut it again as she realised this was exactly the reaction Elizabeth wanted from her. Clearly Elizabeth was going to make it a difficult interview.

'Well, there's no question that for once they've picked the right girl as the Débutante of the Season. It's nice to see that dratted committee get something right at last!'

Elizabeth raised her eyebrows. It was the first time she had ever heard Cynthia Quigland swear, and the fact that it was directed at the organising committee of Queen Charlotte's Ball was even more noteworthy.

'I have to congratulate you, Elizabeth. You're playing those men beautifully. It does get tedious, doesn't it?'

'Yes, it bloody does!' Elizabeth wanted to shock the woman, but when she saw this wouldn't work she immediately changed her tack. 'I'm sorry, Cynthia – I'm probably tired. But it's so boring the way they paw at you the whole time, and think you should feel honoured because they've deigned to descend to your level. If Lord Thompson tries to get me alone in one more conservatory I won't be responsible for my actions. And I don't care if the Right Honourable Thomas Montgomery *is* in line for a junior minister's position when he finishes at Cambridge – I'm still not interested!'

'I'm not surprised: you can do much better than that! Junior minister, indeed! In fact that was why I wanted our little chat today, Elizabeth.' Cynthia looked round as if to check no one was listening. 'I know how tiring it gets, especially when you've already netted the biggest catch this Season.'

Elizabeth looked surprised, but Cynthia carried on regardless.

'Oh, come now, you must be aware that the Earl of Galbraith wants to marry you. I do appreciate that the title and the money are being held in trust for him until he is twenty-five. But it would still mean you'd be a countess in a few years' time.'

Elizabeth stood up, put her hands on her hips and shook her head. 'I'm not marrying Donnie Galbraith, even if he were to be the next King of England. I know who I'm going to marry and I'm going to tell him at Papa's party on Thursday.'

'*You're* going to tell him? Elizabeth, you can't do that!' Cynthia was genuinely appalled.

'Watch me!' Elizabeth said defiantly, and marched out of the room.

On the following Thursday Elizabeth very firmly told Cynthia that she would not be attending either Lady Carroll's luncheon or the garden party at the Spencers'. She wanted to look her best for her father's party; so she had decided to spend the day lazing around at home. It made no difference how much Lady Quigland nagged and pleaded; Elizabeth would not go out.

Her father's guests had been invited for half past seven, and David had agreed to be at the house by seven o'clock. Elizabeth enjoyed getting herself ready that evening and spent two hours in the bathroom and the bedroom. By six forty-five she was ready. Taking a deep breath, she studied herself in the mirror.

Looking back at her was a woman who appeared older than her nineteen years. Bored with the clothes in virginal white and pastels required of a débutante, she had chosen a bronze taffeta and tulle dress. The dress was straight and strapless, sculptured from the taffeta, with stiffened tulle creating a drop-shoulder wrap. Every curve was displayed to its best advantage; below the nipped-in waist the fabric flowed smoothly over her hips. As she turned she could see the deep vent at the back of the dress, filled with the matching stiffened tulle to relieve its otherwise harsh line. With her hair piled on top of her head, and wearing long evening gloves, she could be taken for twenty-five.

On this occasion she decided to be downstairs when David arrived, but timed her appearance to allow no opportunity to go and change once Cynthia Quigland objected to her gown. Cynthia did indeed object but when at exactly seven o'clock the doorbell rang and David was shown in, she was standing at her father's side.

'How do I look, David?' she asked coquettishly, turning slowly in front of him, knowing exactly the impact she was making, and ignoring the expression on Cynthia's face.

'My little girl – all grown up.' Cecil beamed at her, then left her talking with David as the first of the other guests arrived.

As ever Elizabeth greeted her father's guests with charm, accepting the compliments on her successful Season with just the right amount of demurring. Word had also got about that Donald, Earl of Galbraith, had shown more than a passing interest in her, but whenever his name was mentioned – which was often – she managed to appear embarrassed. By nine o'clock, many of the one hundred and fifty guests were positive they had been talking to the next Countess of Galbraith.

Throughout the evening Elizabeth kept close to David, introducing him to everyone as 'the Rouget Corporation's most brilliant asset'. For his part, David felt as if Elizabeth were treating him like an extra bracelet to adorn her pretty wrist; since he was not Donald Galbraith, the other guests could safely ignore him.

'Robert, do look!' Sally hissed in Robert's ear as he spun her round the ballroom. 'Over there.' She indicated with her head to where David was standing with Elizabeth. 'David's face is furious. He's not having much fun, is he?'

138

Robert deftly turned them around so he could see his brother, and laughed. 'Well, it's hardly surprising. No man likes to feel he's being used. It's fairly obvious she's dangling him on a string until she can announce her engagement to the Earl of Whatsit.'

'Galbraith,' Sally finished helpfully. 'And I don't think you're being fair to Elizabeth. In fact I bet you, if it weren't for the money, she'd go for David rather than Galbraith!'

'Poor David. It must gall him to think that all Rouget's money will go to the landed gentry instead of him. Ah well, he had his chance.'

They stopped and applauded the orchestra politely as Robert escorted her from the dance floor.

'That's a terrible thing to say,' Sally remonstrated. 'You're virtually accusing your own brother – and my brother-in-law to be – of being a male gold-digger. I know you don't like him much . . . but surely that's taking things a bit far?'

Before Robert could respond, one of the two other research chemists came over and asked if he could have a dance with Sally. Once again she was whisked off round the room, the starched petticoats of her dress sweeping across the floor.

Robert wandered over to the table to help himself to another glass of punch. Suddenly he spotted two faces at the french window peering in. They disappeared as soon as he saw them but Robert, checking no one was watching, slipped behind the curtain and stepped outside.

'Who's there?' he called sternly. There was a scuffling in the rose garden to the right of the terrace and then a thud.

'Oooh!'

'Sssh!'

He looked over the wall and in among the rose bushes. There he could just make out Edith Jones and Rose Haggerty. Rose was sprawled on the grass, with Edith crouched beside her rubbing her friend's ankle. When she realised who had seen them, Edith gave a sigh of relief.

'Oh, thank goodness it's you, Dr Ghillyand! Anyone else and we'd be in big trouble.'

Robert made his way down the terrace steps and helped Rose to her feet.

All the time Edith carried on talking. 'Please don't tell anyone you saw us. Because of the party the shifts have been rearranged, and Rose and I got the short straw. We start at midnight – which is why rotten old Browning said we mustn't come. I've got a post-op appendectomy to keep an eye on, and Sister Browning says she doesn't want me dozing off. As if I would. So she'd really haul us over the hot coals, even though she's as curious as us. But we wanted to see if we could spot the Earl, Miss Elizabeth's fiancé.'

'Careful, Edith, it's not been announced yet,' Robert said laughing. 'It's only speculation. But I think it's a pretty safe bet by all accounts. Now, look through the windows to the left-hand-side archway from the dance floor. See that good-looking chap in the kilt? That's Galbraith.'

The two nurses followed Robert's pointing finger; then Rose grabbed her friend's arm.

'Come on, Edie, let's go before we're missed. Thanks, Dr Ghillyand.'

''Bye, girls.'

The women giggled as they went off and, smiling, Robert made his way back towards the terrace steps. He was about to run up them when· he heard voices above him. Glancing up, he saw his brother with Elizabeth Rouget on the terrace.

'I am not marrying Galbraith, you idiot. I told you, like it or not, I'm going to marry *you*!'

Oops, thought Robert, and crept along below the wall to the side-terrace steps and back into the house through a different door.

'Where've you been?' Sally asked as he rejoined her in the ballroom.

'I'll tell you later. But I have a feeling Galbraith hasn't won the fair maiden's hand just yet,' he said mysteriously, refusing to explain, and once again swept her on to the dance floor.

Outside on the terrace, a slightly drunk Elizabeth was still blazing at David. '*I* never said I wanted to be a stupid countess, did I? Well, did I?' David shook his head. 'You know it's you I want, and more to the point I know you want me.'

David looked at her, considering what she said. Deliberately he took a cigarette out of his case and tapped it on the closed lid. Elizabeth snatched it from him, and for a second he thought she was going to throw it away. Instead she put it between her lips. When he held out his lighter she drew on it carefully and blew the smoke into the air before reaching up to place it in his mouth. He laughed, and cradled her chin in his hand.

'You've got style – I'll grant you that! Maybe being married to you might be fun after all.'

Elizabeth sidled closer and rested her hands on his chest. 'Think how much you'd enjoy being part of all of this; knowing it would be yours, because as Papa's son-in-law it would be.'

She was aware she was almost begging but didn't mind. David had risen to the bait. All she had to do now was reel him in, but carefully. She waited for a moment, then took her hands off his chest and gave a shrug.

'Well, if you're not interested, I know someone who is. I better go and find Donnie, I suppose.'

'Oh no, you don't.' David grabbed her wrist and pulled her back towards him. 'You're right. I do want you. And thank God you're bright enough to realise that part of wanting you is wanting your link to your father. But since you already know that, what the hell! Of course, you're taking yourself out of the market right in the middle of your precious Season.' He spoke the last phrase with a sneer, determined to have the final word.

'Ye gods!' she exploded. 'Don't you realise I don't care about the bloody Season? I agreed to do it for a laugh, because I was so bored. It's something Papa wanted me to do. It means nothing these days – except to people like Cynthia Quigland who make a packet from sentimental fools like Papa who'll pay to have their daughter "launched". It makes us sound like a fleet of liners. Anyway, I don't see why you should worry. I'm meant to be its great catch.'

David knew she was mocking someone but wasn't sure if it was herself or him.

'Well, if we've agreed, what are you waiting for? Go on, David. Say it. Ask me to marry you.'

David's face clouded over. For a moment Elizabeth wondered whether she'd gone too far. Then coolly she looked at him.

'On one knee, if you please.'

David gave a snort of laughter and threw his cigarette away, grinding it out beneath his toe. 'Let's give them something to talk about. Come here.' He marched her to the french windows and then, when he was sure people were watching them, he went down on one knee. 'Elizabeth, I can't live without you. Please tell me you'll marry me.' It was his turn to mock her.

Elizabeth let a slow smile cross her lips and left him on his knees an instant longer as she enjoyed the sense of control. Then she said, 'I thought you'd never ask.'

The whisper of Dr Ghillyand's proposal and Miss Rouget's acceptance spread round the rooms until it reached Donald Galbraith. Those nearest to him, including Lady Quigland, swore he went alabaster white before he silently left the house followed by Cynthia trying to placate him. However, David and Elizabeth reached Cecil Rouget before the news did.

'Papa, David and I need to talk to you urgently.'

Cecil was about to ask her to wait, when the look on her face made him excuse himself from the group of cabinet ministers to whom he was talking. He led the way to the library. When David formally asked him for Elizabeth's hand in marriage, Cecil was surprised.

'But I thought you were going to marry Galbraith.'

'No, Papa, everyone else thought that. Not me.'

'Are you sure you know what you're doing?' Cecil was as direct in his private life as in business. When he wanted something, like his daughter he asked and usually got it.

'I've never been more certain of anything in my life!' she declared. 'Now, are you going to tell everyone? Or shall we?'

That night Cecil Rouget, knowing how stubborn his daughter could be, said goodbye to an earl as a son-in-law and proudly announced his daughter's engagement to Dr David Ghillyand.

When she heard this revelation, Sally turned and stared at Robert. 'You knew!' she whispered accusingly.

Robert grinned. 'I'll tell you later,' he repeated, and raised his glass in a toast to the happy couple.

On the Friday every débutante and her mother also toasted David and Elizabeth, particularly David, quietly thanking him for removing Elizabeth from the marriage market. The gossip columns enjoyed themselves too and for the next few weeks photographers dogged Elizabeth and David wherever they went. David accepted the attention as calmly as he had accepted Cecil's offer of an allowance to Elizabeth of £10,000 a year.

'I know I'm going to cry!' Violet Chambers peeped over her shoulder to watch her daughter as her father escorted her down the aisle towards Robert Ghillyand. Sally looked radiant, despite getting up at six o'clock that morning. Violet had spent hours making the dress; as Sally walked past her she was pleased to see her daughter had remembered to fluff up the sleeves, although she also noticed that the stiffened petticoat she had borrowed from a neighbour was obviously not being worn.

Through all the fittings Sally had told her mother she wanted the dress to be simple, 'so I can dye it afterwards to make it into an evening dress'. She had finally seemed to compromise by agreeing to wear the petticoat. 'It will also give you something old and borrowed,' her mother had argued. So Sally gave in.

However, on the day she had done as she'd always intended and the dress fell loosely and easily round her feet, the carefully acquired lace on the skirt merging into folds. Yet, to ensure she was wearing something old and borrowed, she had delicately removed her mother's wedding veil from its wrappings and was wearing this under her snug Juliet cap. When Violet recognised it the threatened tears spilled over.

As Violet happily sniffed her way through the ceremony, the sun suddenly burst through the clouds, casting jewel colours of emerald and sapphire, ruby and amber around the couple as it shone through the stained-glass window above the altar. Robert made his vows in a firm voice, but when Sally said, 'I do', her voice had a tremor in it. Not, as their guests thought, with emotion, but because she was trying to suppress a giggle.

'Darling, I was concentrating on you, honestly I was. But when Mum started snivelling I became aware how pompous we all were, and that was it. I really thought I was going to laugh out loud!'

'Well, you didn't, Mrs Ghillyand.'

Robert leaned across the back of the trap to give his wife another kiss. The pony trotted on and the driver discreetly kept his eyes ahead of him. Although Cecil had offered the use of the Manor House for their wedding reception, Sally had politely declined, explaining as gently as she could, without hurting her employer's feelings, that she had always hoped to hold her wedding reception in the same place as her parents, the village hall in Radlett.

It was here that the pony and trap drew to a halt. As Robert helped his bride down, with yet another kiss, their guests spilt out of the doors to greet them. The September sun now lit everything with a golden glow, and nobody wanted to go back into the hall, so they stood around watching as the photographer set up his cameras again to take the requisite group photographs.

Robert had felt obliged to ask David to be his best man but had been more than a little surprised when he had accepted.

Elizabeth had moaned about attending the wedding at all, but David had been insistent and she had left the house with him that morning in a bad mood. However, now she was here she grudgingly had to admit she was enjoying herself. With everyone else she cheered when David brought the chimney sweep up to meet the couple and shake hands with them to give them extra luck, and with everyone else she waved the couple goodbye as they set off on their honeymoon to Studland Bay in Dorset.

As the couple disappeared round the bend in the road, Elizabeth smoothed her gloves back on to her hands and patted her hair into shape. 'Just think, darling, next June that will be us.'

Violet Chambers took the hint, and asked Elizabeth about the plans for her wedding the following year.

'Papa's already secured St Albans Cathedral for us . . . and I'm so excited because Dior has agreed to do my gown, and the bridesmaids', and I can hardly wait. But David insists we have a proper year-long engagement, which I think is an absolute bore, though I suppose I'll have to put up with it!'

Standing outside Radlett church that September afternoon, Elizabeth felt as if the next nine months were an eternity. She looked wistfully down the road in the direction that Robert and Sally had just driven.

As soon as they had celebrated the new year of 1951, Elizabeth became engrossed in her wedding plans. Lists were drawn up; designs for the rooms they would take over in the house were considered; fabrics selected, rejected and reselected; and her trousseau mulled over and meticulously assembled.

'Cynthia, please be a darling and do it for me,' Elizabeth wheedled Lady Quigland. 'I know I embarrassed you last year, but can't we let bygones by bygones? I need someone to come to Paris with me . . . and you know me so well. You'll make sure I don't get it all wrong. And anyway,' she finished lamely, 'Papa wants you to help me.'

It was the mention of Cecil that finally persuaded Cynthia Quigland to help Elizabeth Rouget organise her wedding. After a quiet word with Cecil, a suitable financial agreement was reached. They made several trips to Dior in Paris, and if at any point Cynthia wondered why Elizabeth was marrying David Ghillyand she had more sense than to say anything; she too was enjoying herself.

Part of her duties concerned dealing with the press. As the date approached, the diary editors and society columnists began to follow their progress. By the time Elizabeth's wedding day arrived, several photographers and reporters were huddled round the steps of St Albans Cathedral, together with the usual throng of people who had just come to watch. They were not disappointed. Nearly four hundred guests had been invited and the crowd had great fun spotting famous faces among the congregation that filed into the old cathedral.

'Look . . . isn't that Peggy Ashcroft? I didn't know she was coming!'

'Never mind her – there's Vivien Leigh. Isn't she beautiful?'

'Gawd, there's that Bevan with 'Arold Wilson. Now I'd vote for them. They understand blokes like us.'

'Do shut up goin' on about your politics, 'Enry,' said the fussy little woman standing next to him. '*She's* here. Aah, the dress!'

Dior had excelled himself in his creation for Elizabeth Rouget. Remembering the success of her presentation dress she had insisted on something simple. The white satin fitted snugly down her body to her hips, where it was suddenly swept back to form an elongated peplum over a small bustle. From beneath this billowed lavish layers of tulle. As Elizabeth carefully rearranged her skirts, Lady Quigland's tiara sparkled on her head and her veil fell softly down her back, twinkling with tiny crystals. Her bouquet of gardenias and white roses completed the image.

Once she was certain the whole crowd had admired her, Elizabeth turned to rest her gloved hand lightly on her father's arm and allowed him to lead her down the imposing aisle to David's side.

After the ceremony Fleet Street's best gathered round to get shots of the bridal party and their illustrious guests; the more astute editors had also sent a team to Claridges. The next day every paper carried photographs of what was already being called the 'Wedding of the Year'.

'Mrs David Ghillyand.' Elizabeth held out her left hand in front of her, turning it this way and that, watching the glow from the fire as it moved across her wedding ring. 'I like that.' She walked

145

over to where David was standing. 'Undo me, darling.'

David turned her round and began unfastening the row of covered buttons down the back of his wife's dress. Her skirt flowed round his calves and when she turned to face him, she let the garment slip to the floor. David crossed to the fireplace and leaned on the mantelpiece, watching Elizabeth as she stepped out of the rustling gown. Still wearing her veil she walked over to him. The effect of seeing her in her silk underwear and stockings with the virginal net on her head was too much for him. Without saying a word he scooped her up in his arms and carried her into the bedroom of their suite.

The first time he entered her it was with a brutal passion, but a passion that Elizabeth returned, and together they writhed around on the bed, getting increasingly entangled in her veil. Later David helped Elizabeth bathe, smoothing her body with scented oils in the deep bath-tub. When he made love to her the second time it was a gentle experience for both of them.

Sally dragged herself out of bed, making sure she didn't let the February chill creep under the bedclothes and wake Robert up. He rolled over but carried on gently snoring as she went into the bathroom. She sat down on the side of the bath and swallowed a couple of times, fighting back the inexplicable tears at the news of the King's death, and willing away the nausea. As on the last few mornings she was unsuccessful and a couple of minutes later she was kneeling on the floor, resting her sweaty head against the cool porcelain of the toilet.

She repeated the mental sums she had been doing for the last few days. She was only a little late, but she had never been that regular in the past so had not worried about it. Now it became terribly important to her and she got up and walked in a wobbly line to look at herself in the full-length mirror.

'What are you doing?' Robert yawned and rubbed his eyes as he watched his wife running her hands over her tummy.

'Do you think I'm putting on weight?'

'Nope, and even if you were I wouldn't complain. I like having something to get hold of. Come back to bed.'

For once Sally made an excuse and sent him off to make the morning tea while she had a bath.

As she soaked in the hot water she felt nausea begin to rise again and lay back with her eyes shut. The bathroom door opened and Robert came in with a cup of tea for her. He sat down on the washing box and looked at Sally appreciatively.

'Of course, you'll get much fatter over the next nine months, won't you?' he said in a matter-of-fact voice.

Sally's eyes snapped open and she sat up quickly, splashing water over the side of the bath. 'How long have you known?'

'Oh, come on, love . . . Just because I often appear a million miles away doesn't mean I don't know what's going on around me. I'm well aware that even by your calculations you're about three weeks overdue.' He sounded hurt. 'Now drink your tea. I've put a bit of extra sugar in it.'

Sally took the cup from him. 'Of course I'm not positive . . . Well, not a hundred per cent.'

'My God, Sal, sometimes you amaze me! We work at the best lab in the country and you're not sure if you're pregnant or not. The first thing we're going to do when we get in is run a test on Flopsy and Mopsy and get those bunnies to confirm what we both really know. Now, preggy or not, move it, otherwise we'll never get there, will we?' He got up and left the bathroom, then put his head back round the door. 'Well, I hope you are! It'll be wonderful to have a baby, won't it?'

As Sally dried herself she realised how much she hoped the test would be positive. Eighteen months of married life had suited both of them. It never ceased to amaze her that, although they worked together, spending twenty-four hours a day with each other, the attraction that had been there when they first met was still evident, and growing.

It was a gentle, loving relationship, and Sally held on to Robert's arm, not daring to look for herself as he read the test result.

Robert picked Sally up and swung her round. 'Oh Sal, it's great. We're pregnant!'

'Bless you for that royal "we". But as I'm the only one experiencing morning sickness I suggest you put me down sharpish before I throw up down your back!' And as soon as her feet touched the floor she darted out of the lab to the toilet.

That evening, over dinner, they began to discuss the future. 'I'm not going to stop working, so don't think I am!' she said defensively.

147

'Hey, who said anything about you giving up work? I didn't, did I? Anyway, sweetheart, I'm too selfish to let you stop work. No one else would allow me to get away with what I do in the lab, or the total selfish way I work. No, my mind is made up. Not only will you not give up work, you can even have the baby in the lab!'

Sally punched him playfully on the arm. 'Oh, you. Seriously, though, I might have to. I mean, once I stop working, money's going to be tight, isn't it? Where am I going to have the baby? I could have it here . . .' She looked round her small home. 'Or there's the General, of course . . .' Her voice tailed off.

'Do you want to have the baby here, at the Clinic?' Robert asked her, putting down his knife and fork.

'Well, yes . . .' she said hesitantly. 'But it's so expensive – we'd never be able to afford it.'

'Sally, leave that to me. I'm sure we can come to some arrangement. Besides, Cecil Rouget seems to think the staff are disloyal if they don't use the Clinic. But we'll discuss this some other time.'

She opened her mouth to object, but knew it was useless saying anything to him at the moment. Instead she got up and walked round the table, where she sat on Robert's lap. 'Have I told you how much I love you?'

'Not today, no.'

Over the following weeks Sally's waistline began to fill out and the morning sickness subsided. People were delighted to hear about the baby. In the lab a steady stream of people who 'happened to be passing' came to offer their congratulations and promise Sally that she would soon be blooming with health and vitality. Sally smiled sweetly, doubting every word, but by the time she was four months pregnant the change was astonishing.

She was feeling terrific, and her mood matched the glorious May weather. She seemed to have boundless energy and an increased ability to concentrate. She fitted in with Robert and his needs in the lab more than ever before. And, as they worked side by side, Sally began to understand with even greater clarity exactly what Robert was trying to achieve and was able to prepare chemicals, hand him equipment, and write up notes and results before he asked for them.

Robert and Sally had talked again about where she would have the baby. Despite their positive feelings towards the fledgling National Health Service, both eventually agreed that it might seem disloyal not to have the baby at the Clinic if they could. Robert made discreet enquiries about the costs involved and been amazed at the figures quoted. When he told Sally she had laughed, patted her rounded belly and affectionately told her bump, 'Ah well, poppet, it's Watford General for you.'

Robert said nothing but began to think of how he might raise the money. It wasn't that he didn't trust the staff at Watford General; far from it. He was simply unable to forget that the Rouget Clinic had on call some of the best obstetricians around; and he wanted to give his baby the best start he could.

In the end he spoke to his local garage about selling his car, even though he knew they would need it even more once the baby was born. The mechanic had sucked the air through his teeth and told him that although the car was basically in good condition it would need a bit of work. However, he thought they could give him a good price when he was ready. Robert was delighted; he'd worry about telling Sally after the baby was born; and, since the garage had agreed he should hold on to the car until the last minute, he reckoned he would be able to sell it while she was still tucked up in bed.

The next task was to negotiate with the Clinic administrators about deferring the payment of a deposit. He was planning what he would say to them when he received a message from Clare Grigson that David wanted to see him.

Raising his eyes heavenwards, he shrugged his way out of his lab coat and put on his jacket. Sally smoothed him down, trying to make him appear less crumpled. 'It must be something urgent. What on earth do you think he wants?'

'Who knows.' Robert thought back over the last few months' work, trying to identify potential problems. When Clare Grigson ushered him into David's office, his brother was standing in front of his desk, ready to greet him.

'Robert, come in. Sit down.'

Robert sat in the chair indicated, eyeing his brother warily.

'How's Sally coming on?' David asked as he seated himself opposite.

Robert looked surprised, doubting David had summoned him mid-afternoon to enquire about the progress of Sally's pregnancy, and said as much.

'Actually, you're right, Robert. There is something I want to ask you but it's a bit . . . ah . . . delicate . . . shall we say.'

Robert stared at his brother in silence, frowning.

'It's about those retests you did on the early experiments with the sponge residues.' David picked up a file and began flipping through it. Seeing the look of surprise on Robert's face he smiled at him. 'Cecil gave me this some time ago. I hope you don't mind.' Robert stayed silent. David went back to the file. 'Correct me if I'm wrong . . . but I would say that, judging by this report, it was the experiments you ran with the residues from batch twelve that had the strange effect on you that Christmas.' He gave Robert a copy of the report to study. 'From what it says here, the rats couldn't cope with it either. What I want to know is: how long would it take you to make that stuff again, but this time refining it further? You see, whatever it is, I need it in its purest form so I can give it to my boys in development to work on. I think it has powerful potential and I don't want to let someone else steal a march on us – this information's been sitting around for long enough as it is.'

As David finished speaking Robert was already shaking his head. 'No, David. I'm sorry, but I won't do it. That stuff could be lethal. I'm still not sure if it's hallucinogenic or even carcinogenic. For all I know it could be a potential killer. I'm not prepared to release any of the substance until I'm certain that the negatives don't outweigh the positives – and we both know how long that could take. In fact, the whole project's going to take longer than planned because I'm insisting that Sal stops work on it until after the baby is born. And I've promised her that I won't carry on with the work until she's back in harness.'

'Ah yes . . . Sally. I'm sure she'd see the sense of what I'm saying. Get my lads on to it and you could have enough stuff to keep you going for months by the time she's back next to you.' He lowered his voice a little. 'Besides, I'm not asking *you* to *develop* it, am I? That's my job. I just want you to prepare the basic substance. Look, as you say, it might be harmful – but we need to know *how* harmful, don't we? The sooner we know that, and whether it can be mass-produced, the sooner we can achieve your aim – which is to develop new drugs, life-saving drugs. I always thought that was what you wanted to do – save lives?'

'Of course I do, but –'

'Where's the but? Everything has to start somewhere, and that's

150

what you've done. *You're* the research expert. Now it's *my* turn. Look at Fleming. The penicillin he first produced was a tiny amount but he knew when he had to turn it over for mass-production. Last year they produced over four hundred thousand pounds of the stuff in America alone. Who are you to stop that sort of progress?'

'I don't want to stand in the way of progress. I just want to be certain it's moving at the right pace, that's all.' Robert could feel himself being manipulated but didn't know how to turn the conversation round; how to make his point so David would understand what his work meant to him. It was as if they were back in his flat all those years ago.

David suddenly changed the subject, disarming Robert. 'By the way, I hear you've been asking about costs at the Clinic. Sally would get such good treatment in there, but surely that's a bit rich for you, isn't it?'

'Sally and our baby deserve the best and somehow I'll give it to them.'

David considered this for a moment. 'Look, maybe we could do a little deal . . . You do this for me, and I pay the Clinic bills for you, by way of a thank-you.'

Robert eyed him coldly, hating himself as the thoughts tumbled through his head. Had David finally found his price? Maybe he should accept – at least this way Sally would get the best possible obstetric care. He shut his eyes, trying to think more clearly, and the image of the new equipment being delivered to the Clinic the previous week floated into his mind. The new incubators were the latest from America; supposing their baby should be born prematurely, here it would be sure to have the best chance. A chance that Watford General probably couldn't offer. He opened his eyes with a sigh.

'On condition that no one finds out, and I do it in my own time. Sally finally stops working in the lab next week and, as I've already said, I don't want her near the stuff until we know more about it. Let me wait until she's not around and then I'll do it. That'll also give you time to play the loving brother-in-law, telling her this is your present. Make it an early Christmas present or something.' The sarcasm was not lost on David. 'Don't move. I'll see myself out.'

Robert walked out of the office with a curt nod to Clare Grigson, went downstairs and outside. As he strode back to the lab, despising himself more and more for his weakness, he passed the front entrance to the Clinic and walked straight into Sister Browning, who was talking to one of the staff nurses. 'I'm sorry, Dr Ghillyand.'

'It's not your fault, Sister. I wasn't looking where I was going. Forgive me.'

He hurried on his way, leaving Sister Browning to stare after him because for once, he hadn't stopped for a couple of friendly words.

Back in the lab he took a deep breath before breezing in to tell Sally about David's 'gift'. He found it difficult to look her in the eye, but, since she immediately flung her arms round his neck to hug him, she didn't notice. Robert cuddled her as closely as her bump would allow, but no sooner had he told her than he regretted it, knowing he couldn't back out now.

Elizabeth gave a catlike stretch and lifted the cover from her breakfast tray. 'I'm so hungry I could eat a horse!' she declared.

She tucked into a huge pile of scrambled eggs, mushrooms and bacon, before devouring a pile of crispy toast and marmalade. Then she jumped out of bed and threw open the window, letting the May sunshine and fresh air into the room.

'Oh, Mackers, isn't it a wonderful day?'

Jane MacKay had come into the bedroom to discuss the menu for that evening's dinner party.

'Yes, Miss Elizabeth, wonderful . . . It's even nicer outside,' she said pointedly, not approving of her mistress lying in bed until ten-thirty, since it held up the working of the household.

'All right, I'm on my way. Now, let me have a look at that menu.' With a flurry of her négligé she sat down at her dressing-table and pushed her hair out of her eyes as she scanned the card. 'Not cheese soufflé *again*! No, I know . . . David does love it so. Oh, I suppose it'll do. Thank Cook, and tell Simmons to do what he thinks best with the wine. I really can't be bothered about it all today . . . Oh, there's just one thing.' Elizabeth called her housekeeper back, almost as an afterthought. 'Please ask him to put a couple of bottles of the Dom Pérignon on ice, and be ready to serve it just after the syllabub. That's all.' And she dismissed her again.

Despite her marriage it was still accepted that she would act as her father's hostess when needed. David had grown to hate Cecil's dinner parties because he always felt Elizabeth was playing with him, trying to make him look a fool in front of her father's often eminent and influential guests. This trait had developed in their year-long marriage and stemmed from Elizabeth's boredom.

Since getting married, David had declined invitations to parties and premières, sporting and social events, which Elizabeth longed to attend. At first she went with other friends in an attempt to arouse David's jealousy, but when it had no effect she too began to stay at home, picking fights with her husband, who would usually resolve them by getting up and leaving Elizabeth screaming at an empty seat, thereby increasing her frustration.

Sometimes David would join in and the rest of the household would hear the insults and taunts being hurled back and forth across the room before a silence would descend as they made up their arguments in the bedroom with the same intensity as that with which they fought them.

Tonight's party was going to be different. Elizabeth was planning to win a battle with David before he even knew they had drawn swords; the prospect made her sparkle as she hugged her secret to her. As ever she dressed with care, choosing a sedate calf-length cream shantung dress with a matching stole. David seemed in a good mood that evening, and they chatted as they made their way downstairs.

When the guests arrived, the round of pre-dinner cocktails and chatter got under way. Eventually Elizabeth ushered everyone into the dining-room and the meal began, following its usual smooth pattern.

'Please compliment Cook on the soufflé, Simmons. Quite excellent.' David was feeling contented, particularly since Elizabeth seemed to be behaving herself that evening.

The syllabub was being served; surprisingly, Elizabeth waved hers away. 'I think it's a bit rich for me. I really couldn't face it.'

David looked at her in surprise. He had seldom known her to refuse food, and certainly not at one of Cecil's parties where she would at least take a portion and play with it, acting as if she were eating. 'What are you up to?' he asked quietly.

'I'm not up to anything,' she replied, sounding hurt. 'But women in my condition don't just get cravings for odd food, you know·. . . We can also go off it too.'

The table erupted around them. Cecil moved with surprising agility and was hugging his daughter and laughing and crying with delight at the same time. The other guests smiled indulgently, while David simply sat and stared at his wife.

'Simmons, I want champagne! Isn't it wonderful? I'm going to be a grandpapa!'

Cecil's delight was obvious, and Elizabeth accepted the guests' congratulations demurely, quietly savouring the attention.

Once the visitors had left, Cecil put a protective arm round his daughter. 'My love, I am so pleased, and proud . . . Of both of you,' he added, as an afterthought, putting his other arm round David. 'Now I think you should have an early night, and I'll have to rearrange my diary so I don't tire you out.'

'Papa, I'm going to have a baby, that's all. Keep your diary just as it is. After all, even though I didn't fancy it this evening, I've still got to eat, haven't I?'

'Well, we'll see. Goodnight, my love . . . David.'

Ceil stood at the food of the stairs, watching the couple go up to their room. Elizabeth went in and sat down on the sofa, putting her feet up and crossing her slim ankles. Barely had David shut the door when he turned on her.

'You bitch!' he exploded. 'Trust you to turn such a personal thing into a public announcement. I'd have thought that as the father I had a right to know first.' He paused as a thought crossed his mind. 'I suppose I am the father?'

Elizabeth was out of her seat and across the room so fast that David was taken unawares when the flat of her hand made contact with his cheek. 'You bastard!' she screamed. 'Christ, chance would be a fine thing! We go nowhere, we do nothing. Tell me when I could meet anyone, let alone have the chance of an affair? It's yours all right, and if you've got any sense you'll start treating me properly. Papa is so pleased, and if you haven't worked out what giving him a grandchild will mean, then you're a bigger bloody fool than I thought!'

David eyed her coolly. 'I'm not that stupid. I know damn well what this child means. It secures my future and gives me an even better footing in the Corporation. You may be great in bed, but don't tell me you've forgotten the real reason I married you. What was it you said about my wanting to be a part of all this? Well, you were right, and this baby will help enor-

154

mously. Now I suggest you do what your father told you and go to bed.'

David strode off to his own bedroom, leaving Elizabeth stamping her feet with rage.

Part Three

'I don't believe I'm doing this!' Alex mumbled from her sunbed.

Dan looked up from his book. 'What? Relaxing?'

'No – sitting out in the sun. I spend so much time telling people about the dangers of sunbathing, and here I am doing it. Mind you, I have to admit that for the first time I can understand what people see in it . . . Dan, I think I need more sun lotion. Would you do my back for me?' She reached under the lounger and passed him the bottle.

Dan put down his book and laughed as he took it from her. 'How you can say you're sunbathing I don't know. You've not crept out from under that umbrella. And it must be the third time in two hours I've rubbed this splodge into you. What is it? Factor ninety-five?'

Childishly Alex stuck her tongue out at him as he bent over and began applying the lotion, slowly trickling it on to her sun-warmed skin. Sleepily she was aware of his fingers as they massaged it across the middle of her back and up over her shoulders. When his hand moved back again he gently slipped his fingers down her side and caressed her breast.

'Dan . . . don't.' There was not much conviction in her voice.

'Why not?' he asked softly.

'People will see.'

'No, they won't . . . Now you're well covered, how about a swim?'

Lethargically she eased her arms back into her swimming costume and grasped Dan's hand as he helped her up. Together they picked their way across the sand and shingle to the sea's edge, where the waves were smacking against the beach. They stood for a moment before walking further into the sea, both enjoying the coolness of the water against their warm bodies.

Dan let go of Alex's hand and flung himself into the crest of a wave as it headed towards them. He emerged the other side, tossing water from his hair and yelling for Alex to join him. Cautiously she timed her steps, making sure the undertow wouldn't dislodge her, then finally launched herself with a kick once she was waist deep. With precise strokes she swam to meet Dan. Although they were only a few feet from the shore she discovered she was barely in her depth.

'Here . . . Hold on to me.'

Dan moved towards her and, with his feet on the bottom, wrapped his arms round her. She clung round his neck, laughing. All around her the sea was glinting, a breeze rippling its surface. Suddenly she let go and began swimming towards the boulders at the edge of the bay.

'Race you to the rock!' she called over her shoulder as she struck out.

Despite her head start, Dan caught up and they both crawled up the rock at the same moment. Catching their breath, they sat there enjoying each other's company. Alex leaned back on her arms with her face turned towards the sun, all worries about its ill effects forgotten as she savoured the prickly feeling of the water drying on her skin. Dan watched her, his arms clasped round one raised knee while the other foot dangled in the water.

He leaned towards her and traced a line down her arm with his forefinger. Slowly she turned and gave him a lazy smile, as his touch set off a small series of tremors inside her. Dan took her hand and without saying a word led Alex down the other side of the rock on to the beach of a small bay that was secluded from the rest of the coastline. Silently she let herself be led.

On the hidden beach Dan took Alex in his arms and kissed her. As she responded, she could feel the obvious effect she was having on him through the clinging wetness of their swimsuits. Together they sank on to the sand and Dan peeled her costume's straps down her shoulders. Alex lifted her hands out of the armholes, not taking her eyes off Dan's face, and in a gesture of pure delight she raised her arms above her head. The movement lifted her out of her bathing costume, and Dan bent down to run the tip of his tongue along the line where her tan met the rest of her skin.

To Alex, now lying on the sand, everything was happening in slow motion. If anyone had told her a few months ago that she would be making love in a secret cove on a Greek beach in broad

160

daylight she would have made a joke of it. Now she relished every second. The blue sky seemed to be a towering dome above the high cliffs that curved round the back of the beach. Alex felt as if she were standing on top of the cliff, looking down, watching what was happening. It was if she were two people: one, writhing ecstatically on the sand with Dan; the other a small and insignificant being who was trying to pull her back to reality.

Part of her was bemused by her actions, the other genuinely horrified that she could behave in such a wanton way. But as both Dan and the sun stroked her body she ignored the imaginary reprimanding figure high above her, telling herself simply to enjoy the languor and heightened sexuality she was feeling. She made love to Dan with a passion and abandon he had never experienced in her before, and his body responded accordingly.

Their rhythm matched the surge of the waves, and when the sensations erupted inside her Alex allowed herself the luxury of an involuntary, lusty yell, which the wind immediately carried out to sea. Her cry made Alex feel whole, and the figure frowning at her in disbelief from the top of the cliffs seemed to slot back inside her, rounding her out again. She sat up suddenly, feeling embarrassed, and rolled herself into a ball, her arms clasped round her knees.

'Alex, darling, please don't. There's nothing to be ashamed about. No one saw us. And if you tell me we shouldn't have done it like that I'll never forgive you for cheapening a magical, spontaneous, romantic moment. Ahh . . . !' he finished, holding up a remonstrating finger.

Alex lay back on the sand, trying not to feel self-conscious; after all, Dan had seen her naked and post-coital before. But this time it had been different; she had totally given herself up to her senses and emotions, and her yell had startled her in its intensity. Later she would realise that was the precise moment she had to admit she was in love with Dan.

'You sound like the worst type of tabloid journalist when you speak like that,' she said, in an attempt to hide her confused feelings.

'Please!' he said in mock horror. 'Credit where credit's due. Journalist – yes. Tabloid – God forbid! . . . Have I told you I think you have a great body? No, don't cover it up again!' He leaned over and, placing his mouth on her stomach, blew a loud raspberry against her skin. She chuckled, and the last traces of her embarrassment disappeared. 'Fancy some lunch?'

Alex suddenly realised how hungry she was and reached for her swimsuit. Before they struggled into their damp things, they both walked back into the sea to let the water wash away the grit and sand that still stuck to their bodies. Once they'd swam back to the beach they'd left earlier, they allowed themselves five minutes to dry off. Then they tucked their bags under their sunbeds and headed up the steep twisting path towards their favourite taverna. As they reached the top of the cliff, the wind blew across the ridge and they stood for a moment looking down across the beach before turning down the track to the village.

They ordered *kalamari* and a Greek salad with a half-bottle of retsina and a can of lemonade. Dan mixed the last two together, calling it 'Greek champagne'; Alex had taken a liking to the slightly sweet woody taste of the concoction. The breeze blew under the raffia awning and in comfortable silence they picked at their dish of olives while gazing across the sea to Myrties.

As part of Dan's policy to get Alex to relax before they began asking questions, he had, on their first morning, taken her back towards Myrties and along the little jetty. Here they had jumped on to one of the little cabin boats with about twelve other people and had chugged across the channel to the island of Telendos. It took all of ten minutes, and when they arrived Dan insisted that they stop at one of the waterside tavernas for a drink.

'But we've just had breakfast,' Alex had objected.

Dan had explained that she must learn the Greek way of life; and that meant stopping and watching the world go by over a cup of coffee. Alex had soon understood what he meant, and had reluctantly left the taverna to continue up through the village and down to the beach.

The village itself was tiny, just a couple of closely built streets, but its remoteness gave it a natural charm. They had walked up the slope to the top of the ridge, where the view on the other side of Telendos had made Alex stop and stare. Behind them the water had been smooth and calm, but beneath her on this side the waves rolled majestically on to the shingle beach.

Their first few days had followed the same pattern. In the evenings they would have dinner at one of the local restaurants in Panormos, then take a taxi-bus into the main town of Pothia,

162

where again they would sit at one of the harbour's tavernas and watch the town go about its business. Alex was surprised at how quickly they fell into a pattern, and how soon they began to be recognised and accepted by local people. When she mentioned this to Dan he merely shrugged his shoulders, but she knew he was biting back the words 'I told you so'.

The little boats ploughed their way back and forth between Telendos' small harbour and Myrties' stone jetty. Alex felt peaceful and happy – a contentment she had not experienced for a long time – as she dreamily watched the trails they left in the water. Down there was comparative noise and bustle, but up here the only sounds were the breeze and the crickets and the soft babble of Greek as the taverna owners filled their few customers' lunch orders.

'You haven't been listening to a word I've been saying, have you?'

Alex turned to Dan with a start and shook her head. 'Sorry . . . I was miles away.'

'I was saying, if you feel ready for it, I'd suggest we have breakfast in town tomorrow and start asking a few questions. What do you think?'

Alex sat and pondered. The last few days she had relaxed so completely that, while she hadn't forgotten why she had come to Kalymnos, the reason for her visit had faded into the background. The questions and doubts she'd been carrying with her since February no longer seemed important. They belonged to another world, to another Alex. She was almost tempted to tell Dan that it no longer mattered. However, she knew herself well enough to accept that if she didn't at least try to get the answers she would regret it the moment she returned to London's greyness. 'OK' was her almost reluctant short answer.

After lunch they ambled back down the ridge to the beach again, but the tranquillity Alex had felt during the morning had gone; now she was restless and unable to settle. Dan was aware of her change of mood and found himself reading the same page in his book over and over again. He kicked himself for spoiling the atmosphere between them.

'I'm going for a stroll.'

Dan looked up; appreciating her need to be by herself, he did not offer to go with her. As Alex set off into the late afternoon sun, he put his book on his lap and watched her. She wore a large straw hat and an oversized T-shirt. Far from taking a stroll along the shore, she was walking fast, taking big strides through the shallow water.

You're a bloody idiot, Westbury! Dan told himself. *You take all this time to calm her down and one badly timed question trips her up again. Why didn't you just get on with it without asking her opinion?* For a moment he considered throwing his book down and running after her, putting his arms round her, telling her everything was going to be all right; but he knew that more than anything else Alex needed to be on her own at the moment. He had spent enough time with her to know when she needed a reassuring cuddle or someone to listen, and when she needed to sort out her thoughts alone. Everything about her posture now screamed at him, *Leave me alone!* With a sigh he picked up his book and tried to carry on reading.

As she strode along, Alex found herself fighting back tears behind her large sunglasses. 'It's what you came here for,' she kept repeating like some sort of personal chant. The words seemed to fit in with the noises around her, the breeze and the sea, but shimmering beyond her current surroundings were images of her father, the Rouget Corporation, Vickie's and the various birth and death certificates that had brought her to Greece. She began to slow her pace, finally coming to a halt on a part of the beach which had only half a dozen people lounging under assorted sunshades.

She sat down, just at the water level, with her feet braced against the sand and her knees bent. The edges of the waves licked at her feet, occasionally creeping further up the shore to flow round her before ebbing away again. Sitting there, Alex realised with a jolt that for the first time since discovering the paper in the desk drawer she was able to concentrate solely on what she might find. Other worries – about patients and paying bills, attending meetings and generally battling to get from one day to the next – right now were not only unimportant but distant and unreal; now all the barriers she had built between herself and the truth had gone. All that mattered was the island of Kalymnos and what it might tell her. The enormity of what she was about to do hit her with its full force and her heart began to beat faster.

Alex watched as a little girl toddled along the beach and fell over, catching her knee on a stone. The child burst into angry, painful tears, and her mother ran across the sand to scoop her up. Tenderly she carried her infant back to their towel and kissed and hugged her, gently soothing her young daughter. In a matter of moments the child was wreathed in smiles again and happily playing in the sand, the utter misery completely forgotten as she attempted to build a sandcastle, safe in the knowledge that her mother was close by.

Choked with tears again, Alex turned back to face the sea. *If only it were that easy. I wish I had someone to kiss it better, to make me feel that secure, that loved, that safe.* The ever-present other voice at the back of her mind immediately retorted, *What about Dan?* Despite her sense of dejection, Alex smiled to herself. That morning on the beach had been quite wonderful; she had never felt so free in her life. That she loved Dan she now believed. That he cared for her she also believed; but she couldn't stop asking why. The cynic in her kept reminding her that his interest had originally come about through his journalistic investigations, and she found herself unable to ignore her doubts.

The waves smashed against the rocks at the end of the beach, as her feelings about Dan collided with her renewed fears about what she might discover about herself and her background over the coming days. Her head dropped forward; and, with her elbows resting on her knees, she linked her hands behind her head and finally let the tears flow freely. She hadn't sobbed like this since the night she had sat with Jen and told her what she had found on her father's desk. On that occasion she had felt guilty about weeping and held back, but on this Greek beach, with only the immediate surroundings to worry about, she allowed herself the self-indulgence of a good cry, enjoying the luxury of being able to let all her feelings out.

Slowly the crying subsided and Alex lifted her head, breathing in the clean fresh air. She knew she should have allowed herself to cry like that many years ago, but a lifetime's habit of keeping her feelings to herself had been hard to break. Making love on a beach that morning had seemed the right thing to do; this afternoon, crying had been the right thing to do. In both cases Alex accepted the experience and unquestioningly allowed herself to go with them, each in its own way a part of soothing and healing the anguishes of the past.

'Feeling better?'

Dan's voice was soft behind her. She looked over her shoulder. He was standing a little way off; the bags over his shoulder cast strange shapes on the long shadow stretching behind him in the setting sun. He held out his hand to her. Alex got to her feet and took it.

Neither spoke as hand in hand they walked back along the beach and over the ridge to the harbour. A boat was just about to leave, so they ran the last few yards, jumping on as it reversed out before turning to face Myrties. Automatically they stopped at a bar above the jetty and Dan ordered a bottle of wine. The sun had set while they were crossing the water and now the sky blazed in hues of orange and red. Telendos cut across the colour in a huge black mass, and the lights on the little boats bobbed.

Gradually the startling glow of the sky began to soften and deepen. Alex felt an enveloping calm wrap itself round her. She smiled at Dan, who smiled back and then leaned across to plant a kiss on her cheek. 'I love you,' he said, as if it were a statement of fact that did not need questioning.

These were the first words either of them had spoken for nearly an hour. It was as if Dan had read Alex's mind earlier when she had been sitting on the shore wishing for someone to sweep away her fears.

A few hours before, Alex would have made some sort of self-protecting response; now she just looked at Dan and accepted what he said, nurturing the feeling of peace that came with his words. Here, with Dan, she didn't have to say anything; she could be whoever and whatever she wanted to be.

Pothia harbour bustled with a mixture of tourists, residents and tradespeople. Along the front, mopeds buzzed up and down, often with two people precariously balanced, the back passenger clutching bulging bags of shopping. Street vendors were setting up stalls offering goods as varied as local herbs and spices, polished shells and *koblia*, the worry beads that seemed to grow from the local men's hands as they wound them round their fingers.

The taxi-bus dropped Dan and Alex in the square, and the noise level increased as they walked down the busy narrow streets towards the front. Dan led the way, one hand out behind him so Alex

166

could hold on to his fingertips, allowing them to maintain physical contact with each other.

The night before they had returned to their apartment and drifted through the rest of the evening. They had dined at 'Sun and Surf', where, almost as if sensing the bubble that had wrapped itself around them, both Manolis and Diane had left them alone to eat their meal. After dinner they had not bothered to sit around drinking and chatting with other regulars at the restaurant in the usual way, preferring their own company, wanting to explore by themselves the subtle but important change that had taken place in their relationship. They had walked along the moonlit beach and talked about everything and nothing, stopping occasionally for a gentle kiss. They had gone to bed early but, rather than make love, had cuddled up and contentedly fallen asleep in each other's arms, feeling more intimacy than any passionate intertwining of limbs could have produced.

Now, having reached Pothia harbour, Alex and Dan walked side by side to the Black Rose café. Of the twenty-odd bars, restaurants and tavernas along the front, this, almost at the far end, was the one used by most of the Britons who had, for one reason or another, moved to Kalymnos and now called it home.

'Why this place rather than any of the others?' Alex asked.

'Because they do one of the best breakfast fry-ups anywhere!'

Alex began to protest that she had not come away to eat food she could get in London, but when Dan asked her when she last had a proper English breakfast at home she had to admit she couldn't remember and finally agreed to join him, as a special treat. While they waited for their food they drank orange juice and coffee. Dan was tempted to pick up a copy of the previous day's British newspapers, but Alex wouldn't let him.

'Come on, tell me about the people here . . . the expats.'

'Well, over there . . . that's Harry Robinson – he used to be a master baker until he retired out here a few years ago. Mind you, he still makes the best Yorkshire parkin I've tasted, so long as he can get the Golden Syrup! He comes here most mornings for his breakfast . . . That's Nick. He runs the local disco – usually manages to scoop up a different girl each week! Don't look so surprised. He's very much a night person, and seems less garish behind his console than here in the morning light . . . Those two women there run the local expat newspaper – we might have a chat with them later. But the first person I want to talk to is ... Ahh, here's breakfast.'

With gusto Dan tucked into his bacon and eggs and, despite Alex's comment about 'cholesterol on a plate', she too devoured her food.

'Dan, good morning. How are you?'

Alex was wiping the last piece of fried bread round her plate and looked up at the man beaming down at her. Guiltily, she began getting to her feet, but he put his hand on her shoulder.

'No, don't get up. Sit down and finish your breakfast.'

He called the waiter over and ordered a thick sweet Greek coffee, then sank into a seat next to Dan.

'Alex, this is Papas. He's the man I wanted to see this morning.'

Alex glanced almost shyly at the impressive figure sitting with them. The fact that the local priests owned shops, or could be seen almost any time of the day or night sitting in bars or standing around chatting with local people on street corners, did not make her feel any more comfortable about the fact that Papas was a member of the Greek clergy. His ample black robes covered his rotund form and his greying beard flowed across his chest, parting as he breathed to reveal the crucifix round his neck, while a chimney-pot hat perched on top of his curly long hair.

'What do you want to know?' Instinctively Papas directed his question at Alex.

She felt flustered – the last person she had expected Dan to turn to was a priest – and as a result she sounded abrupt when she answered him.

'I'm looking for two women, Rose Haggerty and Edith Jones. They're probably in their late seventies, early eighties by now. They came here in the early 1950s and stayed. Do you know them?'

The face above the whiskers creased in thought. Unaware that she was doing so, Alex held her breath. Dan wanted to give her hand a reassuring stroke, but, unwilling to break Papas' concentration, he simply sat, leaning forward, waiting for his reply.

'Why are you looking for them?'

Yes! said Dan to himself. As a journalist he recognised that Papas' question meant that the priest did know something about Edith and Rose, but was for some reason unwilling to reveal their whereabouts immediately.

'I need to ask them some questions.' Alex was being defensive.

Dan could have shaken her; if she wasn't willing to give more, they would never get anywhere.

'They came here with Alex's parents – both of whom are now dead – and she wants to know about the time they spent on Kalymnos.'

Alex glared furiously at Dan. How dare he tell this stranger, priest or no priest, about matters that were private to her. Next he'd be telling him the whole story, and then everyone would know about it. In London, where everyone was too busy with their own lives, she had been able to talk to people and expect it would go no further – a mild curiosity one day that would be brushed aside the next. Here, the sort of questions she wanted to ask would whistle round the small community in no time.

'Hmm. Let me see what I can find out for you. How long are you here?'

Dan gave Papas their departure date, and the large man eased his bulk out of the seat. Picking up a newspaper on his way out, he waddled off down the street, where he was stopped by a group of men.

'Bloody nerve. He didn't even offer to pay for his coffee!' Alex was indignant.

'He doesn't have to. Here it's considered an honour to feed the priests. So they get their food and drinks free.'

'That's probably why he's so massive.'

'Alex! That's not like you. Look, I'm sorry he couldn't come up with anything immediately, but it would've been more surprising if he'd been able to say, "Oh yes, first left, second right, and it's the fourth house on the left", wouldn't it?'

'It's not that – it's you. Who the hell do you think you are, telling someone I barely know about my family?'

'Alex, I didn't. You were being so prickly and giving him no information. I had to say something. After all, meeting them is just half the battle. The main thing will be to get 'em to talk.'

'I'm doing it again, aren't I?' Alex asked with a wry smile.

Dan nodded. 'Alex, you've learned to trust me . . . Try and trust other people, too. It's the only way you're going to get anywhere with this, you know.'

'I do know that, Dan, honestly. Believe it or not, yesterday made me feel much better, more in control.' Dan knew she was referring to her sobbing on the beach during the afternoon, as opposed to

169

their love-making during the morning. 'I must admit, I thought I'd got everything into perspective, too. But I don't think I'll manage that until I find out exactly what "everything" is.'

Alex's tone of voice, which previously would have been filled with misery, was now more factual. Dan noted with satisfaction that the slightly panicky edge had gone.

After breakfast they strolled along the front, looking at the boats moored in the harbour, jokingly selecting which of the gin palaces they would have if they could. Dan suggested that they visit the sponge factory. Intrigued, Alex agreed.

Far from being a factory, it was a large, dark, cool, damp shop with huge racks filled with sponges of different shapes, textures, colours and sizes. Groups of tourists followed their guides, while more knowledgeable customers foraged happily among the piles of stock. In the middle, towards the back, sat a weather-beaten old man, his feet lost in a heap of sponges. With a large pair of scissors he was neatly trimming and tidying each one, apparently oblivious to what was going on around him. Behind a narrow counter by the door stood a middle-aged woman, who Alex guessed was the old man's daughter; she was cheerfully haggling with her customers over the price of their purchases. Other local men ambled around the shop looking busy but actually doing very little.

'The dark ones are totally natural and untreated, full of the bodies of the other creatures that live parasitically on sponges, which you must remember are living organisms. The first stage in treating sponges is over here.'

The guide led her group to a huge tank and continued in her sing-song voice the speech she had obviously repeated hundreds of times during the season. Her smile never left her over-made-up face as the group gathered round her.

'Here they are gently soaked in a weak solution of hydrochloric acid. It is the acid that is partly causing the clean smell in here. Too much acid, or the wrong type, and the sponges would disintegrate . . . or something nasty might occur. However, we don't have to worry about that *here* because Kalymnos is also known as "the Sponge Island", since it is one of the main industries and the people have years of experience so know exactly the right strength to use. When they float to the surface they are ready. The next vat . . .'

Again the group shuffled after her.

'. . . is where the sponges are soaked in water to wash away the last of the nasty little creatures and to get rid of any last bits of acid. This can take some time, but when they are clean and yellow they are ready.'

She nodded her head at one of the Greek men leaning against the counter and he ambled over. He rolled up his sleeve before plunging his arm into the vat to pull out the sponge she indicated and wrang it out before popping it into a spin dryer for a few seconds. When it came out it was soft and fluffy.

'Here, isn't that lovely?' The guide stroked the sponge against one of the group's face. 'In England this specimen would probably cost about eighty pounds, but the equivalent cost here on "the Sponge Island" is about twenty. For the ladies, small ones are wonderful make-up sponges – I use one all the time.' ('You're better off without it,' Dan muttered under his breath, referring to her excessive make-up, and Alex dug him in the ribs.) 'They make very good presents for people at home and are easy to pack. You now have fifteen minutes here to make your purchases before we move on. Please gather by the big tree in fifteen minutes. Thank you,' she finished, with an upward lilt of her voice.

'Fancy buying a sponge?' Dan asked.

Alex nodded; it was too good an opportunity to miss. As someone whose idea of heaven was a long lazy soak in a hot bath, a natural sponge was something she had always wanted, but she'd never been able to justify the cost. The large one she had hankered after would have set her back about a hundred pounds.

They moved over to the rack and began jostling with everyone else to get the most attractive sponges. Alex spurned the odd and misformed ones, leaving the other tourists to laugh and joke about their shapes, and picked out a large, open-textured sponge that was almost perfectly round. It was soft and springy. When she showed it to Dan he shook his head and held out a slightly smaller one that was more oval than round, but whose texture was much tighter.

'This one's much better. I'll show you why,' he offered. 'Shield me from Madam.' He nodded and smiled at the woman behind the counter. 'She'll go potty if she sees me doing this, but if you take a sponge and gently pull it between your thumbs it should stay intact and not come away, like this one . . .' He finished triumphantly as Alex's choice began to come away under his pressure.

'A good sponge', he continued, 'will need to be physically ripped to come to pieces and will therefore last a lot longer. Admittedly, it's more expensive, but this one really is a beauty. Let's go and see what we can do on the price.'

Alex bowed to his obviously superior knowledge and, applying the lessons she had just learnt, also picked out a good but smaller sponge as a present for Jen.

At the till, Dan held out their selection to the woman. She was chatting to the old man, who had left his snipping and his seat and was now leaning against the counter. 'Very good quality,' he said in broken English.

'*Nea, poso kani afto?* How much?' asked Dan.

Madam took and felt the sponges. '*Para poli kalo.* You always pick good,' she said to Dan, and gave him a gap-toothed grin. She held up Alex's sponge. 'Eight thousand drachma.' Then she indicated the one Alex had picked out for Jen. 'Six thousand drachma.'

Alex did a few sums. 'That's about forty pounds.' She was delighted and was about to say so when she felt Dan's foot gently applying pressure on hers. She shut her mouth like a trap.

'Too much,' Dan said. 'After all the customers I bring to you!' He was flirting with the woman and Alex watched, bemused, as she softened under Dan's flattery.

'Hokay, hokay.' She raised her hands in mock submission. 'Six thousand, four thousand.'

Dan looked questioningly at Alex as if there were room for doubt. Following his lead, she gave a seemingly submissive nod of her head and said slowly, 'Well, OK', adding quietly under her breath so only Dan would hear: 'You've just saved me twelve quid!' Louder, to the woman, she said, 'Traveller's cheque OK?'

The woman nodded and reached for her calculator to work out the exchange rate, turning it round to show Alex the figure.

Alex rummaged in her bag and got out her book of cheques. She pulled out a twenty and a ten, countersigned and dated them both, then handed them over, tucked inside her passport. The old man was still leaning on the counter, idly watching the transaction; he glanced at Alex's passport and suddenly stood bolt upright. He snatched it from the woman and held it in two hands, looking from the photograph to Alex.

'You Ghillyand?' he asked.

172

'Well, yes,' replied Alex, drawing back from the man and his reaction.

'*Para ghia Mou!* May the Virgin protect me!' he said, and made the sign to ward off the evil eye. 'Take sponges. No pay. Present. Now go!'

'Papa!' the woman cried, trying to stop him giving away some of her best stock, but he had already given Alex back her traveller's cheques and passport and was bundling the sponges into Dan's bag as he moved round the counter and pushed them out of the door. For all his age he was surprisingly strong and they were out on the pavement, Greek curses ringing in their ears, before they had a chance to take in what was happening.

Alex stood staring at her traveller's cheques and passport in her hand.

'What was all that about, do you think?' Dan asked, equally puzzled.

'I don't know, but let's not talk about it here. Everyone's staring. Come on.' She dragged him across the road to a bench and sat down. 'You're going to tell me I'm being paranoid . . . but can you honestly say that the old man's outburst had nothing to do with my name?' She was tucking her belongings safely back in her bag and couldn't see the worried look on Dan's face.

'For once, I'm not going to disagree with you. He definitely came to life when he saw your name. I wonder . . .' Dan's voice tailed off as he gazed back across the road and in through the door, where he could just see the old man in the gloom at the rear of the shop, snipping away at sponges as if nothing had happened.

'What?'

'You're going to hate this, but at some point – not today – I'm going to have to come back and ask a few questions without you . . . No, don't argue. It was you he obviously took a scunner to, and if you're around we'll just get the same reaction. You know I'll have to do this one by myself.'

To Dan's surprise, Alex didn't argue but agreed, provided he did it sooner rather than later.

'Anyway,' she said laughing, 'I got my sponges for free, so maybe I've got something to thank David Ghillyand for after all!' Her laughter sounded hollow and unconvincing.

* * *

'Well, I never thought she'd come looking for us.'

Rose Haggerty rocked gently back and forth, her hands clasped in her lap as she watched Edith Jones shelling peas into a large bowl on the other side of the veranda. 'Anyway,' she added petulantly, '*you* were the one who had to "do the right thing" and go and register it in the first place. If you hadn't, I wouldn't have had anything to send, would I?'

It was almost a logical argument.

'Well, we always knew someone would ask questions eventually, didn't we?'

'We were lucky, Edie, that was all. You know, I never thought I'd hear myself say it but the fact the Clinic never had its own medical staff might have been a blessing in disguise. So why you had to go and register it at all I'll never know. I mean, no one would have been any the wiser, would they?'

Edith put down the peas. 'Because, Rosie, I don't believe in the sins of the father resting on the child. If I hadn't registered it, it would've been as if she'd never existed. I know she wasn't around long. But by registering her coming into this world, and her departing it, we acknowledged that fact. No one else in the family bothered, did they? Besides, it was the right thing to do. It made *me* feel better.'

'You make it sound as if I didn't care – as if it didn't bother me at all. That's not fair. It bothered me a lot – it always has done. It's why I sent the certificate to Mackers. When I read he was dead I hoped she might burn it. I just couldn't do it myself. It would have been as if we'd finally condoned what happened. I know that's silly, but . . . I mean . . . don't you think Alexandra finally has a *right* to know?' Rose's voice was growing shriller as she spoke, and the tremor in it suggested she was going to cry.

'Now, now, Rosie, don't take on so. I suppose you're right . . . but I don't know what we're going to say to her, that's all.'

'What did Papas say she wanted to know?'

'Apparently she said very little. But the young man asked about her parents' time here. Nothing about the Clinic at all.'

'Then maybe it's all right to see her. I mean, we don't know exactly what happened that night, do we? I mean, we had no proof. He just said not to tell anyone he'd gone out. He never told us why.' Rose sounded eager as she momentarily envisaged being able to sit down with Alexandra over a nice cup of tea and have the sort of cosy chat about England that she and Edith enjoyed so much. Edith's next words shattered the image.

'What about Christos?' she asked softly as she eased herself out of the chair and made her way back into the kitchen. The only sign of her own disquiet was the white gnarled knuckles tightly gripping the edge of the bowl.

Rose began rocking the chair faster. 'We don't have to tell him she's here, do we?' she asked hopefully.

Edith came back through the door and walked round the chair to face Rose. She put her foot on the runner and the chair jerked to a halt, tipping Rose forward so that she was looking straight up at Edith.

'We won't have to tell him. If they're asking around town for anyone who knows us, then Christos is sure to hear about it, isn't he? How do we know he won't send her up here? After all, it would be an easy way for him to avoid the issue, wouldn't it?'

Rose's lower lip began to tremble and her eyes filled with large greasy tears. 'Edie, I'm scared. Could she send us to prison? We're too old to go to prison, aren't we? What's going to happen to us?'

'I don't know, Rose. But I hope this has taught you a lesson. Next time you want to do something silly like send old bits of paper home, you'll talk to me first!'

Edith sounded as if she were scolding a naughty child for scrumping apples, not a woman in her eighties who might have pulled the whole fabric of their lives down around their ears.

Christine, the holiday rep they had met at Kos airport, was sitting at the bar chatting with Manolis when Dan and Alex walked in. She raised an arm and beckoned them over.

'Knew we'd meet up here eventually. How are you enjoying Kalymnos, Alex?

Alex was surprised that Christine had remembered her name in all the hubbub at the airport. When she commented on this Christine laughed.

'It goes with the job. Every guest always remembers my name but seems to forget that I have anything up to twenty-seven new ones to learn each fortnight, so over the years I've taught myself a few tricks of the trade. Mind you, I may be good with names, but money . . . !' She turned back to Manolis. 'OK, so you've got eleven of my lot with you tomorrow, which we've finally agreed is a total of one hundred and thirty-two thousand drachs. I'll book the cabs and make sure they're down by the *Splash* for nine-thirty.'

'That's a thought.' Dan leaned across Christine. 'Room for two more tomorrow, Manolis?'

'Of course. Tomorrow is special . . . only my special friends. Last week I take fifty-five. Too many, many too many. Tomorrow only twenty, OK?'

Alex gave Dan a questioning look. 'Now what are you letting me in for?'

'You'll love it, won't she, Chris?' Christine nodded. 'Manolis does a leisurely round-the-island trip which involves skimming over the waves, visiting little hidden bays, drinking ouzo, eating, drinking again, eating barbecued *souvlaki*, drinking –'

'I get the picture!' Alex held her hands up in mock surrender. 'Sounds lovely . . . going nowhere and all day to do it.'

Manolis grinned at her and his eyes twinkled under his baseball cap. 'Dan, I like this lady. She is my sort!'

'Hands off, you old Casanova – I saw her first.'

Alex laughed. It was a long time since anyone had even jokingly sparred over her and she had to admit she liked it.

The next day they were the first to board Manolis' boat, *Splash II*, at her mooring in the marina. She was an elegant wooden schooner and the gleaming polish of her woodwork was a tribute to the regard in which she was held. Manolis explained that, although the *meltem* – the local hot wind – had blown itself out overnight, it would still be a bit rough, so they would have to cling to the coastline.

'Kettle is on. Come have a coffee and we wait for the others.'

The little cabin was very comfortable with a surprising amount of room. It was also well decorated, with various shells and nautical items. A kettle bubbled away on a small two-ring hob. The radio played softly in the background and behind the table two men played backgammon adding, to the comfortable feeling in the cabin. Manolis introduced everyone to his crew, 'actually my brother and nephew, but today crew', and laughed his huge laugh as they waited for the rest of the group. They didn't have long to wait, and two taxis pulled up at the marina to disgorge a group of cheerful tanned people.

As soon as they were on board Manolis did a quick head count.

'Everyone ready?' To a loud chorus of 'yeses' the *Splash*'s engines sprang to life. As the 'crew' weighed the anchor and secured the gangplank, everyone settled down around the decks of the boat.

Alex and Dan sprawled on sun mattresses on the cabin's roof, where they not only had a good view of the rugged coastline but could also join in conversations with Manolis and the other passengers. They were a lively group, and by the time the ouzo bottle and mid-morning snack of feta cheese and tomatoes on bread came round it seemed to Alex as if she had known these people all her life. Happily she lay back on the mattress.

'Not worried about the sun today, then?' Dan teased her.

She couldn't be bothered to reply and with a vague wave of her hand closed her eyes again, but pulled her hat over her face. She drifted contentedly with the swell of the boat, feeling the throb of the engines. Manolis gauged the mood of his passengers perfectly, telling them local tales and legends as they passed various points along the rocky coast.

They laughed with him at his stories of the bishop who had his own private nunnery to serve him; the pilot who had built his own telecommunications centre which he was not allowed to use because it interfered with all of Kalymnos' broadcast and shipping frequencies – and stories about caves and smuggling and the people of the villages they passed. Gently his rounded tones and almost perfect English washed over Alex. She was on the verge of dozing off when Dan woke her.

'Look, Alex, up there!'

He was pointing up the steep cliff rising on both sides of the boat. Alex blinked a little to adjust her eyes to the bright light and at first could not see what had made Dan so excited. Finally her eyes focused and as she stared up the sheer rock face she could see mountain goats bounding up and down and across seemingly impossible terrain. One little kid had obviously managed to climb down the rock but had got itself stranded and stood bleating on the edge for its mother, which obligingly came and got it.

Ahead of them Alex saw a small natural harbour.

'This Vathi,' Manolis explained. 'It is deepest channel here and Vathi is at the bottom of Green Valley, which goes along top of the island. During and after the war, Vathi was used many times to smuggle secrets across water to Turkey, but you do not worry – now it is quite safe.'

The Greek's loathing of his near neighbour was evident, and although his passengers found Manolis' feelings about Turkey disagreeable they had too much respect for their host and his country to say anything.

'We take one hour here and then go.'

The gangplank was lowered and everyone trooped off the boat. Some people immediately went to one of the harbour tavernas for coffee, while others, Alex and Dan among them, chose to meander through the small village and explore some of the shops before sitting down in the shade for a cool drink.

'What do you think was smuggled?' Alex sucked noisily on her straw. 'I mean, what do you think they had here that was worth smuggling? I know it's got a lot of agricultural land, but I didn't think there was much here.'

'Who knows? Actually one thing they used to manufacture in a big way here were cigarettes. You don't hear much about it these days, what with the anti-smoking lobby – that's even reached as far as Greece!'

The sound of a klaxon rent the air, resounding round the high walls of the channel. 'Come on. That's for us. Manolis might seem to take this trip easy but he really works to a fairly tight schedule.'

They were last back on the boat; the other passengers were leaning over the bows yelling for them to hurry up.

After her doze earlier Alex felt like staying awake, and as the sun climbed higher she sat under the awning chatting quietly to Manolis and his family. He told her about the sponge divers and what a remarkable group of men they had been. They used to dive to the bottom of the sea, without air tanks. Holding their breath for minutes, they would hack the sponges off the rock, putting them into large nets over their shoulders before swimming back to the surface with their haul. It was considered a matter of honour to stay down as long as possible; and many of the old divers had to retire after they got the bends by surfacing too quickly, thinking they could defeat the ocean. Once this had happened they were no longer any use at the bottom of the sea and nowadays could be found cluttering the bars and tavernas around the island. You could always spot the divers by their crooked arms or bent legs and stooped posture.

'We went into the sponge factory and I got a beauty. Dan showed me how to pick out a really good one. The prices were great, really cheap compared with home.' Alex bit her lower lip as she deliberated; then, checking that Dan was still snoozing on the cabin roof, she turned back to Manolis. 'Actually something very odd happened.' And she told him about the old man's reaction when he saw the name in her passport.

'So what is your name that is special?' It was a natural question.

'Ghillyand.'

As she answered, Alex observed Manolis' face closely to see if he reacted oddly or showed any sign of recognition, but his face wore his usual jolly expression and he shrugged his shoulders dismissively.

Alex was disappointed. She was not sure what she had expected, but she had hoped for some sort of response. With a sigh she turned and looked over the stern of the boat, watching the wake foaming behind them, flinging up sparkling white beads of water to catch the sunlight.

It was mesmerising; she didn't know how long she sat there thinking about nothing as she studied the shapes in the water. When the spray began to subside she looked up. They were approaching a small island and Manolis was easing the *Splash* carefully to its mooring. On the right a path wound up the hillside to a tiny church at the top. The beach was stony, and an old wooden hut with a rotting sail boat leaning against it stood in the shade of a twisted olive tree. On the left was a small stone house, outside which a group of people were sitting. As usual the men played cards or backgammon and fingered their worry beads, while the women, all dressed in black, with aprons on and scarves tied under their chins, bustled around preparing a meal. They greeted Manolis warmly, who announced the party would stay here for a while.

Dan and Alex decided to visit the church and climbed up the deceptively steep path to the top of the hill. The church was even smaller than it appeared from the boat, but before they went in they explored the area behind it, where they'd been told there was a monk's cell. Sure enough, the cool stone building round the well in the centre of the courtyard revealed a blanket neatly rolled in the corner and a plate and jug next to a Bible on a bare table. A few goats also wandered about; their bleating echoed round the courtyard.

They walked towards the church door; out of respect, Alex

179

wrapped her sarong round her legs. When she looked inside she was overcome by emotion. She would never have regarded herself as a religious person. At school she had suffered the required Scripture lessons that the law demanded, but attended church only for weddings, christenings and funerals. Had she been asked she probably would have declared herself an agnostic, saying she lacked the arrogance to state definitely there was not anything there, but likewise refusing to accept there was.

As she entered that simple little church, she didn't exactly discover a belief in God, but she found for the first time that she could understand people who had a plain unquestioning faith. It was something to do with the ornate little altar and its burning candles, the herb-strewn floor that released the scent of rosemary and thyme as she crept inside, and the dull glow of the golden chalice under a cracked dark picture of the Madonna and Child. The whole church could not have been much bigger than twelve feet by eight, but at that moment it was more majestic and spiritual than the large cathedrals or abbeys she had visited.

Alex had a sudden urge to cross herself, but felt it would be an insult to the people who prayed here. Instead she fumbled for her purse and scooped out all the coins, dropping them with a clatter into the bowl where a few other coins had been placed. As she went to leave, she looked again at the altar and, not for the first time, found herself saying, 'Please God . . .' – and this time she meant it.

Dan was leaning over the wall, chewing a blade of dry glass and looking down the hill. 'Hmm. Got you too, I see. The first time I came here I couldn't quite believe this place. There's something about it that's really . . .' He tailed off. For once even Dan couldn't find the words.

Alex untied her makeshift skirt and tucked her arm into Dan's as they walked down the hill. 'Peaceful and honest,' she finished for him.

'Honest. Yes, that's a good word for it. You know, maybe there's a feature in this; religious experiences – where and when.' Dan caught Alex's eye. 'I'm not mickey-taking, but if I thought for one moment you'd had a genuine religious experience I swear I'd dump you in the sea head first!'

Laughing, they made their way back to the beach and hobbled over the pebbles into the sea. Side by side they swam out to the low harbour wall, where they gazed down through the crystal-clear water at the sea urchins that clung to the rocks and the shoals of little fish that darted in and out and around their toes. Then they rejoined the rest of the *Splash*'s passengers, who were now sitting in the shade chatting. Glasses of retsina were pressed upon them and their Greek hosts began asking them about their opinions of Greece.

National pride was much in evidence, and, whether because of the retsina, the tiny church or the general atmosphere, Alex found herself telling one of the women that she had lived on Kalymnos when she was a little girl. This resulted in much hugging and kissing and questions in a mixture of Greek and English about where she had lived and what she remembered.

Everyone was disappointed when she explained that she had been barely eight months old when she and her father had gone back to England in 1953.

'No mama?' asked a woman who seemed to be the daughter of an aged female who was sitting in the far corner.

'No. She died in an accident here, which is why we went back to England. But my nannies decided to stay on. That's why I've come here. I want to find them.'

The woman translated, and as she did so a mosquito buzzed round Alex's head, making her wave her hand at it and turn away, so she did not see the look that crossed the old woman's face. Dan did see it. He picked up his beer can and took a swig from it, asking casually, 'You wouldn't know where we could find them, I suppose?'

Again the woman translated. This time her mother scrambled to her feet and shuffled inside the house, muttering oaths to herself as she slammed the door behind her.

'Dan . . . ?'

Before he could answer, Manolis had risen to his feet. 'Leave to Manolis,' he said, and ambled into the house after the old woman. A few minutes later he reappeared, grinning from ear to ear. 'They live in Linaria. Where?' And in answer to his own question he shrugged his shoulders and spread his hands, indicating he could not tell them more than that.

'Linaria?' said one of the group. 'We're all going there to the Sunset Café for a drink this evening. Why don't you join us?'

It was a kind invitation from a group of people with whom Dan and Alex both felt comfortable; even if Dan had wanted to decline the offer, Alex wouldn't have let him.

Dan observed her as she talked to the others, noting how relaxed she had become. Her shoulders were no longer tense, and despite her efforts to avoid the sun her skin was golden. Her eyes shone, and when she threw her head back to laugh at a silly joke, her enjoyment was real. The prickly Alex was still there, threatening to reappear any minute; but it was as if she had been turned inside out. The vulnerable Alex who was usually buried deep inside was clearly on display, while the spiky Alex had been pushed down inside. Dan suspected that when they returned to London she would change back again.

That evening, when they arrived at the Sunset Café in Linaria, the rest of the group were already there and had saved two extra seats by heaping them with cameras and bags, ready for their new friends. The café itself differed little from any of the others in the neighbourhood, with its plastic seats and tables, but its position made it unique. Perched above Linaria beach, it had the most stunning view of the bay. Bougainvillaea hung over the white-washed sea wall, below which the water lapped against the shore like silk. In the distance the multi-coloured lights of a taverna set into the rock took on a fiery glow in the fading light. As the sun began to set, the café filled up as people gathered to watch the nightly spectacle.

Although everyone carried on chattering, they barely glanced at each other, keeping their eyes on the sky, watching the last red sliver sink below the horizon. Somebody aimed a comment at Dan, who turned his head to make a suitable retort; as he did so he became aware of two elderly women standing a little way down the road. Their heads were close together and, although like every-one else they seemed to be watching the sunset, Dan could have sworn they kept looking over to their table.

He got to his feet, saying, 'Won't be a minute, my next one's a beer', to indicate his intention of returning. He glanced at Alex, who had caught up with their drinking partners and was getting decidedly tipsy. She was also still engrossed in her conversation. Nonchalantly he stuck his hands in his pocket and strolled down the road, appearing to be stretching his legs. As he walked past the two women they seemed to draw together, but he ignored them. No sooner had he gone past them than he heard one say to the

182

other, 'There, Rosie, I told you not to worry.' It took all of Dan's willpower not to jump into the air, punching the sky with his fist in his delight; instead he carried on strolling down the road until it petered out on the beach. Still keeping an eye on the women he made his way along under cover of the wall, ensuring as he went that he kicked plenty of sand into his shoes. He came to the short flight of steps that led back up to the road, where he waited for a few minutes.

When he felt the time was right he head up the stairs, glancing over his shoulder at the blaze of colour that now lit the sky. As he had anticipated, he arrived back on the road close to where the women were standing. He sat down on the wall and removed his shoes, tipping the carefully gathered sand out of them.

'Magnificent, isn't it?' he asked casually as he replaced his shoes before standing up and giving the women one of his most becoming smiles.

'Yes, it hasn't been this good for weeks. Of course, the winds do make a difference. When they blow they seem to dull the colours somehow.'

'You sound very knowledgeable. You must have been here before.'

'We live here, up there . . . have done for over forty years . . . so we should know something about it, shouldn't we?'

With a feeling of surprise Dan realised they were flirting with him and if he wasn't careful he might lose this opportunity. He didn't mean to blurt out his next question with such force, and his tone was rougher than he intended.

'Actually, I was hoping you might help me. Would I be right in saying that you're Rose Haggerty and Edith Jones? If so, a friend of mine would love to have a chat with you.'

The women grabbed each other's hand and stood staring at him with looks approaching horror. Rose's face crumpled and her lower lip began to quiver. Edith felt her friend's reaction and turned on Dan.

'Now look what you've done. What business it is of yours who we are? We haven't done anything to hurt you. Go away, leave us alone!' As she spoke her voice grew increasingly strident until the people at the café turned to peer down the road to see what was going on.

Alex, realising Dan was somehow involved, got to her feet. Her drinks made her a bit wobbly but she ran down and joined the little group.

'Dan, what's wrong? What are you up to?' Alex eyed the small group.

'Alex, I'd like you to meet Edith and Rose. This is Alex – Alexandra Ghillyand.'

Alex stood and stared at the women, who stared back, not knowing what to say or do. Mechanically she held out her right hand. 'Hello . . . I was hoping to bump into you.' It was the sort of comment you would make to someone you met when shopping in the local high street, not to people you had travelled several hundred miles to find.

Automatically Edith took Alex's hand and gave Rose a nudge to make her do likewise.

Alex discovered she was trembling as she shook hands. 'I want to talk to you. Please may I?' It sounded feeble but her underlying longing and hope rang out in every word.

'We'd rather not.' Edith turned Rose round and tried to take her away from Alex and Dan, but Alex began to speak again.

'No! Please don't go. You don't know how far I've come to talk to you. There's so much I don't know . . . don't understand. I know you can help me. You wouldn't have sent that certificate if you didn't want to help. I don't want to hurt you, I just want to know the truth. Surely I'm entitled to that, after all this time?'

These last comments, which so closely reflected what she had said a few days earlier to Edith, made Rose turn back to face them, dragging Edith round with her.

The look of pure need and raw emotion on Alex's face was almost a tangible thing that reached out and wrapped itself round the two older women as they contemplated her. Rose tugged at Edith's arm and instinctively the two women moved towards Alex, making clucking and soothing noises as they would at a small baby.

Dan knew it wouldn't take much to persuade them, but he also knew that if they felt pressured or rushed they would refuse to say even one word. He took a small notepad and pen out of his pocket and scribbled a note of their address. 'Here, this is where we're staying. You can always leave a message with Sylvie if we're not there.'

Dan held out the note and reluctantly Edith took it from him, glancing at it before folding it once and putting it in her pocket.

'We'll let you know. Come on, Rosie . . . Supper will get burnt.'

Rose raised a papery hand to Alex's cheek and gave it a stroke, saying quietly under her breath, 'Robert's little girl', before scuttling after Edith, leaving Alex and Dan watching until they turned round the corner.

Alex dragged her hand across her brow, swaying a little as she did so. 'I think I'm a bit drunk.'

Dan held out his arm, and thankfully she slid in underneath it, holding him round the waist as they went back to the café. Sheepishly she avoided everyone's gaze, sitting down and reaching out for her drink, not because she particularly wanted it but because it gave her something to do. By now the sky's flaming colours had totally mellowed into a rich purple and silently Alex stared at the bottom of her glass, the thoughts once again whirling round and round in her head. Suddenly her head shot up and she grabbed Dan's arm, making him slop his drink over the edge of the glass and on to his neighbour's lap.

'Hey, Alex!'

'Dan, didn't you hear her? Didn't you hear what she said?' Alex was now standing up, gazing down the road in the direction that Rose and Edith had gone.

'Alex, sit down. You really are smashed, sweetheart, aren't you?'

'No, I'm not – well, yes I am – but she called me Robert's little girl. Not David's, but Robert's! I'm so squiffed I didn't realise it. Dan, what did she mean?'

If Alex had had her way, they would have spent the next day sitting on the patio outside their apartment waiting for a message from Edith and Rose. Dan, however, persuaded her that it would be better for both of them if they went out. Reluctantly, Alex let herself be taken into Myrties and Massouri to rummage round the shops. She expected to find the usual tourist traps but was instead enchanted to discover the local pottery and jewellery made by the people of the villages. They stopped for lunch and by the time they got to the apartment laden with blue and green pots and a hand-made silver bracelet, which Dan had bought as a present for her, it was mid-afternoon. They were unlocking their door when they heard a scuffling on the stairs behind them and Sylvie's head appeared over the wall.

'For you. Message. Telephone.'

Alex almost dropped all her parcels in her haste to snatch the paper from Sylvie. She read it and turned, grinning at Dan. 'They say they'll see us tomorrow afternoon at three.' She wrapped her arms round his neck and gave him a hug.

The next day, the start of their second week, dragged along slowly until Dan finally agreed, 'Yes, we can begin to make a move.' It was five to three by the time they made their way up the rough, dusty path to the address they had been given. Doubts about whether they would easily find the house were unfounded, for the moment they saw it they knew it had to belong to Edith and Rose. As if to confirm their thoughts, the two women were sitting on the veranda at the back of the house when they came round the last curve in the path.

The geranium pots neatly arranged inside the low wrought-iron fence and the swathed, tied-back curtains at the windows screamed their Englishness at them. Dan held open the gate for Alex and shut it carefully behind them. Alex waited until Dan was standing next to her before ringing the bell, then reached down to hold his hand. They heard footsteps inside and Edith opened the door. Her greeting was formal but not unfriendly, and she shooed them through the house, which had been decorated in an English style that looked out of place among the exotic surroundings, to the small veranda where Rose was sitting in her rocking chair.

They took the seats indicated and accepted the offered glass of cold lemonade and home-made shortbread, making polite conversation as they settled. Finally none of them could carry on the pretence that this was a purely social call and, surprisingly, it was Rose who turned the subject round.

'You want to know what happened?'

Alex nodded.

'What do you already know?'

Alex thought for a moment, trying to organise her thoughts before she spoke, slowly at first and then more quickly as she became more confident.

'I know that two girls called Alexandra Marie Ghillyand were . . . apparently . . . born within a few weeks of each other at the Rouget Clinic . . . That their parents were David and Elizabeth Ghillyand, and Robert and Sally Ghillyand. Mrs MacKay told me Robert and Sally's daughter died, but I'm still trying to find out what happened to Robert and Sally. I think they went away or

186

something . . . but where I don't know. Mrs MacKay wouldn't tell me. She said *you* would have to do that.'

Alex paused, awaiting a reaction from the two women, who were both avoiding her eyes. She sighed and ploughed on.

'I know the other baby girl died of aortic atresia. As a medical doctor I fully understand what that means. I know that I – and everyone else – always believed I was David and Elizabeth's daughter, but I can't be . . . can I?' After all this time the question was surprisingly easy to ask.

Rose rocked to and fro in her chair, while Edith sat upright in hers, eyes bright as she finally returned Alex's look.

'You are Alexandra Marie Ghillyand – don't worry about that. No, don't say anything.' Edith held up a hand to stop Alex interrupting. 'Let me explain.'

As the weeks passed and Elizabeth's pregnancy began to grow more obvious she became increasingly difficult and petulant, resenting the bulk she was having to carry with her. She was also not pleased when David told her he was again going to Greece.

'I'll tell Papa you can't go. That I need you here,' she said sulkily.

'Elizabeth, you misunderstand me. I don't just need to go, I *want* to go. Anyway, if I don't go now, I'll only have to go later, and believe it or not I want to be here when this baby is born.' He walked over to her and wound a curl of her hair round his finger, 'Despite everything, I do actually care about you and this . . . our baby,' he corrected himself.

He took her in his arms and kissed her before he left the room. She wanted to call him back, to ask him to hold her, to prove to her that he meant what he said, but she refused to beg, so miserably she let him go.

David returned to his office, but instead of reading the reports in front of him he sat staring out of the window. *Damn it all, why can't we talk like two sensible adults? Why does she have to turn everything into such a bloody battle?* With a sigh he turned back to his paperwork.

Two days later David made a point of accompanying Elizabeth when she went to the Clinic for a pre-natal check-up. The obstetrician, Mr Chiltern, greeted Elizabeth warmly.

'Radiant as ever, and I am delighted to see you, too, Dr

Ghillyand. We do like our fathers to be involved, and aware of what is going on, don't we, Sister?' Sister Browning nodded her head. 'Now, if you'd like to wait here, I'll just disappear with Elizabeth and check that all is going well, as I'm sure it is. While I'm doing that, please would you get Edith and Rose? I think, as you're both here today, it's as good a time as any for you to meet your midwives, don't you?'

Beaming at everyone, Mr Chiltern fussily escorted Elizabeth into the consulting-room.

'Just as I expected,' he said when they rejoined David. 'Everything is doing beautifully, and I think we can now give you a revised delivery date of just before Christmas. What a lovely present that will be for everyone, won't it?' He beamed at them all again.

David found the man's attitude excessive and was about to say something when a knock at the door stopped him.

'Come in,' called Chiltern. Edith and Rose entered the room, Rose looking decidedly sullen. 'Good, glad you could be found. You already know Elizabeth and she's going to be having her baby here with us, which is lovely. Dr Ghillyand, we really are very lucky having these two here, you know. Difficult to find good SRNs outside the NHS who have got their Midders as well.' It was clear Mr Chiltern was not an admirer of the new National Health Service. 'One of the reasons I'm always so pleased to be called into the Clinic. Good girls, these, and we've worked together before – haven't we, girls?' He sounded as if he were talking about the prize cows in his personal herd.

The two nurses, accustomed to his manner, nodded, not knowing what else to do.

'Yes, we're a well-established team and between us we'll make sure everything goes well, won't we, girls?'

They nodded again. Rose swallowed hard but Edith timidly answered Chiltern's question.

'Yes, we will. And we're ever so pleased about the baby.'

Rose nodded for the third time.

Elizabeth stared at the two women and rolled her eyes. 'Oh God. Not you two again! Honestly, David, there's hordes of nurses here. Why do I have to get those two?'

'Because, as Mr Chiltern says, they're the best resident midwives the Clinic's got. I mean, we wouldn't want you to go into labour and have someone you didn't know in attendance, would you?'

'I suppose not.' Elizabeth crossed her ankles and began flicking at her gloves in a bored manner.

Quickly David jumped in. 'Please forgive Elizabeth – she's just feeling a bit tetchy. I think it's delightful you'll be looking after my wife. After all, you know each other already and you did such a good job in getting her back on her feet after that awful flu.' His words, even though they weren't sincere, had the desired pacifying effect on everyone present. After a few minutes' polite conversation the two nurses left the room and returned to the staff lounge to let their colleagues know why they had been summoned.

'Why did it have to be us?' Rose asked no one in particular, after they had broken the news. 'It was bad enough when she was in here before, but pregnancy doesn't seem to have improved her any – spoilt madam!'

'Oh God, how awful!' Jean voiced the others' opinion but the note of relief in her voice was obvious. She stirred an extra spoonful of sugar in her tea before dropping the wet spoon back into the sugar bowl.

'Mind you,' said Mary. 'You've only got yourselves to blame. I mean, you were the ones who wanted to do the extra training, and look where it's got you!'

'Come on, Mary – that's not fair,' remonstrated Eileen from the depths of the one comfy armchair. 'You would've loved to do your Midder – you just weren't bright enough.'

'That may be so. But I tell you what – if getting to be a midwife would have meant looking after Lady Muck then I'm glad I didn't do it!'

'I will not have you referring to Mrs Ghillyand as "Lady Muck",' said Sister Dobson from the doorway, making the group of nurses jump to their feet and attempt to tidy themselves up. The Clinic's four sisters had their own small sitting-room and rarely conde- scended to visit the nurses' room. 'In fact that's why I've popped in. To let you know that just because Nurses Jones and Haggerty are to be Mrs Ghillyand's midwives it doesn't give the rest of you good-for-nothings the right to leave her total care to them. When she is our patient she will get the same attentive care as everyone else who is with us at that time. Do I make myself absolutely clear?'

'Yes, Sister,' they chorused, not sitting down again until their superior had left the room.

'Who does she think she's kidding? Elizabeth Rouget, getting

189

the same treatment as everyone else. Do me a favour. I mean, if she didn't demand full room service herself then that cold stick of a husband would. I tell you, those two are as bad as each other!'

Eileen picked another biscuit from the tin a grateful patient had left them. 'You know what gets me?' she said through a mouthful of crumbs. 'How different those two are.'

Edith glanced up from the small gas ring in the corner where she was waiting for the kettle to boil. 'Which two?' she queried, pouring hot water into the pot as Rose fetched the milk.

'The two Ghillyand brothers. I mean, I get the feeling that David Ghillyand doesn't want to know, but you'd think Robert had invented being pregnant, he's that excited about it. You know, I think he rather wishes he had medical training so he could deliver the baby himself.'

'I think it's sweet,' Rose observed, sitting down with her cup of tea.

'You would!' said Jean. 'But could you imagine David Ghillyand wanting to be anywhere near the delivery room, even if he had trained in medicine? Test-tubes are about that man's limit.'

The door flew open and three more nurses walked in. 'Come on, you lot, it's nearly four. Time you were back out there.'

There was a mad dash for Eileen's comfortable armchair when she got up and followed Edith and Rose out of the door. They carried on discussing the two sets of prospective parents as they went back to work. Their feelings about David were confirmed half an hour later when he walked into the sluice room, where Rose was working.

'I wanted another chat,' he said nonchalantly. 'Just to confirm in your minds how important this baby is. Despite what you might think, I want this baby very much.'

Rose blushed, thinking of her earlier conversation with Edith.

'Good. I see you understand me. Please make sure your colleague gets the same message.' He gave a terse smile and went out, leaving the sluice room door swinging behind him.

Although Sandra Huntsworth was a capable lab assistant and technician, Robert found himself more aware of her presence than he had ever been of Sally when she had been working beside him. Initially he thought that it was because he was missing Sally, but he eventually realised it was not just the change in his personnel but the fact that, unlike Sally, Sandra had to be asked for everything.

'I suppose what I'm trying to say is that I've been taking you for granted, haven't I?' He carried on rubbing Sally's back as he spoke.

'No, darling, of course you haven't. It's just that I know how you work and what you're going to need. I must admit, if I didn't know that, I'd have problems too. But it's easy for me because I know the way you think. I expect Sandra finds it difficult because you never say anything when you're working . . . Quick! Here, feel.'

Tenderly she took Robert's hand and placed it on her bump. When the baby stopped kicking she carried on as if there had been no interruption.

'There's nothing else for it, darling. You're just going to have to be more aware, and remember to ask Sandra for what you need, instead of expecting her to know.'

Robert thought about what Sally had said and the next day began making an effort to make Sandra's job easier. When he and Sally had worked together they often didn't stop all day, but with Sandra he made a point of taking a proper tea break, and became a regular sight in the canteen, which he and Sally had only infrequently used.

Sometimes Edith or Rose would be having lunch at the same time, and often Robert would be invited to join them. Ever since they had discovered it was on the night that Robert had given them a lift to the cinema that he had proposed to Sally, they had felt proprietorial about the couple. They were genuinely delighted that they would be looking after Sally's delivery and told Robert so each time they saw him.

Robert would thank them and settle to his lunch, sometimes reading the paper and sometimes pretending to read it so that he could listen to the chatter and gossip on which the Rouget set-up seemed to thrive. The tables full of people buzzed with talk.

'Well, I just don't know what to do, Susan. I think it's a downright liberty to expect me to type up all those stupid notes again. I didn't mind doing it the first time, but to just assume I'll do it again is a bit much. You know, when I started I felt a bit underhand, giving those extra copies to David Ghillyand, but considering Robert just sends that upstart Sandra over with the notes, and

191

hasn't even got the manners to thank me for doing the work, I don't feel so bad about it this time.'

Hearing his name mentioned, Robert glanced up and saw David's secretary, Claire Grigson, having lunch with Cecil Rouget's Susan Wilmot.

'Why don't you go and tell Robert Ghillyand that it's got to stop? I mean, I know you said Sally had asked not to let him know what was going on, but that was ages ago, when she was busy too. Now she's just sitting at home, she's got plenty of time to type those notes up herself, hasn't she? Why should you carry on doing it? Honestly, Clare, they've no idea what we have to put up with, do they? I think you have every right to feel put upon and I'd tell him if I were you. Talking of which, do you know what my Roger asked me to do? Well . . .' And the conversation continued on more personal subjects.

Thoughtfully Robert stirred his coffee. He had not given any notes to Miss Grigson for typing. In fact, he had never asked where the typed notes came from. It had always been down to Sally, and now Sandra, to check he had everything he needed. So which notes were being passed to Clare Grigson, and why did David want a copy of them?

When he got back to the lab he looked through his various folders of notes. Most were neatly written in Sally's legible hand-writing, or more recently Sandra's straggly but clear scrawl. Sally had typed some of them, but these were easily spotted because of the mistakes and typing over. Then he noticed that the one set of notes that were perfectly typed, as if by a professional, were the notes on the sponge experiments. Why on earth had he not noticed sooner? Sally would have said it was because he read with-out looking. Until now he had not understood what she meant.

Over tea that afternoon he made a point of asking Sandra about the notes. 'You know, I haven't said it before, but I do think you're doing a great job. It can't be easy taking over for a few months, as you are. How do you keep up with it all?'

'I just do. You learn to.' Sandra appreciated Robert's praise but didn't want to ruin things by saying anything she shouldn't.

'I tell you where you're really quick – that's in getting the notes typed up. I must admit I could have done without the extra sponge work, but with your help we got that out of the way nice and quickly, didn't we?'

Sandra glowed with pride. 'Well, actually, I can't take the credit for that. Your brother told me that Miss Grigson had helped in typing up all your original notes – and that if I needed her to do it again while I found my feet then I was to let him know. He said I didn't need to bother you with it, as it happened like that before. I hope . . . I haven't done anything wrong . . . have I?'

Robert had a frown on his face and he ran his hand across his forehead. 'To be honest, Sandra, I don't know. I don't suppose any notes are still being sent over there, are they?'

'No – all those notes were completed weeks ago. What have I done wrong?' She sounded panicky.

Robert put a reassuring arm on hers. 'You've done nothing wrong. Now calm down. Just promise me two things. First, if any similar offer is made, you'll tell me straight away, even if it's Mr Rouget himself who makes it.' She nodded, her eyes wide. 'Second, that you don't tell anyone that this typing was done outside the lab. Everything that goes on here is highly confidential, and if anyone finds out we're not containing work we'll both be in trouble.' Again Sandra nodded and, considering herself chastised, excused herself.

Robert felt guilty about making empty threats. Since it didn't really matter where the notes were typed; he almost ran after Sandra to tell her he didn't mean it, but stopped himself. Something was going on and he wasn't sure what. Awful thoughts were beginning to form in his mind and he needed time to put them in order, to make sense of them.

He began to spend longer in the canteen, listening avidly to the gossip, gradually putting a picture together. As the image crystallised he became more concerned until, at last, he made up an excuse to talk to Miss Grigson.

'May I?' he asked as he took his lunch over to her table. She nodded in surprise. 'I've been feeling bad about all that work you've done for me. I should have said thank you sooner.'

'You're welcome . . . Oh, but I didn't think you knew about it.' She slapped her hand over her mouth, remembering how she'd promised David not to tell a soul.

Robert was about to lie to her, but common sense told him this would get him nowhere. 'Well, I *didn't* know until I heard you and Miss Wilmot talking about it the other day.'

Clare Grigson buried her head in her hands, the unflappable

exterior crumbling in front of his eyes. 'Please don't let on you heard me! I promised your brother I wouldn't tell anyone. You won't say anything to him, will you?'

'I won't,' Robert reassured her. 'But I wondered if you'd answer a few questions for me . . . hmmm?'

Clare agreed, dreading what he was going to ask and surprised when he enquired about the dates of David's trips to Greece. He asked her a few more questions about some of David's regular correspondents before thanking her and again assuring her he wouldn't tell anyone what she had done.

That evening he finally confided in Sally.

'Oh Robert – don't be so ridiculous! That's an awful thing to say. Look, I know you and David don't always see eye to eye, but that's quite an accusation you're hurling at his head. Besides, where's your proof?'

Robert opened his mouth to say something and then changed his mind.

'Ah-ha!' Sally cried triumphantly. 'I knew it . . . you haven't got any proof. I must also say I'm surprised at you, especially when he's being so nice as to pay our bills at the Clinic. No, don't look at me like that.' She was getting quite angry; if her bulk had allowed her, she would probably have been pacing their small living-room. 'I'm disappointed with you. I know David and Elizabeth can be bores, but they are family and I think this gesture proves it and . . .'

Suddenly she was crying. Full of concern, Robert went over to her.

'Oh, Sal, I'm sorry, I didn't mean to upset you. It's just that I am really worried. Come on, darling, please don't cry. I can't stand it.' He took out his handkerchief and held it to her nose. 'Blow,' he instructed.

As much as he wanted to carry on the conversation, sharing his suspicions with his wife, he decided it would be better to let the matter drop. It was Sally herself who next brought the subject up a few days later.

Although Robert didn't know it, Sally's tears hadn't been caused by her being emotionally wobbly on account of the pregnancy but by a nagging thought that she had the proof he needed. After all, she herself had given Miss Grigson the notes to be typed up, and it would have been very easy for David to obtain a copy.

'Do you really think that's what David is doing?'

Robert was surprised, because the question didn't relate to any conversation they had been having, but he immediately knew what she meant. 'Yes, I do.'

'Who else have you talked to about this?'

'No one. Why?'

'If you're really that concerned, why don't you go and talk to Cecil about it? He always says he's there to be talked to, that he likes it when his staff come to him. You know how much he likes to play the father role. So do as he says and talk to him. I'll come with you, if you like.' She made the offer sound as casual as she could.

Robert was startled. He could tell Cecil about the purified residues he was preparing for David, but he didn't want Sally to find out about his deal with his brother, nor that he knew about her deal with Clare Grigson. In the end he arranged to see Cecil by himself.

If Cecil was surprised that Robert had asked to see him, he didn't show it when he shook hands with him. 'Now, what did you want to see me about?'

'It's rather difficult to know where to begin.' Robert stumbled over his words like a nervous schoolboy.

'Come now, I'm a reasonable man, and I'm not going to eat you, am I? Out with it, out with it.' And he gave Robert an encouraging smile.

Cautiously Robert began to speak, telling Cecil about his fears about David. As he continued, Cecil stopped fidgeting and concentrated on what he was saying. When he had finished, the older man stood up and walked over to where Robert was sitting. Placing his hands on the arms of the chair he leaned over him, and spoke in a quiet, but tight voice.

'Dr Ghillyand, I have never heard such rubbish in my life. Your precious residues are indeed being used as David told you – for drug development, of which I am well aware. I am also aware that David is paying your bills out of the kindness of his heart, and love and concern for you, his brother and sister-in-law and your child. And this is how you repay him – wild accusations designed to glorify yourself. There is no glory for you, Robert, only my repugnance. Now get out!'

Cecil's contained rage was more terrifying than his angry outbursts and as quickly as he could Robert left. By the time he reached the door, Cecil was sitting at his desk writing busily and did not even raise his head when Robert said a polite 'Good morning' as he left.

'Oh, Sal, it was awful . . . I know it sounds crazy, but I'm positive I'm right. Now I wish I hadn't said anything. I feel like a traitor and I have a horrid feeling I'm not going to be allowed to forget this.'

After Robert had gone, Cecil had put down his pen and sat back, considering what had been said. That Robert was bright was common knowledge, as was the fact that he and David merely tolerated each other – something Cecil found hard to understand. When his father and brother had died in the trenches the loss had gone deep, and even now not a day went by when he didn't miss them. No, Cecil couldn't understand the evident antipathy between the Ghillyand brothers. However, what Robert had said was serious, and Cecil knew it needed to be checked. He wasted no time in talking to David, whose look of horror was more than enough to confirm what Cecil already knew.

'David, I'm sorry, but I had to ask. You can see that, can't you?'

David nodded. 'Look, this might sound mad, Cecil, but are you sure it's not Robert who's up to something? I mean, it wouldn't be the first time someone tried to point a finger at an innocent man to throw a smoke-screen round his own activities, will it?'

'What do you suggest? I don't want to sack him – he's too good.'

'No, I agree with you. The trouble is, no one knows what he gets up to in his lab, do they?' Cecil shook his head. 'So why not put someone else in there with him, to keep an eye on him?'

'See to it, David, and get them to report to you. You can keep me informed over dinner. By the way, do you think Elizabeth is up to another dinner party?' And with this problem resolved Cecil turned the conversation to domestic matters.

David let him talk on but excused himself as soon as he could, not wanting Cecil to see how bothered he was by Robert's accusations. The fact that Robert had got close to the truth was what had produced David's early look of horror. He wasn't sure how Robert had worked it out. After all, hadn't he commissioned the extra work in Greece himself? Only a few men knew what was going on in the old olive-pressing shed behind the main plant. None of them had had cause to contact England, so he should have been safe. If Cecil ever found out about that . . . *No*, thought

196

David, *I'm going to have to watch Robert and make sure I have a few handy answers for Cecil in case I should need them.*

'Sal, I can't take much more of this. The man virtually sits on my shoulder all day, asking me stupid questions. It's bad enough having him there, but the way he flirts with Sandra makes her jumpy. Would you believe, she actually managed to slip and break a centrifuge today? That takes talent.'

'Darling, I'm sorry. Oooff.' Sally held her stomach as the car went over the rough surface of Tykes Lane.

'What for? Are you OK?'

'Yes . . . I'm fine . . . Keep driving. Well, I'm the one who suggested you talk to him. If I hadn't, you'd still be boss in your own lab, wouldn't you?'

'It's not your fault. Sal, are you sure this is a good idea?' he said as she gave another groan.

'Look, this baby is nearly two weeks late, and I don't know about you but I want to hold the infant before I'm forty! Now we're not doing anything wrong, just helping nature along a bit, that's all. Besides, it was Edith who suggested letting the air out of the tyres and driving up and down a bumpy road. It's an old midwives' trick for inducing labour. Keep driving.'

Robert shook his head and did as he was told. Sally didn't know what he had expected but when, an hour later, they were still driving up and down the rough road even she decided to give in.

An hour later she told Robert to get her bag. He hadn't had time to refill his tyres with air so the short ride to the Clinic was also a bumpy one. As she walked carefully up the steps she felt a flood of warm liquid run down her legs. She stopped in amazement and looked at the small pool spreading beneath her bump.

'Your waters broke, have they, love? Come on, let's get you sorted.'

Edith Jones tucked an experienced hand under her elbow and led her into the Clinic, where a wheelchair was waiting for her. She collapsed heavily into the seat and Edith was about to push her up the corridor when Robert grabbed the wheelchair.

'At least let me take her to the delivery room,' he pleaded.

'I shouldn't, you know, Dr Ghillyand. It's very irregular.'

'Go on, Edith . . . please.'

197

'I don't care who bloody well gets me there – just push!' Sally instructed from her seat.

'No, darling, that comes later!' Robert joked, and Sally laughed as he took the handles of the wheelchair.

However, at the delivery room door Edith took over. This was her domain, hers and Rose's, and Mr Chiltern's of course, but mainly it belonged to her and she was not letting any prospective father through the door, even if he was the Head of Research for the Rouget Foundation. On that she was adamant.

Robert refused to leave and in true form prowled the carpet of the waiting-room. A couple of times he curled up on the sofa, but most of the time he simply waited, feeling utterly helpless, and completely useless. Every so often someone would come out and he would grab at a wrist to check that all was going well. He was always reassured but after eleven hours he was worried. An hour later he was certain that they were keeping something from him. Half an hour after that he got up, and with great deliberation straightened his tie and left the waiting-room.

This isn't on! he told himself. *After all, if something has gone wrong then I have a right to know!* He paused for a second at the door before pushing it open. Rose was the only one who looked over her shoulder as the door opened.

'Dr Ghillyand!' she said in a shocked voice. 'You can't come in here – not now!'

'That's the right shoulder . . . and here it comes!'

'Robert!'

A sound like a splutter and then a cry suddenly hit the air.

'It's a girl, a smashing girl! Here you are, Sally.'

The blood-stained, mucus-covered baby was placed on Sally's tummy. She looked at her daughter in wonder.

'Robert,' she whispered. 'Look.'

'It's highly irregular having a father in the delivery room. We haven't even cleaned her up yet!' protested Edith, but no one was listening.

Robert stood next to his wife, tears streaming down his face. 'I thought something was wrong,' he explained. 'But it's not, is it? It's wonderful. Oh, Sal!'

Gently Edith took the baby from Sally and weighed her. 'Seven pounds and six ounces. Lovely!' she declared. 'Now, Dr Ghillyand, do please go away and let us clean up your wife and your daughter.'

She added with a smile, 'You can see them both again in about five minutes.' And this time it was his elbow she held firmly in her hand as she led him out of the room, chatting as she went. 'Have you decided on any names yet?'

'Oh yes, we agreed that weeks ago. She's Alex, Alexandra Marie Ghillyand.'

'If I have to listen to another person cooing about that bloody baby I shall go mad!' screeched Elizabeth through her teeth at the maid who had brought her lunch. 'It's bad enough that I'm stuck in this dump without having to put up with all that stupid babbling. What the hell do you call this?' she finished as the cover was removed from her tray.

'It's tomato soup, with a bit o' boiled fish, peas, potatoes and crumble for afters,' said Lily helpfully.

'I can see what it is, thank you very much. Where's the salt?'

'You ain't allowed any. It says so in the kitchen.'

Lily was backing towards the door but she was not quick enough and Elizabeth's plate caught her shoulder as she disappeared out of the room. A few minutes later the door opened again and Sister Browning, followed by Edith and a timid Lily, swept in.

'I have told you before, Mrs Ghillyand, that I will not tolerate this type of behaviour. If it weren't for you being confined to bed, I'd make you get out of it and clear this mess up. However, Lily' – Sister Browning turned to the maid and gave her one of her rare smiles – 'I'm sorry that Mrs Ghillyand is creating so much extra work for you, but I'd be most grateful if you could tidy this away.'

She turned her attention back to the bed. 'And as for you . . . Nurse Jones has already explained that you have had to come to the Clinic early because your blood pressure has shot up. Too much salt will exacerbate this, so until further notice, which could well be the last six weeks of your pregnancy, you will be not only on a salt-free diet but also eating as simple a menu as possible.'

Elizabeth opened her mouth to speak, but Sister Browning carried on.

'Mrs Ghillyand, we are all well aware how you feel about your pregnancy, and all of the nursing staff. You have made that quite clear. Nevertheless, it is our job to ensure your continuing good

199

health and the safe delivery of your baby, and that is exactly what we are going to do. Of course, it would be easier if you decided to co-operate with us, but if you choose to make your stay an unpleasant one there is nothing we can do about it!'

Behind the group at the foot of the bed the door opened and David walked in. In a glance he took in the scene, with Lily on her hands and knees cleaning up the mess on the floor, the broken crockery and the tray around her. He sighed. Elizabeth's tantrums were getting worse.

'Not again, Sister?' He totally ignored Elizabeth, who was sitting, her arms folded across her chest, sulking in her bed.

'I'm sorry, Dr Ghillyand.'

'It's not your fault. Let me talk to her alone, please.'

David held the door open as the sister shooed Edith and Lily out of the room. He shut it firmly behind them before pulling a chair to his wife's bedside.

'Elizabeth, this has got to stop. This baby is too bloody important to be put at risk because of your stupid, selfish behaviour.'

'That's all you care about, isn't it? The baby. You don't give that for *me*, do you?' And she snapped her pudgy fingers sharply under his nose, making him pull back from her.

'Now you come to mention it, no, I don't. It's hardly surprising, is it? Just look at you. It's bad enough you've blown up like a barrage balloon, but I'd have thought, Elizabeth, you might at least have attempted to comb your hair and keep your face looking decent.'

David pushed the chair back and left the room as Elizabeth hurled yet another missile from her bed. It hit the back of the closing door with a resounding thud before it fell to the floor.

Sobbing, she turned and buried her face in her pillow. Curling her hands into tight fists, she pummelled the pillow on either side of her head, her body shaking with misery and rage. After a few minutes she calmed down and rolled over again. Cautiously she picked up her hand mirror and inspected her face. As much as she hated to admit it, David was right. The pregnancy, which in the early days had made her look like a sleek, thoroughbred race-horse, now made her bloated and huge. Her tears had not helped, since her face was now also blotchy and her nose red. Pathetically she rubbed the back of her hand across her nose and under her eyes, which stared back at her from swollen cheeks.

'I'll show the bastard. He got me in this mess and, my God, when I get this thing out of me, he won't know what's hit him!'

Sandra sat on her stool watching Robert as he prowled around the lab. That he was unhappy was evident, and that the cause of his unhappiness was Mr Stockley was equally evident, but what Sandra couldn't understand was why. As far as she was concerned, having Mr Stockley working in the laboratory was a bonus. It wasn't that she disliked Dr Ghillyand – nobody could do that – it was simply that he wasn't very talkative, and Sandra found the long silences tedious. Since Mike Stockley had taken over the bench on the far side of the lab, there had been much more chatter during the working day and Sandra was enjoying the mild flirtation between them.

Robert sighed. The work he did was not secret by any means, but he was accustomed to working by himself without being watched. Although he knew Sandra meant no harm, he had overheard her gossiping with Mike Stockley often enough to know that inevitably work, including *his* work, was often the topic of conversation. He knew he couldn't stop them talking to each other, but their seemingly innocent conversations somehow made him feel threatened. Besides, the freedom he had originally been given to conduct his own research had gradually been eroded; all he was now working on were projects dictated to him by other people. He was increasingly uncomfortable at the Rouget Foundation.

'I feel as if I'm being spied on in my own lab. There's some feeble excuse about no space, and Stockley's in with me,' he complained to Sally when he visited her at the Clinic. 'I don't like it, Sal. If it was just you and me I wouldn't mind so much. But now we've got little Alex . . .' He leaned across and gently stroked his daughter's downy head with one finger as she sucked happily at her mother's breast. 'Somehow she makes it all different.'

Sally sat in the armchair smiling down at Alex. Looking at them, Robert felt a lump rise in his throat.

'What's the matter with you?' Sally asked, bemused.

'You'll laugh, but looking at you two in that classic position has got me all emotional. You know, up until now, when people said they'd do anything to protect their family I always thought I knew what they meant, but now I know I wasn't even close. God, if anything happened to you two . . .' He shut his eyes, not even daring to imagine what could happen.

'Charming! You mean, by myself I didn't matter, but now we have this little poppet it's all changed?'

Robert began to protest at her misinterpretation of his comment when he caught the teasing twinkle in her eye. 'You know what I mean,' he said, laughing.

'Yes, I do. But seriously, Robert, are you really that worried?'

Robert thought for a moment before replying slowly, 'Yes . . . Yes, I am. I can't say exactly why . . . I just feel that something is going on. I'm still sure that David is involved and what I told Cecil is right. In fact, come to think of it, all this has started since I spoke to Old Man Rouget. It's too much of a coincidence.'

Alex finished her feed and Sally began tidying herself. She winded Alex, gently rubbing her back, then eased herself out of the chair and made her way to the crib at the foot of the bed. As she tucked Alex into her cot she carried on the conversation, using her business over the baby as an excuse not to meet her husband's eye.

'You know what you said about needing proof? Well, I think I've got it,' she said guiltily. 'When we had to redo those tests, David said I could get Miss Grigson to type up the notes for me. I didn't mention it to you at the time, because it didn't seem important, and anyway it got me out of doing all that extra paper-work.' She stood up and looked at Robert across the crib.

He shifted uncomfortably on the edge of the bed. 'Sal . . . actually I knew about that. Not at the time,' he added hastily, 'but I found out recently. I didn't say anything as I didn't want to upset you before Alex was born.'

He looked so miserable that Sally went and sat next to him, hooking her arm into his and resting her head on his shoulder. He rubbed the top of her head with his cheek and could just detect the slightly sweet-sour smell of her milk.

'There's something else you should know,' he added. Sally stared up at him. 'This room and everything here . . . David wasn't just being kind. He gave me . . . We did a deal.'

'What sort of deal?'

Robert haltingly told her about the extra work he had done, reproducing the residues for the Rouget Corporation, and about David's plans for development. Sally sat and listened in silence. When Robert finished she reached up and kissed his cheek, before getting up to lean over Alex's crib again. Robert followed her and stood at the other side, and they both looked down at their daughter.

'Sal, I think we should leave.' Robert didn't take his eyes off Alex.

'I think you're right. What do you intend us to do – resign?'

'No. If we do that, David will try and stop us. After all, we both know we're right, don't we? To David we're the threat now. No, as soon as you and Alex are fit, I think we should just go. Quietly and without any fuss. How do you fancy Australia?' he finished in a half-joking tone, trying to lighten the atmosphere.

'Wherever.' Sally bent over the crib, tears streaming down her face as she gazed down at Alex, who slept peacefully. She didn't look up as she added, 'There's only one thing I want to do before we go.'

'What's that?'

'I want her christened, here at home, in Radlett, before we go. I know it's irrational but at least she'd have some link with home, with England. Please, Robert, let me have her christened. Just quietly, no fuss, no big ceremony. Just us.'

Finally Robert just nodded his head, understanding the enormity of what he was asking Sally to do, and why she needed to give their daughter some link, however tenuous, to home.

'Hello, Dr Ghillyand? It's the Clinic. Sister Dobson. We thought we should let you know that Mrs Ghillyand has been in labour for some time.' It was clear from her tone of voice she didn't approve of the fact that David clearly didn't know his wife's contractions had started much earlier. 'What's that? Yes, of course we know she's not due for another month, but premature deliveries are to be expected in cases of toxaemia, and as you are well aware Mrs Ghillyand has been in a highly agitated state for the last few days. Now, your *wife* – a heavy emphasis was put on this last word – 'is asking for you. May I tell her you're on your way?'

'I suppose so.' David dropped the receiver back into the cradle. He drained his whisky glass in one gulp and rang for Simmons.

'Please get me my raincoat, Simmons. Mrs Ghillyand has gone into labour and I'm needed at the Clinic. I'm expecting a call from Mr Rouget in America. Tell him what has happened and not to worry. I will contact him as soon as his grandson is born. Don't wait up . . . I have a feeling it's going to be a long night.'

'Very good, sir, and, if I may, the best of luck.'

'Thank you, Simmons.'

David knew he should be experiencing some sort of excitement or emotion, but all he was feeling was irritation that he had been dragged away from a quiet night in front of the fire to face the torrents of rain and icy gusts of wind outside, combined with an uncomfortable night on a sofa at the Clinic. He was tempted to phone to say he would stay at the house until the last minute, but his common sense told him that this would enrage Cecil when he found out, and that life with Elizabeth after the birth would be even more difficult. Reluctantly he turned up his coat collar, put his head down and ran through the rain across the gravel to his car.

When he arrived at the Clinic he turned the car round and parked it at the front, with the keys in the ignition, and left it facing the road. He then ran up the steps and pushed his way through the doors. Sister Dobson was waiting for him.

'Good evening, Dr Ghillyand. Leave your coat here and I'll get one of the orderlies to dry it out for you.'

David shrugged his way out of the wet coat and followed the sister down the corridor.

'I'm afraid Mrs Ghillyand is having rather a bad time of it. She's moved into the second stage of labour now. She actually began having contractions at two o'clock this morning, but it didn't seem worth bothering you at that point.'

This last statement was made in such a nonchalant tone that David stopped in his tracks.

'Do you mean to tell me my wife has been in labour for seventeen hours' – he glanced at the clock – 'and no one thought it worth telling me?'

David was furious, mainly because he was suddenly overcome by a wave of genuine concern for Elizabeth. He knew he hadn't been kind to her during the last few weeks, and even though the Clinic was luxurious she had had a miserable time. If anyone had asked him at that moment what his feelings were for his wife he would have emphatically told them he loved her.

It was probably the only time during his married life that he felt like that about her.

When they reached the delivery room Sister Dobson called for a gown and made David put it on before he went inside. As he walked in the door, Elizabeth raised her head from the bed.

'Where the hell have you been?' she screamed. 'I'm in agony here and you can't even be bothered to . . . Oh, my God!'

Her face scrunched up with pain and her knees automatically bent up. Her shoulders tightened and her head lifted forward again to meet her body as it was pulled by another contraction.

'I'll wait outside, if you don't mind.'

David left the room and shakily took off his gown. Despite their many fights, he had never seen Elizabeth's face so contorted and he found the raw pain difficult to cope with. He took out his case, removed a cigarette, and tapped it a couple of times on the lid before putting it in his mouth and lighting it.

He walked over to the window and stood gazing at the rivulets of rain scurrying down the glass. The wind tossed the bare branches of the trees in the moonlight, which came and went as the clouds rushed across it. As he stared out of the window a thought crossed his mind. Determinedly he walked down the corridor and ran up the flight of stairs to the sister's office. He could see the strip of light under the closed door and without knocking he barged his way in. Sister Dobson looked up in surprise.

'Dr Ghillyand, is everything all right?'

'Where is he? Where's Chiltern?' David had suddenly realised that the obstetrician wasn't in the delivery room.

'Ah, yes. We caught up with him in York at five o'clock. He was there for a symposium. He is on his way back and, weather allowing, will be here as soon as possible. Your wife is in good hands, you know. Haggerty and Jones are highly competent midwives.'

'I don't care if they are "highly competent".' His voice dripped with sarcasm. 'Chiltern is meant to be looking after my wife, not those two . . . two overgrown housemaids! He should have been here!'

'Dr Ghillyand, don't you think you're being a bit unreasonable? After all, the baby isn't due for another month.'

'Yes, and you yourself told me that premature deliveries are not unusual when a pregnancy has followed the pattern Elizabeth's has. For God's sake, why don't you try and get some other obstetrician in until Chiltern gets here? Also please remember that, apart

205

from being a senior member of the Corporation's staff, I also happen to be your employer's son-in-law!' And he banged his way out of her room, leaving the sister decidedly ruffled.

David went back to staring out of the window, feeling better after exploding at Sister Dobson. He ignored the activity going on behind him as people scurried in and out of the delivery room. He kept his eyes fixed straight ahead of him.

Silently Sally helped Robert put the cases and the few household belongings she wanted to keep into the car. She picked up Alexandra's carry-cot and, while Robert held an umbrella over both of them, placed it gently on the back seat of the car before turning to look for one last time through the rain at the small house that had been their home since their wedding in 1950.

'Come on, darling. Of course it's difficult, but you know as well as I do we can't do this any other way.' Robert put an arm round Sally and purposefully pushed her towards the car.

'Knowing you're right doesn't make it any easier. Leaving like this makes me feel as if *we're* the ones who've done something wrong. Ah well.'

Sally concentrated on smoothing her gloves on to her hands as Robert held the door open for her. She settled herself in the passenger seat and twisted round to tuck the blanket more firmly round the still sleeping baby in the back seat. As he opened the driver's door, Robert paused also for a final look at the home they were leaving behind.

'It's only bricks and mortar.' He gave Sally a peck on the cheek and started the car. Or, rather, he tried to start the car.

'Robert, it can't play up! Not tonight. Not now!' Sally sounded incredulous.

'Don't worry, it's fine . . . Once it catches it'll be OK. The rain will help cool it down so it doesn't overheat, and at least the weather will mean there won't be much traffic on the road, particularly at this time of night. Damn you, start!'

As he cursed the car, the engine sprang into life. It spluttered a little as he reversed on to the private road that led off the vast estate, so he began pumping the pedals, pushing the petrol through the engine. The car shot forward. To encourage it, Robert put his foot down on the accelerator. He had to concentrate hard to see through the driving rain as it was swooshed from one side of the window to the other by the wipers.

'Funny how important moments in our life seem to be accompanied by rain, isn't it?'

Robert knew Sally was making conversation because she was nervous, and he had to admit that he too would be happier once they were out of reach of the Rouget Corporation. Since they had decided to leave, both of them had been tense and irritable, but any doubts had been swept aside over the last few weeks.

After Alexandra's birth at the end of October, Robert had taken a few days off. He was owed some holiday and he said that he needed the time to complete the nursery. The truth was, he couldn't bear to be parted from his daughter. When they had first come home, Robert would stand in the small bathroom watching in rapt adoration as Sally fed and bathed Alex. In the end Sally had objected to being what she called a 'sideshow'. On one memorable evening she walked into the bathroom, handed the baby to Robert and said firmly, 'Your turn.' At first he had been terrified of the tiny creature but since she was obviously just as happy with her father washing her as her mother he soon relaxed, and quickly became less scared of her smallness. In the end Sally virtually had to push him out of the house and back to work.

When he walked into his lab, Sandra was talking with Mike Stockley. With a guilty air she disappeared when Robert walked in, and he soon found out why. In his few days' absence Stockley had more or less taken over in the lab. Not that it was his fault; it was quite clear that Mike, who was happy to be a company yes-man, had been given little choice in the matter. Robert was informed that everything he did now had to go through Mike, and that included requests for materials. The *carte blanche* that had been so attractive had been completely withdrawn.

Robert did a slow boil until he could stand it no longer. He tried to make an appointment to see Cecil but was refused, always being referred to David. Finally, and in sheer frustration, he agreed to see his brother. The meeting had been a short one. Not only had David remained seated throughout the whole interview; he had also never once stopped his writing, nor lifted his eyes from his paper until Robert had finished speaking. Then he had fixed him with a steely look and spoken just five words, 'I don't like being crossed', before returning to his work.

More than anything else, this had convinced Robert and Sally that their time at the Rouget Foundation was over.

Rose Haggerty came out of the delivery room. They hadn't been able to get another obstetrician and it had been a tough birth. She had a slight worried smile on her face.

'Dr Ghillyand, you have a daughter. She's had a few little problems, but nothing to worry about. However, Mrs Ghillyand is a bit upset, and we'd be grateful if you'd come and see her straight away.'

David stood for a moment, the thoughts tumbling through his head. A daughter? A girl? This baby was meant to be a boy, a son and heir to secure his position in the hierarchy of the Rouget Corporation. Cecil's views on women in business were well known, and the thought of David taking over with only a girl to follow him would be unthinkable to Cecil. Ah well, the next one would be a boy. He followed Rose into the delivery room.

'David, David, they've taken my baby! I want my baby! Where is she?'

Edith and Rose had managed to clean Elizabeth up a bit and although her hair stuck to her forehead she was neatly propped on her pillows in a fresh hospital gown. She was looking round wildly, clawing at the bedclothes.

'Where is she, David? Why have they taken her? Something's wrong, I know it is. I want my baby.'

By now Elizabeth was screaming, and the huddle in the corner by the baby's crib broke up as Edith came over to her.

'Now, now, Elizabeth, everything is fine. Just fine. Baby had a long journey and is recovering slowly, that's all. Now you roll over like a good girl and let me give you something to make you sleep and feel better.'

There was something in Edith's tone that made Elizabeth do as she was told. The midwife neatly and quickly wiped an area on her bottom before applying a syringe and smoothly pushing the plunger down.

'Morphia,' she explained to David, who was sitting by Elizabeth, clumsily stroking her head. 'Everything's fine, you'll see.'

'No, it's not,' she continued to argue, but her words were slurred as she began to drift to sleep.

'Take her back to her room and let her sleep it off. Dr Ghillyand, please could you wait a moment?'

The group round the crib continued to whisper. David watched as Elizabeth's bed was pushed out of the door. When he turned to face the group Edith and Rose were standing in front of him.

'We need to talk to you for a moment.'

'Not in here.'

David cast an eye round the delivery room, wanting to be outside its confines where everything was clean and smelt of furniture polish, not soiled with the messy aftermath of the birth of his daughter and the smells of carbolic.

He led the way back to the waiting-room and sat down. Edith and Rose remained standing. Edith inhaled through her nose and took a small step forward.

'Dr Ghillyand, Mrs Ghillyand has had a difficult and protracted labour and it would appear that if she had gone to term she could well have suffered a stroke. It would be inadvisable to consider another pregnancy.'

As this information sank in, David realised his hopes for a son were now in complete tatters. Edith continued in a rush, as if she wanted to get all the bad news out of the way as quickly as possible. The fact that David scared her didn't help her sound as compassionate as she would normally have done.

'As you know, the baby was born prematurely. It does look as if she's having breathing problems and she's a bit on the blue side, indicating some sort of circulatory difficulty too. We're doing all we can but we thought you should know.'

David glanced stonily from one woman to the other. Without saying a word he stood up and pushed between them towards Elizabeth's room. *No!* he said to himself. *It's bad enough it's a girl, but if she dies then I'll lose all of it. Oh Christ, Elizabeth, you silly cow!*

He had to blame someone and Elizabeth was the obvious choice. He sat down in the armchair beside her bed and watched her. As she cooled down and her hair dried out it sprang back into its own soft curls, which now partly spread round her pillow. Her face was still puffy and her fingers swollen. As her chest rose and fell, he could see the glint of her engagement and wedding rings on the chain round her neck, where she had placed them when she became too bloated to continue wearing them. The only sound was the

209

rain and wind and the gentle ticking of the clock.

David must have dozed off because he awoke with a start. Elizabeth was also awake and lay staring at the ceiling, whimpering like a kitten and plucking at the edge of her sheet.

'I want my baby. Where's my baby?' She repeated the words over and over again, crooning them to herself. Suddenly she sat bolt upright in the bed and began to yell. 'She's mine! I want her! Where is she? What have you done with her?' This last question was directed with pure venom at David, but before he could answer she lay down again, went back to her crooning and stared glassy-eyed at the ceiling.

There was a knock on the door. Rose timidly put her head round to ask David if she and Edith could have a quiet word. She glanced at the bed and noted Elizabeth's gentle singing. David got up and followed Rose into the corridor where Edith was waiting for him. He knew something was badly wrong.

'I am sorry to have to inform you that your daughter died this evening, at ten forty-seven.' David looked at the clock; it was now eleven seventeen. 'We did everything we could . . .' Edith's voice tailed off, halted in its platitudes by the expression on David's face.

That's it, he thought. *All of it, everything gone.* 'What about Elizabeth?' he asked, almost as an afterthought, as if it were something he thought he should ask rather than something to which he actually wanted to know the answer.

'We'll tell her if you want, but I'd suggest we leave it until the morning.'

All three looked at the closed door, as if they could see through it.

'No, I'll do it. Now go away, you pair of idiots. I knew Chiltern should have been here.'

He went back into the room, where Elizabeth was still crooning to herself, 'I want my baby. Where's my baby?' He leaned across the bed, putting his hands either side of her.

'She's dead.'

Slowly Elizabeth's eyes turned to focus on his face. She blinked a couple of times before letting out a huge scream and lifting her fingers in an attempt to scratch his face. The door flew open and Rose stood there.

'I think she needs sedating again,' David said as he stood up and left the room. He didn't bother to pick up his coat but walked straight outside. He carefully took out and lit another cigarette, cupping his hands round his lighter to keep the tobacco dry. He leaned on the bonnet of his car and felt the rain trickle down his collar. As he stood there a beam of light appeared from down the road. It grew stronger, and with it the sound of a car's engine. The next thing he knew, an old Rover P2 shot past him with two people sitting in the front.

What the . . . ? he thought to himself, recognising the car and licence-plate as Robert's. Without thinking he threw his cigarette down into the gravel and screwed it out under his toe before jumping into his car and starting the engine. Flicking on his lights, he set off after Robert's car.

Alex moaned and Sally turned round to check she was all right. A light shone in her eyes through the rain-splattered back window. 'Robert, there's a car behind us.'

'I know. It's been on our tail for the last few minutes. I'm going to pull over and let it pass – it's blinding me.'

Robert directed the car to the edge of the lane and noted that the car behind them did likewise. Puzzled, he applied the hand-brake and looked over his shoulder.

'There's someone getting out and coming this way. Maybe he's lost.'

Sally also squinted at the man walking towards them.

'My God! It's David. For Christ's sake, Robert, get out of here!'

He didn't need telling twice. Slamming the car into gear, he put his foot down hard, urging the car forward. There was a bitter taste in his mouth. He didn't know why but he was scared, very scared, and a quick glance at Sally told him that she too was terri-fied. Their fear seemed to feed off each other's and, as if Alex could sense it too, she woke up and began crying. The headlights behind them seemed to be getting closer and Robert crouched lower over the wheel as they came round a bend and straight into the wind. Ahead of them was the bridge over Tykes Water and a few yards beyond that the turning on to the main road. Once there, they would be off private land and David would have to slow down.

Behind them David kept his eyes fixed on their rear lights, pushing his roadster closer to them all the time. He didn't know why he was following them, only that they had to be stopped. How, he didn't know, but they had come too close to the truth and David couldn't risk being exposed. They were slowing down by the road and David did likewise, drawing to a halt a few yards behind them.

Ignoring the rain, he got out of the car and began walking towards the Rover. Suddenly the rear lights flared and the car jerked forward and back on to the lane. David swore and ran back to his car, setting off after them. He had to catch them before they reached the A41. If only he could overtake and get in front, he could block their way.

The lane curved round and the rain beat against the windscreen. They drove between the large oaks overhanging the lane which, for a brief second, acted as a wind-shield. The rain cleared and in that moment, as if in slow motion, David watched as the car ahead of him lost control. It took the left turn on to the bridge too quickly, its wheels spun on the scree that made up the surface of the lane as if it were trying to get a grip. Then it seemed to glide into the stone column at the end of the balustrade and bounce off the bridge to end up with its nose facing down the bank at an angle. Seconds after he saw the impact, the noise of the crash echoed back at him in the wind – that and the noise of a horn blaring into the night.

David stopped the car and for a few minutes just sat, gripping the wheel, trying to catch his breath. He smoothed his hand over his hair as he got out of the car and, trance-like, walked towards the other vehicle. He peered through the window. Robert was slumped over the steering wheel, his torso pressed against the horn. The window was smashed and David reached in to push his brother back into his seat. As he did so, his hand touched something warm and viscous. He gave Robert's shoulder a push. The horn ceased, to be replaced by a squelching sound. Robert had been impaled on the steering column. As he hit the back of the seat his head lolled to one side; he seemed to be staring, wide-eyed, at David. Looking across at the passenger seat he could see Sally. She was twisted round, as if she had curled up sideways against her seat and gone to sleep. It was only the fact that the left-hand side of her face was a pulp where it had smashed against the windscreen that told him she was not asleep.

David stepped back slowly into the piles of sodden leaves that covered the ground. He had wanted to stop them, yet not like this. He began to retch, bitter bile coming into his mouth. Unable to stop himself he bent over, then began to puke, his stomach contracting and pulling until it had disgorged its entire contents. Exhausted, he leaned against a tree, catching his breath, gathering his wits about him.

I'm safe! was his first thought, quickly followed by the certainty that no one must know he had ever been here. Frantically he scraped together a pile of leaves and dumped them over his vomit; then slowly he made his way back to his car, carefully examining the road for any tyre marks. He was lucky; the rain had instantly washed away the tracks left by his car but the skid marks from Robert's car could be clearly seen. He stood upright and gulped great dollops of fresh air, lifting his face to the rain, letting it wash over him.

I must get back to the Clinic, tell them I was distraught, tell them anything! No, David! He stopped himself. *Think, man. Be calm. Panic now and you lose everything.* He began to walk slowly back to his MG. As he did so he heard a sound, quietly at first but growing louder: a baby crying. He spun on his heels and moved rapidly back to the Rover. There, wedged behind her mother's seat, still in her carry-cot, was the baby. For a moment David was tempted to leave her there, to let her perish with her parents. Then an idea began to form itself out of the fog in his mind. He reached into the car, careful not to disturb anything, and eased the baby out of her cot, leaving that and the blankets behind.

The child stopped crying and blinked at him. He stared back.

It's madness. It won't work. Why not? Who's to know? Elizabeth won't. I can deal with those two. Do it. What have you got to lose? What have you got to gain? Round and round it all went in his head as the baby bawled in his arms. Suddenly he made his mind up. Tucking his arms tighter round the baby, he returned quickly to his car and drove back to the Clinic.

At half past midnight David's MG Midget once against came to a halt by the front entrance of the Rouget Clinic. He parked the car, checked that no one was watching, got out and went round to the passenger seat, from which he carefully removed a swaddled bundle.

As he crept along the corridor towards Elizabeth's room he kept his eyes and ears open. When he arrived he placed his bundle on the armchair, wedging it in with cushions so it wouldn't fall off.

He rang the nurses' bell, hoping that one of the other night staff wouldn't answer.

He was relieved when Edith answered the call. She was surprised to see David standing there. Then she made a move towards the bed but David stopped her.

'No, Edith,' he said quietly. 'I was the one who rang the bell, not Elizabeth. I need to talk to you and Rose now, where no one else will overhear us. Pick that up.' He indicated the bundle on the chair.

'My God, it's a baby!'

'I know. Now come on.'

Expertly carrying the baby, Edith led the way back to the nurses' room and Rose, who also exclaimed when she saw the infant that Edith was carrying.

'Who else apart from you two incompetent idiots know that Elizabeth's baby died this evening?'

'Well, we had an emergency in, and what with that and everything else ... No one. We haven't had a chance to do anything about it. The body is still in the chapel of rest,' Edith finished.

'Right,' said David through gritted teeth. 'With the way you two have behaved this evening, trying to handle a difficult birth you couldn't manage, I could get you both struck off and make sure you never work again. Do you understand me?'

Rose attempted to object, but David brushed her aside. 'When ... If,' he amended. 'If Cecil Rouget finds out that you killed his only grandchild, your life won't be worth living.' He spoke quietly and firmly, but his voice was menacing.

The two women visibly paled. Rose's eyes filled with tears, and again she tried to explain. 'We tried to get a doctor – honestly we did – but no one was available. So we did all *we* could.'

'Exactly, all *you* could. Which wasn't enough and clearly proves your negligence in your duties as midwives. Now, this baby here' – he pointed at the bundle Edith was still holding – 'needs a mother. Her parents were killed in a crash earlier tonight. My wife is demented and clearly needs a child. This one is three weeks old. Elizabeth is so befuddled she won't know the difference, and I'll need you two to ensure nobody else realises what has occurred. If it gets out and you try to implicate me in any way, I shall deny it, and I guarantee that people will listen to me rather than you.'

Edith looked at the baby, peeling the blanket away from her face. Her eyes opened wide as she recognised the child. 'My God! Isn't this Dr Robert and Mrs Sally's little girl?'

'Correct – but, as I said, they've just been killed in a road accident and little Alexandra now needs parents. She might as well have us, don't you agree?' Again his voice was threatening. 'Now, where's my daughter's body? Is it still in the chapel?'

Wordlessly the two women nodded. David got up and as he left them said, 'Don't forget to change all other relevant charts and get her a name bracelet.'

'What shall we call her?' It seemed a ludicrous question, but David realised that by asking it Edith was signalling her acceptance of the situation.

'Call her what the hell you like. You can give her a bloody number for all I care.'

The baby gave a little mewing noise and Edith looked at her again before facing up to David. 'Then I think she should keep the names her parents – her *real* parents – gave her. Alexandra Marie.'

David spun round on his heel and glared at the nurse. 'Don't be so bloody daft. No one will accept I've given my child the same names as my brother's. That's just plain stupid.'

Edith felt a sense of injustice flood through her. How dare this man deprive this child of everything, even her name. 'I'm sorry, Dr Ghillyand, but those are the names she was given and I think she has a right to keep them.'

Looking at Edith standing up to him he had suddenly had enough. 'What did they call her again?' He groaned as he heard the names. He had wanted to call her Cecilia or Cecily after Cecil but now knew that would be impossible.

'I'll tell Mrs Ghillyand the names if you want me to?' offered Edith, getting braver, but David snapped back at her and all the courage she had discovered vanished as quickly as it had arrived.

'I think I can talk to my own wife, thank you very much. You go and try to look after this brat better than you did the other one and let me deal with Elizabeth.'

Dan looked from Edith to Rose and suddenly his expression changed. 'You agreed to a baby swap?' he said incredulously.

Rose leaned towards him and put her hand on his. 'You don't understand, do you? It was David, who he was, what he was like. The man was bad, do you hear me? Bad. We couldn't have done anything else, could we, Edie?' She turned rheumy eyes to her companion.

'Robert and Sally are dead?' Alex asked in a whisper, as if Rose had not spoken. Dan's hand shot out to hold Alex's but she ignored him, staring down at her fingers as she twisted them together in her lap. 'I didn't know. I'd hoped they were still alive, gone abroad or something . . . I don't know. Just something.'

'I'm sorry, I thought you knew what had happened to them.' It was Edith's turn to look distressed as she appreciated the dreadful manner in which this young woman had learned who her parents were and that they were dead. 'We don't know how the accident happened, but we think David had something to do with it – we don't know what exactly. After she was told her child had died Elizabeth went a bit mad. David left the Clinic and when he came back he had you. He told us to say you were Elizabeth's baby and we didn't know what else to do but agree. Your name is the right one, though. It's what Robert and Sally had decided to call you. I insisted on that. I made sure you kept the right name.'

Edith was desperately trying to make amends and this was all she could hold on to. Alex gave her a watery smile before looking at Dan.

'Dan, they're right. David was a tyrant. Maybe you can't understand it but I can.' Alex pulled her seat closer to Edith and Rose, making Dan suddenly feel excluded. 'Go on. What about the other baby, David and Elizabeth's real child? What happened to her?' Alex and Dan listened intently as Edith, with interruptions from Rose, told them what they knew of that night.

After the post-mortem had been quickly performed by a tired visiting pathologist, the baby's body had been stitched together and placed behind a screen in the chapel of rest. Shakily Edith and Rose dressed the waxy mutilated body of David's own daughter in her cousin's clothes before he grabbed her body.

'You haven't seen me since I left here after the baby was born – do you understand me?' Silently they both nodded. 'See there's no one around. Go on!' he urged in a loud whisper.

216

Leading the way, Edith crept down the corridor, checking round corners and beckoning David on. When he got outside the rain had stopped, but the air was still heavy with moisture. He put his bundle on the seat next to him and set off once again to the bridge. Everything was as he had left it.

He made sure he parked the car on the road where it would not leave any tyre marks and, getting out, took the body with him. He made his way to the car and was about to reach in to put the body into the carry-cot when something stopped him. He unwrapped the blanket from around the baby's head and for the only time looked at his daughter. Her translucent eyelids were closed under a wrinkled, eyebrow-less brow, giving her a startled expression. For a split second he hesitated as a surge of feeling went through him, but it was so quick he avoided acknowledging it. It wasn't too late; he could still go back and put everything right. He gave himself a shake and almost roughly replaced the blanket before placing the body in the car. Not sure quite what to do next, he shut the door and walked a little way off the road, lighting a cigarette as he went. As the flame on his lighter flickered in the damp air, he paused, his cigarette unlit. He turned and looked at the damaged Rover, and then at his lighter.

Replacing it in his pocket, he went to the car and slowly walked round it, examining its precarious angle and taking mental measurements as he did so. He knew what he was going to do. Not wanting to get any incriminating dirt on his jacket he took it off and put it in his own car. He then returned to the Rover and, flexing his muscles, began to rock it on its nose as it faced down the bank. The rocking picked up momentum and the car began to shift from one axle to the other until, with one final effort, David was able to let it swing with a dull thud on to its side. Robert's body slumped against Sally's as the glass in the side window shattered against a rock buried beneath the leaves.

David stepped back and studied his work. He was satisfied that the final resting place of the car tallied with the damage to the bridge's wall. It would be clear that the car had skidded and ricocheted off the wall to end up in its current position. Rolling up his shirtsleeves, David made his way to the car bonnet, which had been bent into a sharp angle from the impact. He slipped his bare arm into the gap and began feeling around. After what seemed like hours, his probing fingers settled on a smooth upended bowl. He withdrew his hand and searched the ground for a suitable stick, which he then inserted under the bonnet, aligning it with the bowl. As if he were using a billiards cue he drew the stick back and rammed it forwards, breaking the glass fuel bowl. The smell told him he had succeeded. As he strained his ears he could hear the rest of the petrol flowing up the fuel lines out of the smashed bowl and over the engine.

He knew that Robert had been having trouble with dirt in the carburettor, which was why he had fitted the Wipac bowl in the first place, so that he could check the sediment levels. He could feel that the car had been overheating; if he wasn't careful the engine might still be hot enough to ignite the petrol. He stepped back and went into the wood where he began kicking at the piles of leaves heaped among the roots of the old trees until he found a dry stick. Again his lighter flickered in the dark and he held it against the stick, praying for it to catch. It smoked a bit and then crackled into flames. Checking the wind direction, David hurled it at the Rover and then rapidly stepped back. For a moment he thought it had missed and gone out when it hit the wet undergrowth, but then he saw a tongue of fire beneath the car. He moved back towards his car, and as he reached in to get his jacket there was a hollow boom and the whole vehicle was engulfed in smoky flames.

Without looking back he drove home.

The next morning he was woken early by an apologetic Simmons, telling him that some gentlemen from the police wanted to see him. He checked in the mirror for any telltale signs of the previous night's activity. Then he arranged his face into a suitable expression and went downstairs.

For David, the hardest part was reacting in an appropriate manner when the police informed him that they had found the Rover, complete with the charred remains of his brother, sister-in-law and their baby. 'Or at least, sir, that's who we believe them to be. There's not that much we can identify. We're checking dental records and the like, so you don't have to worry about a formal identification of the bodies.'

At this David had looked genuinely relieved. He had then explained that the night before he had been at the Clinic, where his wife had given birth. Suitable congratulatory remarks were delivered and, after agreeing that the midwives could confirm this

– 'Just routine, sir; we don't expect anything untoward' – he let Simmons show them out.

He phoned the Clinic that morning to check that Elizabeth was all right and was told by Rose that she was still sedated. David waited until late afternoon before visiting his wife. When he arrived he found Edith, who explained that she and Rose would be taking it in turns to care for Elizabeth and the baby, so at no time would anyone else have to go near them. David was suitably grateful but also went to see Sister Dobson to insist that Elizabeth be moved home as soon as possible, and that Edith and Rose nurse her from there.

Although unhappy about the move they couldn't argue, but it was two days later before Elizabeth was well enough to see David. When he walked into her room he noticed that much of her puffiness had disappeared and she was once again wearing her rings. She was still dopy but managed to sit up, helped by Rose and David, and to hold the baby for a few minutes when they brought her in. David held his breath as she stretched out her arms, but he needn't have worried. Elizabeth was in no state to notice that this child was far too old to be hers. When her head began to drop over the baby's, Rose quickly grabbed her and took her back to the nursery. David was about to creep out when Elizabeth jerked awake and called out to him.

'David, David! They've taken my baby! My baby's dead!'

He sat on the edge of the bed and took her hand. 'No, she's not. She's gone back to the nursery.'

'No, no, no! She's dead. They told me. You told me. She's dead!'

'No one told you that. How could they? She's alive and very beautiful. It's Robert and Sally and *their* baby who have died, not ours.'

'Robert and Sally?' Elizabeth stared at David, a vacant expression in her eyes. 'Robert and Sally and their baby?' she repeated again slowly.

'Yes,' David explained. 'They were killed in an accident the night our baby was born. That's why I thought it would be nice to give our baby the same name they had picked for theirs. Alexandra Marie. What do you think?' As he was talking, David watched Elizabeth for a reaction.

Still heavily drugged, she woozily bit her lower lip as she

219

considered what he had said. 'You want to call our baby Alexandra Marie, like their baby?'

'Yes, I do. We both do, don't we?' He gently stroked her hands.

'My baby's not dead?'

Again David reassured her, but Elizabeth would not be pacified and eventually he rang the bell and told Rose to bring the now screaming infant back to Elizabeth. When the baby was placed in her arms, David was pleased to hear her softly croon 'Alexandra Marie' at the child while she held her and rocked her.

It was a scene that would be played out many times over the next few weeks, as Elizabeth slowly regained her strength and sanity. She again queried the choice of names but David had told her she had chosen them herself when she had heard about the accident. Although Elizabeth had wavered, David had been able to convince her when he showed her the other baby's birth certificate. 'As next of kin it's been down to me to sort through their things.'

'What about your mother? Couldn't she do it? It would give you more time to be here with me ... I mean us.' Elizabeth carefully adjusted what she said to include the baby.

'Mother is too old, you know that. Besides, I'm glad she hasn't been able to be here. It's too distressing, finding things like a dead child's birth certificate. It was a sweet thought, calling our baby after theirs, and when she's older we can tell her about the rest of her family and show her this.' He held up the certificate and then folded it carefully into his wallet.

Elizabeth shrugged. She was still too tired to think straight and although some early feelings of affection for the baby were beginning to stir she wasn't yet sufficiently interested in the baby to argue. By the time Cecil returned from America she was still weak, but out of bed in the living-room. It was there that he met his granddaughter for the first time.

'Are you saying David actually *killed* his own brother?' Dan broke the silence that had settled over the group after Edith had finished speaking.

'No!' It was Rose who answered. 'Just that he went back to the crash with the body. We know he did something and it was important that we vouched for him, saying he left the Clinic after your

'. . . I mean the baby's . . . birth – but we don't know quite what. Any more than we know what he did the night your mother . . . I mean Elizabeth . . . died.'

Alex's head snapped round. 'Hang on. Is there something I don't know about Elizabeth's death?'

'Rosie, don't you ever learn when not to say anything?' Edith again sounded like a schoolmistress rebuking a child.

Alex stood up and walked round the back of her chair, creating a barrier between herself and the rest of the group. She gripped the chair tightly and spoke slowly, carefully enunciating her words. 'I'm sorry, I need some time to take all of this in. Forgive me.'

'It is getting late. Why don't you come back tomorrow and we'll carry on then?' Rose gave Edith a surprised look at this extended invitation, but Edith just shook her head and hissed sideways at her, 'Christos!'

Alex had had more than enough for one day, but, even more than before, she needed to know the rest of what had happened. She accepted the invitation and let Dan lead her back down the dusty path, a protective arm round her shoulder.

'A nice girl. I like her,' proclaimed Rose.

'So do I, so do I,' replied Edith, cross that she had not given Alex her seal of approval first.

Alex and Dan did not say much as they walked back to their apartment.

'OK?' asked Dan, giving her a squeeze as they walked along.

Alex nodded. 'It's odd. I spent so much time lately, trying to work it all out, and you guessed it months ago, didn't you? I am my own cousin, aren't I? I wonder what sort of life I would have had if they had reached wherever it was they were going. I wonder if the dead baby would have hated David as much as I did.'

'Alex, you'll never know. I hate it when you put yourself through this sort of mangle, and this time it really is unnecessary. You're you, and that's quite good enough for me.'

'She's a lovely girl, David. Lovely. Pity, I had hoped for a boy, family name and all that, but we have time for a son and heir, don't we?' David had yet to tell him that this would be the only baby he and Elizabeth would be having. 'Cheers,' said Cecil, and raised a glass of champagne to his lips.

David sipped his drink, wondering what it was Cecil had wanted to talk to him about. He had tutted his sympathy about Robert and Sally but it was done in such a perfunctory manner that David knew he was just following convention.

'You probably are wondering why I wanted to see you . . . mm?' asked Cecil, as if he could read David's mind. 'It's about our Alex – nice gesture to give her her cousin's names.' David glanced away. 'She may not be a boy, but she is still a Rouget. Needs looking after. I don't believe in giving babies money – too much for their parents to worry about. Instead, I am giving you thirty per cent of my stock in the Corporation.' Cecil sat back in his seat, waiting for David's protests about his generosity and thanks.

Instead David said nothing, which Cecil took as a stunned silence. In fact David was working out the value of the shares.

Thirty per cent! It's a big slice, but to hell with sons and heirs. What about me? It's time you named me as your successor, you old bastard! Thirty per cent? After all I've had to endure with that stupid daughter of yours! The thoughts went round and round as coolly he thanked Cecil, using the grandiose terms he knew the man expected to hear.

'Another thing . . . I'm worried about Elizabeth. She's not herself. She's had a bad time. She needs a change of air. So I have decided that for the next year you will be running our Greek plants – from Greece.'

At this David sat up; to be based in Greece for a year would be perfect.

'You can maintain the development of the sponge work and look after Elizabeth as well. It's all arranged. You leave in two weeks. William Smythe has been notified and Maria is finding you a home and staff.'

David thought rapidly. 'As far as staff is concerned, how would you feel if we took our own nannies? Elizabeth will never be able to cope with that long journey and the baby, so we'd need someone with us for that, anyway.' David made the request sound as light as possible. For a moment he thought that Cecil was going to refuse him. 'Alex knows Edith Jones and Rose Haggerty, from the Clinic, so I'd like to take them. I'm sure Elizabeth would agree.' He pushed the point.

'But David, they're nurses, not nannies!' Cecil objected, knowing that even though Matron wasn't his concern she would still make her feelings known and make life difficult.

'Yes, I know, but surely it's better for Elizabeth to have people with her she knows, and who know the baby?' Cecil considered for a moment before agreeing, on the proviso that David told Matron himself.

When Edith and Rose heard the news they weren't happy. The last thing they wanted to do was go to Greece – effectively to give up nursing and become nursemaids. David, however, made it clear they had no option. It was in January 1953 that the family and its small entourage set sail from Southampton.

'When we arrived we were amazed. The house – sorry, villa – was the most lavish we'd ever seen. It had a huge living-room, and the bathrooms! There was the blue one covered in dolphins and all the fittings were like big shells, even the . . . you know!'

'Rose, Alex doesn't want to hear about the villa, do you? No. So, when we arrived everything was lovely. Elizabeth seemed to be getting better and better, but then David began to spend nights away and Elizabeth started going sort of strange again. She took to creeping about and listening at doors. On more than one occasion we found her listening in on the phone extension when David was taking an important business call, didn't we, Rosie?'

Rose nodded. 'And you, poor mite, were as good as gold. Elizabeth was actually glad we were there and despite some of her odd behaviour I actually felt sorry for her. You know, she tried hard to be a proper mother to you, really she did, but she didn't know one end of a safety pin from another.'

Edith chimed in, 'Honestly, Alex, she really did try to feed you and bath you but she just couldn't cope. It was sad.'

A yell, greeting them, stopped Edith in mid-conversation. Alex shaded her eyes as she looked down the path, waiting to see who would emerge round the curve.

'My God! It's the man from the sponge factory!' Dan was more surprised than Alex. He hadn't managed to return to find out what had caused so much excitement and it looked as if he was now going to find out anyway.

'Good afternoon, Christos.' Edith answered his yell and gestured for him to come round the side of the house and on to the little veranda. His stooped frame moved slowly but steadily until he was sitting with them. He took off his flat cap and twisted it in his hands. Edith said something crossly to him in Greek and then made the introductions. Rose leaned forward, saying in a loud whisper, 'He doesn't understand much English but we'll translate for him.' Alex nodded.

'Why is he here?' asked Dan. Alex glared at him.

'All in good time, Dan, all in good time,' said Edith. 'Where were we? Ah, yes. Elizabeth said David was having an affair – she suspected Maria Eropolos. So she set out to have what she called "my own bit of fun". I think she found what she was looking for too. The atmosphere was awful, and then suddenly it got better, didn't it, Rosie?'

'It was as if they'd called a truce ... going out every night, spending time together, just like two newly-weds. It was lovely to see. Elizabeth looked like she did the year she came out. As if her worries had stopped, you know. Love rekindled. That sort of thing.'

Edith tutted and gave Rose a disparaging look. Then she picked up the story where she had left off.

William Smythe and Maria Eropolos had done their utmost to find a suitable villa for David and Elizabeth. It was a large airy building in Elies, just off the main road, and reached through a wrought-iron gate by a long flight of shallow marble steps beneath an arbour of grapevines. Outside were several terraces and patios, some in quiet corners providing shade all day long, others were filled with sunshine from dawn to dusk.

As well as the master bedroom and *en suite* bathroom, the villa boasted two additional main bedrooms and bathrooms. There was a large sitting-room, a dining-room and a study, for David, leading off the entrance hall. Under the main terrace, a further suite of three bedrooms with a shared bathroom provided the perfect nursery for Alex and her nannies. A cook and general maid lived in a small annexe at the back that was hidden behind pomegranate trees and hibiscus bushes. The villa, only a five-minute walk away from the sea, lay within easy reach of both the main harbour of Pothia to the south and the village of Myrties to the north.

In England, Elizabeth had played at running the combined household in the Manor House. In truth, with its well-oiled wheels it effectively ran itself under the guiding hand of Mrs MacKay and Simmons. The prospect of looking after a home properly for the first time did not delight Elizabeth, as she told Maria when she visited the villa on her first morning in Greece.

'The trouble is, my darling Maria,' said Elizabeth from the sofa, where she sat covered by a light blanket, 'while I think you've been very clever in getting this for us, I simply don't think I'm well enough to manage it myself. I'm still horribly weak – and that dreadful journey . . .' She gave an affected shudder.

'I know, it's awful.' Maria placed a cigarette in a holder and lit it elegantly. 'That's why Spiros and Anna are here. They know the house. You relax and they work.'

Both women smiled, with the empathy of the wealthy. Maria made sure that everything was in good order and gave instructions that Madam was not to be bothered; any domestic problems should be referred to her. Elizabeth let her know how grateful she was and also how tired, before Maria, taking the hint, made her excuses and left.

As soon as she was out of sight, Elizabeth pushed the blanket off her lap and jumped to her feet. Grabbing a hat, she set off to explore the place that was to be their home for the next year. There were few villas around here and theirs was easily the biggest. Odd clusters of small one-storey houses could be seen in olive groves, half covered by jasmine, while in the distance, closer to the church, were larger buildings. There were two beaches nearby, separated by a large rock that had an odd little house hewn out of it.

Elizabeth walked along the shore for a while, swinging her hat and enjoying the feel of the sand between her bare toes and the weak winter sunshine on her head. She longed to stay there all day, but she knew David was due to return for lunch and she thought it expedient to be there when he got back. Reluctantly she retraced her steps.

'So what do you think?' David asked as he shook out his napkin and placed it on his lap.

'I think I'll like it – especially if you come home for lunch and a siesta every day.'

Elizabeth gave David a knowing look from under her eyelashes. She had regained her figure quickly and, with it, most of her old self-confidence. She again believed in her ability to attract David and played with him as a cat does with a trapped mouse, teasing him one moment, rebuffing him the next, claiming she was still too weak to accommodate him; then altering the pattern and succumbing just often enough to maintain his interest in her.

'Elizabeth, as much as I would like to, it won't be possible.' Seeing her eyes begin to glint, David quickly continued, 'Not every day. But let's see how it goes, shall we?'

For the first few weeks David did manage to join Elizabeth every day on the terrace for lunch – usually a light meal with freshly caught fish. In the early days they both relaxed together but as time went by Elizabeth began to hope that David would not come home; not because she didn't want to see him but because of Alex.

Although she was a happy baby, whenever Elizabeth came close Alex would pull away and start to cry. Much to her own surprise, Elizabeth found it distressing. Having been brought up in a grown-up world, Elizabeth had little experience of young children before and was scared of the life that was now her responsibility. She would never have gone so far as to admit openly she loved her baby – but she did, passionately. However, the more she tried to look after Alex herself the clumsier she became.

Feeding and bedtimes became a trial of wits, with both mother and child becoming more and more upset until eventually Edith or Rose would quietly take over, soothing Elizabeth as much as the baby. One day when David had returned to work after lunch, Rose came across Elizabeth lying face down on the baby's blanket sobbing her heart out. She coughed politely but Elizabeth didn't respond. Rose crouched down beside her and put a calming hand on her back, making Elizabeth jump. 'What's the matter, Miss Elizabeth?'

'Oh, Rose!' Elizabeth cried, hurling herself into the older woman's arms. Rose had little choice but to sit there stroking Elizabeth's hair as slowly she stopped crying. '*You* believe I love Alex, don't you? You know how hard I try and how difficult I find it. David says I'm just lazy and don't care . . . but I do, Rose, I do! It's not my fault I couldn't feed her myself, is it?'

'Of course you care. And Edith and me, we know how much you try. You wouldn't take so much care if you didn't feel anything, would you?' Rose felt uncomfortable at the sight of Elizabeth expressing such genuine emotion over Alex. 'Maybe that's the trouble . . . Maybe you try too hard. I mean, she's a small *person*, that's all – not a china doll. Of course you have to be careful with her . . . but, if you ask me, babies are cleverer than we think. I bet they know if Mother is unhappy and they sort of catch it, don't they?'

Elizabeth raised her head and dragged the back of her hand under her nose; for a moment she looked no more than a child herself. 'What am I going to do, Rose? If David doesn't see me being a good mother he'll . . . he'll . . .' And she was off again, crying into Rose's lap, unable to voice her fear that David would leave her. Eventually she cried herself to sleep. Rose left her on the blanket in the shade of a tree and crept off to talk to Edith.

When Alex's bedtime came round again, Elizabeth was no less agitated. Ashamed at having shown her feelings in front of the servants, she was more waspish than usual, making Alex howl even louder. For a tormented hour Elizabeth refused any help from the nannies, who stood helplessly watching as things went from bad to worse. Eventually they managed to put the baby to bed. As Elizabeth was about to go and change for dinner Edith stopped her.

'What do you want?' Elizabeth asked, trying to push the woman away.

'Well . . . Rose and I think we might be able to help you get things right – with Alex and Dr Ghillyand, I mean.'

'I don't need any help with my husband, thank you very much. And certainly not from two spinsters like you.'

It was a spiteful barb but in an odd way it made Rose and Edith feel better: this at least was the Elizabeth they knew.

'Oh, go on then. What is it?'

'How would it be if me and Rose look after the baby until Dr Ghillyand comes home for lunch. As soon as we see him we'll give her to you, and when he arrives you'll be playing together. Alex won't have time to get cross, and we'll take her away for her nap once he's had the chance to see you.'

Elizabeth reflected for a moment; then a flicker of a smile crossed her face. 'Do you think it would work? Won't he realise what's happening?'

'Why should he? Anyway, it'll make it much nicer for you because you can make sure you look beautiful for him when he gets home, can't you?'

That made Elizabeth's mind up for her. David had been complaining lately that she was neglecting her appearance, and Elizabeth reckoned there were too many lovely girls around to risk letting David stray.

Tentatively they tried out the plan the next day. It was carefully orchestrated. Spiros stood lookout on an upper terrace, scanning the main road for David's car. When he shouted down below to the nursery, Edith or Rose carried Alex out while the other followed, arms full of blankets and toys. By the time David's car deposited him at the wrought-iron gate the scene was ready for him. He looked mildly surprised at the scene of tranquil domesticity that greeted him but it was so much better than a sulky Elizabeth and bawling, red-faced baby that he said nothing.

The scheme worked so well that day that it became part of the household's regular routine. Invariably David would make his way up the shallow steps out of the midday sun under the arbour to find his wife and daughter playing there. If Alex had an odd elderly expression on her pudgy features he didn't notice it, nor did he have time to do so, for no sooner had he appeared than Elizabeth would kiss the baby lightly on the brow, summon whichever of the nannies was hovering and hand the child over to her, saying lightly, 'I think it's time for Alex's nap, don't you, Nanny?' And the baby would be whisked away as quickly as she had appeared, leaving Elizabeth free to lavish attention on David. Whether David believed it Elizabeth didn't know or care. So long as he could never accuse her of being a bad mother she was satisfied.

Once Elizabeth had finally delegated all her daughter's care to the nannies, the only other time she spent with Alex was at the end of the day after Edith and Rose had bathed her and got her ready for bed. She and David would go together to the nursery to say goodnight. At weekends, when David was home, she would tell him that she spent all week with their darling daughter and therefore wanted to devote this time to him. David never questioned her; the less he saw of the baby the happier he was about her. If he didn't see her he could forget she even existed.

It was a silly game, but one they both played with consummate skill, never sure quite who was deluding whom, Elizabeth acting the role of wife and mother, or David the attentive husband and father. It was not to last.

They had been on Kalymnos for six weeks when David

announced he had to visit another of the Rouget Corporation's plants, and would be away overnight.

'Work is work, I suppose.' Elizabeth sounded petulant as she carried on playing the game. She fussed over David's large suitcase and started to pack it for him, despite his protests that he wouldn't need all the items she was piling into a heap on the bed. 'Don't be silly, David. Pyjamas, dressing-gown, shaving gear, two clean collars and ties – I assume you will be wined and dined this evening? – underwear and handkerchiefs. Of course you need all of this.'

'Elizabeth, it's very informal. I wasn't intending to wear a suit – just slacks and a shirt, with a sweater to keep off the evening chill – that's all,' David protested.

'My God! You'll look like one of those smelly men down at the harbour. If you think I'd allow my husband to represent the Rouget Corporation dressed like a sailor you've got it wrong!' She was growing angry, not understanding his objections.

'That's what this fuss is about, isn't it? Nothing to do with whether my clothing's right for where I'm going, but whether it will let down the Rouget name. Well, listen, sweetheart . . . See these?' He grabbed her left hand, holding it up and pointing to her engagement and wedding rings. 'These mean that you're no longer a precious Rouget – you're now a Ghillyand. No longer regarded as Cecil's daughter but as my wife!'

Elizabeth snatched her hand away from him. 'May I remind you that you married me because I was a Rouget? You wanted what was mine by rights, you've got it by association so pack your own bloody bag!' Sweeping the pile of clothing on to the floor, she stormed out of the room.

David bent down to pick it up. He poured himself a small whisky from the decanter on the tray by the chaise-longue and drank it, before he smoothed the clothes, put them back in the cupboards and replaced them with the garments he had mentioned. It was a much smaller bag that David carried out of the villa that evening.

The next day Elizabeth's mood had not improved, and everyone else kept out of her way. She tried to place a telephone call to her father, to tell him how badly David had behaved, but the operator couldn't make the connection. By the evening her temper had worsened into a shimmering rage. That night, when David returned exhausted from his trip, she hurled all her anger at him as they changed for dinner, screaming about her boredom, the fact

229

that he neglected her, leaving her virtually a prisoner in the house all day because the local people could not speak English.

'And I'm fed up with your indifference towards me!' On and on she went. 'Christ, you don't even love me any more, do you? You never did!'

'Well, Elizabeth, yesterday you reminded me I married you for who you are, because you're Cecil's daughter. Well, my dear wife,' he said, his voice dripping with sarcasm, 'you were absolutely right. It's the only reason I married you, and don't you forget it!' He made to leave the room but Elizabeth moved faster and slipped between him and the door, standing with her back to it, holding it shut.

'Whatever the reason you married me, I am still your wife. And if you want to maintain your special position with the *family* business I suggest you start treating me as such.'

She looked up at him, a defiant expression on her face. David reached down, caught her round the waist and, with a rough firmness that was reminiscent of the first kiss he had given her on the terrace at Elstree, he pressed his lips hard against hers. As she began to respond and her arms came up round his neck, he pulled away from her and gave her a cold smile.

'No, Elizabeth. That was to show you I do know what my duties as a husband entail. It might be better if you tried to remember your duties as a wife.' He pushed her to one side and opened the door, turning as he went through to add conversationally, 'I've got to go away again next week. Two nights, this time. See you downstairs for cocktails in five minutes.' Then with her temper still bubbling he left the room.

Feeling foolish and unsatisfied, she gaped after him from the doorway as he whistled his way down the stairs.

It was to be the first of many such rows – rows which, depending upon where the battlefield was, could be heard through the entire villa. Edith and Rose tried to avoid their employers when they were in full flight, and certainly kept Alex out of their way. Aware that the child was neglected, the two women did all they could to compensate for what was, in their eyes, an almost parentless existence.

'Poor little Alex,' Rose crooned, supporting the baby in her left arm and trickling water over her tummy as she kicked her legs and gurgled happily in her bath. 'No visit from Mummy and Daddy tonight? No, there won't be. Daddy's away, isn't he? Yes, he is, and when Daddy's away Mummy ignores you, doesn't she? Yes, she does.' Alex put a tiny fist in her mouth and blew raspberries at Rose.

'Rosie, do be quiet. She's better off when they don't visit her. It's not as if they're even her parents after all, poor mite.'

'I know, Edie, I know. But it doesn't mean we can't love her, does it? It's easy now, while she's little, but what's it going to be like when she's older? She'll need someone to turn to, someone who's on her side – and that's us. After all, someone will have to tell her the truth one day.'

Edith spun round on her heel from the shelf where she was folding nappies and walked over to Rose, who had taken Alex out of the bath to dry her in a large towel and cover her in talcum powder. 'Rose, we've got to forget all of that. It's dangerous even to refer to it. Do you hear me? It's dangerous. Now, don't ever mention it again, and let's get Baby into bed.'

Silently, and suitably cowed, Rose did as she was told.

That night, when she went to her own bed, she took out a small key from its hiding-place and with her hands burrowed into an alcove behind a picture on the wall. She drew out an old tin box and opened it. Pushing aside her passport and other items she had placed in there for safe-keeping, she pulled out a long piece of paper. Unfolding it, she studied the death certificate for Alexandra Marie Ghillyand, then murmured under her breath:

'I promise you, Alexandra, one day, when the time is right, and when you're old enough, you'll know the truth.'

David strolled over to the window, took a cigarette out of his case and lit it. William Smythe's office over the Customs House gave a magnificent view of Pothia harbour out of one window and the open sea from the other. David drew on his cigarette as he took in the sight of the ships and boats that steamed or chugged their way to their moorings or cast off to return across the water with their passengers and cargoes. Slowly he walked across to the other window. By squinting, when he looked across the harbour wall, he could make out Turkey in the far distance, shimmering in the heat.

The noise of the customs officers arguing with a group of

fishermen about their haul, both declared and undeclared, drifted up to him. He smiled to himself as the argument grew more and more heated before it settled down when a deal was struck.

'Sorry to keep you, David. Damned bureaucrats. Go on through – he's just leaving.'

David let himself be shown into William's office. Despite its white walls it was decorated in a style more suitable to a City of London firm than one based on a small Greek island. It was furnished with leather Chesterfields and heavy oak furniture; a large, dark print of the Port of London hung above the desk. A uniformed man was standing with his back to the door, stuffing a sheaf of papers into his briefcase.

'Mr Smythe, thank you. The Police Department are most grateful for your assistance in this matter. Anything we can do to be of mutual help, please let me know.' The police captain spoke almost perfect English. He gave William a smart salute, and with a bow in David's direction left the room, shutting the door firmly behind him.

David sat down, indicating with a wave of his hand that he didn't require the whisky William was offering. 'Too early for me.' It was only ten-thirty. He carried on smoking as he watched William pour himself a glass and noted the way his hand shook slightly. William seated himself behind his desk and took a gulp at his drink.

'That's better. This heat is too much for me, you know. Thins the blood. Nothing a Scotch can't put right, though.'

'Quite.' David stubbed out his cigarette in the crystal ashtray and leaned forward in his seat, his elbows resting on his knees as he made an arch with his fingertips. 'Well, have you considered the offer?'

William flushed a little. 'It's an interesting offer, and I'm seriously considering it. But how do I know I can trust you to make the payments?'

David smiled to himself. By asking the question, William had indicated that he had already reached a positive decision; now it was simply a question of sorting out the details.

'Because, my dear William, you know what I am doing – not totally I grant you, not the merchandise – but you know enough, and that gives you potential power. But the power I have is greater. You see,' he added casually, 'I know the details of the business you were just conducting with the Chief of Police. If that got out, it

232

could make life difficult for you, very difficult indeed. Just think of the effect it would have on Maria if she ever found out – and what that in turn would mean to your life style. Somehow I can't see you rotting in a Greek jail. It's not as if I'm asking you to set this up for nothing, is it? I think you're just going to have to trust me, don't you?'

William had flushed an even deeper red above his collar and a sheen of perspiration covered his face. He fumbled in his pocket for his handkerchief and mopped his brow. He was clearly playing for time.

'I . . . I don't know what you mean . . . The business I was discussing with my previous client was a family matter and – '

'Please don't insult either of us by lying, William. Admit it, I've seen through you. Acknowledge that the fact we both have something on each other guarantees our mutual security. I won't upset the applecart for you, and you won't do it for me. Now, have we got a deal?' David sounded more insistent as he asked this final question; he was getting bored. Playing mind games with William was too easy.

'Yes, David, we've got a deal. I'll make the arrangements and let you know what they are when we get together for dinner on Thursday. I take it you and Elizabeth will be joining Maria and myself?'

'We wouldn't miss it for anything . . . Don't worry, I'll see myself out.' David stood up and, as he left, added, 'One other thing, old boy. Go easy on the old booze. Too much and it addles the mind . . . makes you imagine things, you know.'

The secretary, overhearing Dr Ghillyand's last remark, silently agreed with him. Lately some of Mr Smythe's behaviour had been most peculiar.

David's trips became ever more frequent and occasionally he was away for two or more nights at a time. Elizabeth became increasingly bored. She began spending her afternoons on the beach, where she quickly became popular with the local Greek men. For a while she flirted with them, enjoying the control she could exercise over these bronzed, muscular men, laughing as they literally fell over themselves in their attempts to please her. She toyed with the idea of taking one of them as her lover but decided she couldn't be bothered; the intrigue would become tedious and the men were so young that there would be no fun in it.

Much as she was loath to admit it, she missed David. She missed his sullen company, their fighting and their passionate love-making, which was taking place less often because when David was at home he usually complained of being tired. After a few months he had instructed Spiros to move his things out of their shared bedroom and into one of the other main rooms. 'After all, Elizabeth, we never shared a room in England. Why should we here?' She had picked up a shoe that Spiros had dropped and thrown it across the hall at him in her fury.

'Papa, David doesn't love me any more. I want to come home. Please let me and Alex come home . . . please, Papa. Don't you want to see your little granddaughter?' She used every ploy she could to persuade her father to allow her to return to England, but he refused.

'My love, David is working very hard for me at the moment. That's why he's over there, and your place is with him. I miss you too, and would adore to have little Alex with me, but I think you should stay there. It's cold and wet and windy here – you need the sun and fresh air. England can't give you that. No, you must stay in Greece.'

Their weekly conversation followed this usual pattern, leaving Elizabeth frustrated. What she didn't know was that when David spoke to Cecil Rouget once a week from the office he would indicate, without specifying in so many words, that Elizabeth was making a recovery but still seemed depressed. He voiced his worries at the way she sometimes appeared to lose touch with reality, imagining things.

'It's not so bad that I can't cope, but I'm glad we're here. There's less to confuse her.'

Cecil listened to his son-in-law's concerned talk of his wife and, even though he longed to let her come home, he agreed with David that England would make her worse. Each time Cecil spoke to Elizabeth on the telephone he would make soothing noises, but would dismiss her complaints as signs of the mild paranoia to which David referred. His conversation with David reassured him that his daughter was in good hands, with a man whom she not only loved, but who clearly loved her in return.

If Cecil had seen Elizabeth he might have questioned David;

she had never looked so fit or healthy. The sun had turned her a deep golden brown and brought out the red highlights in her hair. All the swimming and walking had firmed her body; she glowed with health and energy and she knew it. Which was why she couldn't understand David's behaviour towards her.

Elizabeth lay in her bath, soaking in the local scented jasmine oil, luxuriating in its smoothness and relishing the sensation of the sand being washed off her body and out of her hair. She climbed out of the bath and patted herself dry before wrapping a silk dressing-gown round her. It clung to her still damp skin and she walked back to her bedroom. Anna had closed the shutters to keep the room cool, but the evening sun crept between their wooden slats to lend the room a soft light. Elizabeth made her way to her dressing-table. There, as her robe fell open, she caught sight of herself in the full-length mirror.

Gazing at her reflection, she slipped the silk off her shoulders and let it fall softly to the floor. She reached up and released her hair from the towel she had wound round her head and the chestnut curls, already almost dry, cascaded over her shoulders. She watched the woman in the mirror as she ran her hands across the fullness of her breasts, enjoying the feelings as the palms of her hands rubbed against her nipples and down over the white expanse of her belly, marvelling at the contrast of the golden skin of her arms against the whiteness of her body where the sun had not reached it. Her fingers stroked the inside of her thighs.

David had entered the room as Elizabeth had dropped her towel. She was so rapt in her own reflection she hadn't noticed him. He stood there, mesmerised, admiring the curve of her back, the rounded white buttocks and tanned legs, enjoying her as she enjoyed herself. It would have been so simple to tell her that he needed her, to show her, but instead he wanted to hurt her, to keep her at a distance.

'Most erotic, sweetheart, but I'd prefer it if you concentrated on getting dressed or we're going to be late.'

Elizabeth started, and grabbed her robe from the floor, clutching it to her. 'Get out! Get out!' she screamed, stamping her bare foot on the floor.

David went.

Furiously Elizabeth dressed. *How dare David spy on me like that?* she asked herself. *He shows no interest in me for weeks, and then he behaves like some common peeping Tom. If he wants it now, that's tough. He'll have to beg for it! I'll show him. I'll pay him back somehow.*

A week later she was walking across the hall when the phone rang. She went to answer it but it stopped after the first ring. She gave a shrug and was about to carry on when she heard David's voice speaking urgently and quietly. Usually, when the telephone rang at the villa, even if he was sitting by the extension, David would leave it ringing, preferring to let Spiros, Anna or Elizabeth answer. It was odd not only that he had answered it at all, but that he had answered it so quickly. She crept towards the door to his study and listened hard.

'. . . madness to try tomorrow. There will be no cover. It'll be too quiet. Wait until the next night.' There was a pause while, presumably, he listened to the other end of the conversation before he continued, 'Because the boats will be going out and it will be busier. Easier to lose ourselves in the crowd and not be noticed.' Another pause. 'Fine, fine . . . but make sure you're not late when you phone me tomorrow. If you mistime it, anyone might answer. You cut it very fine today.' As the receiver rattled back down, Elizabeth sprang softly away from the door and glanced at her watch. By the time David emerged she was sitting on the terrace with her sunglasses on, reading a magazine, a drink in her hand.

Her mind was racing. *The bastard. He's got a mistress. No wonder he keeps going away for overnight trips. Doesn't need much clothing? Huh! She's probably got it all there for him. It's that bitch Maria Eropolos. It must be. Well, dear sweet lady, next time you two meet I intend to be there too!*

'Hello, darling. You look tired. I'll get Spiros to get you a drink. *Spiros!*'

David sat down and gave a silent thank-you that Elizabeth was in a good mood. 'Sweetheart . . . I've got another overnight business trip coming up. The night after tomorrow. I'm sorry.'

It was all Elizabeth could do not to pour her drink over his head.

Next day she pleaded a headache and stayed in her room. Five minutes before the expected call she crept downstairs, waiting in the bend of the stairs until the phone rang. As before it rang just once. This time she knew David had answered on the extension and quietly she made her way to the hall table. Carefully she lifted the receiver.

'Meet at Vathi, ten o'clock at the Fishers Taverna. You will be met by the captain of the *Odyssey Two*. He knows where to take you, and you'll be quite safe. He's been paid to keep his mouth shut, and his fear of not getting his money means he can be trusted.'

Elizabeth could not believe her ears. David had actually got someone else to make the arrangements for him. A man was acting as go-between! For a split second she thought she had recognised his voice, but the thought did not stay with her long enough to crystallise. She had to admit it was clever of him to think of using a boat as a meeting-point. Well, she intended to confront Maria and David together – once she had the evidence.

On the following day David left for work with his small bag. Elizabeth didn't even bother to make sure she was up in time to see him off. Instead she watched him from behind the half-closed shutters of her room. All day she prowled around the house, savouring the anticipation and anxiously looking forward to her evening's outing. *At last,* she thought, *something to do! Something that's different!*

At eight-thirty she changed from her dress into a pair of navy slacks and a jumper, and tied a scarf round her head before slipping out of the villa. No one saw her leave. In the darkness she made her way down to the village square and casually strolled into the local taverna, as if she had gone out for a walk and was stopping by on her way home. Women didn't usually drink alone at the taverna but enough local people knew her to greet her warmly and to accept her behaviour as that of a foreigner. She allowed a young lorry driver to buy her a drink and flirted with him. By nine-fifteen she had secured her lift across the island to Vathi.

The old pick-up truck bumped along the rough road and Elizabeth skilfully kept the driver at arms' length. As the road wound down the valley towards the top of the village, the rock face rose above them. Suddenly a large group of people appeared in their headlights and the driver sounded his horn, trying to make them move out of the way.

'Don't worry . . . this is fine. Thank you, it's so sweet of you to bring me all the way over here.' She fluttered her eyelashes at the truck driver and brushed his cheek with her lips. Before he knew what was happening his passenger had opened the door, jumped out and disappeared, leaving behind a young man who felt he had been cheated.

Elizabeth mixed with the crowd who had come down to the harbour to watch the fishing boats leave. Keeping to the deepest shadows, as much as possible, she walked towards the Fishers' Taverna. She craned her neck, trying to see if David had arrived. It appeared she had got there first, when suddenly she saw him. He was wearing an old pair of trousers and a rough sweater, not dissimilar to the clothes worn by the men who were about to go out on the boats; round his neck was knotted a scarf, and an old battered cap covered his head. Stealthily Elizabeth followed him. He was deep in conversation with two men. As one of them turned round, the light from a lantern swinging on a boat fell across his face. It was William Smythe.

She hung back, watching, while David and the other man leaped down from the harbour on to the first boat, making their way to its stern to pull the *Odyssey Two* towards them on her mooring rope before they lightly jumped aboard.

William stood on the harbour wall and raised his hand. 'Good luck!' he yelled.

Somehow Elizabeth knew he wasn't referring to the size of catch they might net. Both men on the boat were too tense and lacked the camaraderie of their fellow sailors. The engines began to throb and the little boat reversed out of the harbour with all the others. The air was full of the stench of stale fish and diesel fumes. The men yelled across to each other as the flotilla set off to the fishing grounds – a bastion of maleness working with and against the elements, threatening and threatened by their surroundings. Slowly the voices and the sounds of the engines faded away and the crowd of women, old men and children did the same.

Elizabeth moved closer to William and then changed direction slightly so that he would notice her. He looked startled and she arranged her features into a look of pleasant surprise.

'William! How nice. I didn't think this was your sort of thing – waving the men off to wish them luck! Where's Maria?' she added wickedly.

He glanced round nervously. 'Well, one likes to do one's bit. What brought you over to Vathi?' He ignored her query.

'Well, David's away overnight, up at one of the plants, and I always get bored when he's not around – I miss him so much. So when I heard the boats were going out tonight I thought I'd come and join in.'

'William, darling – over here!' They both turned round to see Maria leaning out of the window of her car, waving to them. 'Everyone get off all right?'

Elizabeth frowned to herself. What was the bitch doing here when she should have been with David? Apparently she had drawn the wrong conclusion. But, if David was innocent, why had he not told her he was going out with the fishing boats? She was perplexed.

When David returned the next day she made no reference to the fact that she had seen him in Vathi and as the days went by she realised that neither William nor Maria had mentioned it to him either. She became increasingly curious, especially as the timed phone calls to the villa continued. She learned to recognise the signs, learned to be around when the telephone rang and also learned, as had Robert and Sally, exactly what her husband was doing.

Edith had been translating as Christos spoke. At first he seemed frightened, but as he gained confidence the words poured out of him. More than once Edith had to ask him to slow down or repeat what he had said. It was patchy, but bit by bit they pieced it together.

Christos had been a young man when David and Elizabeth arrived on the island. He had recently married and, according to the local custom, on his wedding day his father-in-law had given the bride and groom their first home. His wife came from a good family and therefore the home wasn't just an extra floor built on top of her parents' house but a brand-new building of their own. His wife's family (at this reference to them he had spat noisomely on the floor, causing Rose to wrinkle her nose in disgust) made it clear that they thought their only daughter had married beneath her.

Christos was determined to prove them wrong. He was a hard-working man and not only used his boat to catch fish, but would go sponge-diving as well, seeking the deepest grounds to pick the best sponges possible. It was still not enough, never enough for his in-laws. He let it be known that he was willing to take on more work.

One evening he had been out with his friends when an English-man approached him. Christos knew who the man was. Maria

239

Eropolos was a famous woman on Kalymnos and everyone knew that William Smythe was her man. Smythe began to talk to Christos of adventure, of a special job that needed doing, of high risks and high rewards. Christos was interested and, when he asked how much this special job could earn him, he was amazed. It was more money than he could have earned in ten years. He told Smythe he was his man. Smythe agreed to pay him half his money in advance, and suddenly Christos could afford to give his wife all she deserved – a new kitchen, an extra room on the house for the baby she was now expecting, new clothes. It was wonderful. Until he heard what the job was.

At first David's captain stayed with the other boats, but when they turned south-east and began to spread out he set an easterly course. Neither of the men spoke as the little boat chugged across the sea, bucking and pitching with the waves. Ahead of them, looming up out of the water, was a huge land mass, its blackness blocking the starry sky. In the light of the half-moon they could just make out the rocky outcrops along its shore. A few other boats could be seen, and the captain reset his course to avoid them until, tracing a serpentine route, they reached the shallows and the captain leaped into the water to haul his boat up the beach. David followed and helped heave the boat towards a rock where it could be moored.

When the boat was secured, David clambered on board again and from his small bag took out his clothes. Quickly he changed from the Greek fisherman's garb into clothes that wouldn't associate him with Turkey's nearest western, and most hated, neighbour. Then he jumped back on to the beach, timing his jump to avoid the waves and land on the rough shingle above the watermark.

'If I'm not back by six in the morning then leave without me!' He barked his instructions in Greek to the captain, who nodded.

David made his way up the shingle and on to the road. For a second he could be seen silhouetted against the sky as he reached the top of the slope before he disappeared again. Headlamps of a car, which had obviously been waiting for him, were switched on, and it drove away.

The car followed the coast road and came to a stop at the junction with a dirt track. To the side of this was a pole that had been stuck in the ground. It had once stood upright but now it was at an odd angle and its battered sign pointing to 'Turgutreis' seemed to point down at the dirty soil around it. David got out of the car, felt in his pockets for his cigarette case and, reassured, gave a curt nod to the other occupants before setting off, on foot, down the path.

David had to pick his way carefully in what little light the half-moon provided. The windmills on the hillside cast eerie shapes against the sky as their sails sighed in the gentle night wind that wafted the scene of citrus trees towards him. When, towards the bottom of the track, he passed a few low houses, he took a torch out of his pocket and used it to light his way. David passed a small mosque and followed the noise of laughter and music; although it was nearly midnight, the small village was still very much awake.

He had been told there would be a wedding and it was clear that the entire village was still celebrating. People were dancing around a monument to the Turkish admiral, Turgutreis, their colourful costumes setting off the collars of coins around the women's throats and the fierce-looking daggers tucked into the men's belts. He made his way to the *kahve*, the coffee-house to the right of the main square. A glass of raki with a small jug of water was placed before him. He poured one into the other, watching as the alcohol in the anisette turned a cloudy white. A young boy ran past him, dodging in and out of the throng, carefully balancing tiny cups of sweet Turkish coffee on a tray suspended on chains from his fingers.

David summoned him. *'Iyi aksamlar. Nerede Mehmet?'*

The boy stopped and came towards the table. 'Mehmet?' He queried the name.

'Mehmet,' David repeated firmly and took a cigarette out of his case, tapping it on the lid before lighting it.

A man looked up from a table opposite where he was smoking his hubble-bubble pipe. *'Istiyorum banolu bir oda* – Want a room with a bathroom?' It was more a statement, than a question.

'What is the price? *Fiati nedir?'* David gave the expected reply and the man inclined his head towards him, inviting him to join him at his table. Picking up his raki and water, David moved across and sat down opposite Mehmet.

Like other men of the village, Mehmet was dressed in the traditional embroidered clothing of trousers and a short boxy jacket over a striped shirt which had long tails of the same cloth hanging from each shoulder down his back. On his head was a bright red,

241

softly pointed hat with a long tassel, and round his waist was tied a wide sash of tightly woven fabric covered by a pointed scarf. Between the sash and the scarf, an ornate, vicious-looking short dagger was tucked. David eyed it cautiously as he finished his cigarette.

Mehmet watched him over the top of his narghile as he smoked, letting the air bubble over the water in its small pot-belly. He stopped occasionally to pick at one of the small *mezeler* dishes spread on the table before them. With another nod of his head he indicated that David do the same. Not wishing to offend his armed host, David did as he was told.

Suddenly a yell came from the centre of the square and David turned in its direction; when he turned back, Mehmet had risen to his feet and was adjusting his dagger in his belt. He raised his hand to warn David to stay in his seat and left him as he went to join the other men in the square.

An expectant silence fell over the crowd and they moved to the edges, allowing their men space to perform. A jangling was heard, quickly joined by the sound of a stringed instrument and some sort of hollow drum. Slowly the men began to bob and weave and sway in time to the music; stamping first this foot and then the other as they held their arms in the air; dropping first to the left knee and then to the right. The music got faster and so did the men. David rose and peered over the heads of the crowd watching the spectacle. When it finished he went back to his seat, which was where Mehmet found him when he too returned to the table. He didn't sit down, nor did he say anything, but once again gestured with his head to let David know that he should follow him.

Mehmet led the way into the building, pushing aside the richly coloured rug that hung in the arched doorway as a protection against the mosquitoes. David blinked as he moved into the gloominess of the room, which was heavy with the scent of the dancers' sweat and smoke from the meats and fish grilling on an open charcoal fire at the back of the room. No women were inside the *kahve*. David followed his host to a secluded table in a stone alcove. Here they sat down again and David could see why he had picked this table, for it provided them with an unimpeded view of the entire room. A boy came over, and baklava and more Turkish coffee were ordered. David had forgotten how much the Turks adored their sweetmeats.

At last, in a somewhat guttural voice, the man spoke. His English was good. 'So you did come. Have you got the information?'

This time it was David's turn to remain silent as he once again took out his cigarette case. Offering it to Mehmet, he held it open for him.

Mehmet glanced up and let his hand be guided by David's eyes towards the cigarette he should take. He took two. When their order arrived Mehmet used the boy's fussing as an opportunity to tuck one cigarette into the top of his soft leather boot. When the boy left the table Mehmet was happily smoking the other one.

'So, you like our dancing?'

David nodded, all too aware of the dagger glinting in the sash.

'We are good as we dance the Zeybek. It is our symbol of courage and heroism. It shows our love of our country and that we will do anything to protect her. One day she will again conquer the world, and when she does she will remember her friends.'

'Does she remember her friends of today as well of those of tomorrow?' David asked the question in an equally soft voice.

'Yes. When I have checked the information, your money will be transferred.' Mehmet went to lift the cigarette to his mouth but David put a hand on his arm and stopped him.

'You have half the information there. You will get the rest when the money has been transferred.'

Mehmet's face clouded over and his free hand moved to the hilt of his dagger.

David sat back in his seat. 'Kill me and you'll never get the rest of it, will you? Now do be sensible. Once I know I have the money, then I will return with the rest of the details. If I'm prepared to risk this journey again, you should be prepared to trust me.'

'Trust!' Mehmet spat the word across the table. 'You speak of trust, but you do not trust us! You prefer to play games. I had hoped for more from an Englishman, but I see you have spent too much time among those Greek barbarians to know the real meaning of honour.'

David gave a low snort of laughter. 'There is no room for honour in our sort of commercial arrangement, my friend. It's simply a matter of seller and buyer. I have the goods, you have the money. The rest of the transaction will take place once each of us is satisfied that the other has fulfilled his side of the bargain. Now, as much as I have enjoyed our fortuitous meeting tonight, I must, sadly, leave you.' The irony in his voice was not lost on Mehmet. 'When everything is ready, contact me through the usual channels and I shall, at great personal risk, return. I recommend that it is someone else who helps me find a room next time, my friend. *Allahais-marladik.*'

'*Gule, Gule,*' replied Mehmet tersely and returned to his pipe.

Casually David sauntered out through the smoky atmosphere and back into the freshness of the night. Outside the festivities continued. The younger women had joined the youths in the square but now they were dancing to the latest imported American records and Rosemary Clooney's voice blared out from an old wind-up gramophone. The flamboyant clothes seemed out of place against the words and music that made them twirl and stamp their feet in delight. As David made his way round the edges and under the shadow of the great admiral, a young woman darted towards him and grabbed his hand, pulling him towards the dancing. David shook his head and tried to pull away. Angrily the woman stamped her foot, and in a second two men with daggers in their belts were at her side.

They listened as she explained wildly that the man had refused to dance with her. David suddenly realised how excessively drunk they were and for a moment thought they were going to turn on him or, worse, make him dance. He glanced at his watch. It was nearly two-thirty; he would have to hurry if he were to make it back to the boat in time to catch the tide. Seeing him check the time, the two men turned in disgust. One bit his thumbnail at him, while the other pursed his lips and spat in his face, directing a foul oath at the man who had so insulted his sister by refusing to dance with her.

David didn't respond, hoping that the other men, who were just as drunk, hadn't witnessed the incident, fearing that they would also come to help defend the girl's honour. He waited until the trio had returned to their friends before wiping the spittle from his face. Once again he slipped into the shadows and retraced his steps back up the path. As before he used his torch until he had passed the mosque and the final few houses.

Beyond this point he again had to feel his way, since he didn't want to risk the pinpoint of light being seen and arousing suspicions. He stumbled a couple of times; putting his hands out to break his fall, he scratched them in the rough scrub and gorse growing out of the rocks. Finally he made it to the top of the path. The car was waiting for him, its driver sitting in the passenger seat with his feet propped on the steering wheel, his arms crossed on his chest and his cap pulled down over his face, snoring. Violently David shook him awake, putting a hand over his mouth to stop him yelling out loud. Sheepishly the man moved across and started the car.

Fifteen minutes later David was back on board the *Odyssey Two*, heading out of Turkish waters into Greek.

'OK?' asked the captain, delighted to be leaving the rough shore behind him as he made for the harbour and soft sands of his homeland.

David was in the little cabin changing back into the fisherman's clothes he had worn earlier. 'It went well, but I have to come back again.'

'*No!* I will not go back to those waters. You told me just once. Just *once*. If they catch me, then . . .' He made a slicing gesture with his hand across his throat.

David came out of the cabin, tying the scarf round his neck. 'Don't worry, I'm not asking you to do it for nothing. I'll pay you next time what I'm paying you tonight.'

'No! No! I do not worry about the money. I am now a traitor to my country. I am full of shame.'

'Tonight has made you a traitor. Next time you do this crossing it won't make you into anything you are not already. Anyway, I have hidden a small memento from my visit on your boat.' The captain looked petrified. 'If you don't take me back I shall tell the authorities that you have been smuggling, and where they can find the proof. So we have a deal, don't we?'

The captain nodded, knowing he was trapped.

It was a week later that David received notification from his bank in Switzerland that a large sum of American dollars had been deposited into his account. A few days after that he once again told Elizabeth that he would be away for a few days. She made her usual objections but David ignored them as ever.

This time the departure from Vathi was a little harder, for they didn't have the shield of the other boats going out to the fishing grounds. It was therefore agreed to delay the crossing until the

245

small hours of the morning. The engine seemed to echo round the channel as it chugged out of the harbour, but, apart from one old man who grunted in his sleep and rolled over again to carry on snoring, no one was disturbed. The sky was beginning to lighten to a dirty grey as they drew close to the Turkish coast. This time the captain was more circumspect about where he moored and found a cave where he could hide the boat. As before the car was waiting, and in the half-light of the approaching morning it drove to the top of the track and the crooked sign.

Going down the path was much easier than on his previous visit; the increasing light enabled David to make out the rocks and pot-holes in the surface. By the time he reached the small mosque the sun was appearing above the horizon, bringing with it the promise of a clear, hot day. The religious men of the village, most of them elderly, were shuffling their way to morning prayers.

David hung back, not wanting to be seen to be coming from the roadway. He waited until their voices could be heard calling out before he cautiously continued. This time, when he entered the square it was almost quiet. It was the day of the weekly market, which was why it had been selected for the trip, and a few people were setting up their stalls and laying out their wares. Fresh vegetables, from glossy aubergines and crooked green beans to shiny red peppers and angular green chillies, were set alongside barrels of cracked wheat and rice, and the scent of cumin and cinnamon mingled with the sharp tang of vinegar floating from the assorted pickle barrels.

David joined the villagers as they took advantage of the cool of the morning to do their shopping. The level of noise increased until the women yelling their wares from the market stalls mingled with the shouts of the men placing bets on the outcome of a throw of dice. David stopped at one of the fruit stalls to buy some apples, not because he wanted them but because the bag would make him less conspicuous. Slowly he moved round the market-place, stopping here and there to look at produce but not buying. Finally he came to a stall set up outside a shop selling tooled-leather bags and belts. He began an innocent-sounding conversation about what the woman had for sale before she offered to show him the rest of her stock inside the premises. He followed her through the shop to the small courtyard out at the back where a man sat stitching the pieces of a bag together.

246

'My name is Aziz. You have the rest of the details?' the man asked.

David nodded.

'Good. Come with me.'

Aziz put down his tools and wiped his hands on his large calico apron, which he then removed. He led the way into a house at the other side of the courtyard, where he sat down at the kitchen table. A woman brought them sweet apple tea and small, delicate pastries, then left, understanding that she wasn't needed when men were talking.

'The first part of the formula you gave Mehmet is good – it has been tested. What you have today tells us what to do next, yes?'

'I told Mehmet you would have the rest of the information when I received my money. I've got my money now . . .' David shrugged. 'So I will keep the rest of the bargain.'

He reached up and took off his old beret, turning it inside out to reveal its lining. He felt round the edge until his fingers found a small hole and carefully began to ease away the threads. When the hole was big enough he wriggled his little finger inside and hooked out a small rolled-up piece of paper. He uncurled it and handed it to his host.

'With this you will be able to use the sponge residues to create the necessary solution. Make sure your workers do not inhale any of it; it doesn't take much to cause an effect. What it could do to a whole town is unthinkable. I tell you, the idiots who discovered it gave themselves a very bad time. In fact, you might say it ultimately led to their deaths.'

Aziz studied the paper closely before nodding. 'It is good. It is very good. Tonight it will go to Istanbul. Magnificent Istanbul – it is in two parts the world. This paper arrives Istanbul Europe but it leaves Istanbul Asia, and then across to friends in Russia. Russia friend of Turkey. Russia one great power knows other great power.'

'I don't want to know,' David interrupted him. 'Our agreement was that I would deliver the goods into Turkey, which I have done. If you want to sell them on to Russia that's nothing to do with me. I've kept my part of the deal. As far as I'm concerned it's over. I had information you wanted. It had a price; you met that price; I sold. What you do with it now is up to you.'

Aziz smiled, and raised his glass of tea. 'Now, you will be my guest. We go to the baths. Tonight you dine with my family and tomorrow we do not know each other.'

David smiled back, not wanting to let Aziz know that given a choice he would rather leave immediately. However, once he reached the bath-house he was almost pleased that he had had to stay.

Mustapha was a huge bulk of a man and his body gleamed with the heat of the steamroom. His fingers found every knot in David's body and with what felt like steel-tipped fingers he kneaded his way into them, easing the tense muscles. It hurt at first and there were moments when David visibly flinched as the large man found a particularly tender spot, but slowly, despite his sense of vulnerability lying naked on the marble slab, David began to relax and his thoughts drifted as he rolled to lie on his back.

Mustapha smiled knowingly to himself as he could see the effects David's thoughts were having on his body.

He poured a little scented oil on to David's stomach and the smell wafted into his consciousness. It made him think of the smell of the sun on the fig trees behind the main Rouget Corporation plant on Kalymnos, and in his mind he followed the path round the back of the building, to the smaller shed. His shed. David felt as if he were floating, floating round the shed looking down on the hand-picked team he had drawn together to work secretly for him in developing the residues. Never mind what Cecil wanted. Cecil was as bad as Robert. Robert and Sally. In their car driving to get away from him. Fear. Crashing. Hurting.

Mustapha covered him in hot towels.

David was back in the shed in the stifling heat. No windows; everyone had to think the shed was empty. No one must suspect he was working on Robert and Sally's discovery as well. No one must know he wanted the control that it gave him. Sweat dripping off him as the hut grew hotter. The men beginning to feel the effects. Responding as David scared them, seeing how far he could go. Putting a handkerchief over his nose. Not being able to breathe.

David woke up with a start. Part of the towel had covered his face and he spat the corner of the wet cloth out of his mouth. He blinked as he glanced round the steamroom, aware that he must have called out, since the other men were looking at him. He hoped his words had been in English. Slowly the men settled down again and the sounds of slapping and pummelling resumed.

David relaxed once more, but this time his thoughts were

sharper. What was he going to do with the discovery? It was all very well for Cecil to want to lead the way in producing new painkillers but Robert and Sally had been right. Used as a controlling drug, poriferase was worth a lot more. 'Poriferase,' he murmured to himself, letting the name slip through his lips. It was a good name, a solid name. Silly that it came from something as light as a sponge. *Spongos*. Part of the family of *Porifera*. His lips formed the word but very little sound escaped. David smiled sleepily as the name of the new drug – his drug – went through his mind. Cecil might be a shrewd businessman but he was a fool. Someone was going to develop the stuff first and it might as well be the Rouget Corporation as anyone else. Ah well, what did he care? He'd made his money but at the same time had also managed to keep the original formula.

No one would ever think to look in the shed. Certainly no one would dream that such a loyal employee as Dr David Ghillyand, the boss's son-in-law moreover, would be working on his own, in an opposite direction to the rest of the company. It was all too easy. Sponges were bought for the development work at the main plant, and David simply paid the suppliers a few drachmas more to buy extra sponges for him. Easy. Easy to take them into his own little shed and get his team working on them. Easy. And the idiots were so grateful for the extra money they didn't argue. *Fools!* he thought contemptuously.

Easy, all so easy. He smiled to himself. Once he was out of Turkey he could relax.

Christos had had to take his little boat illegally out of Greek waters into hostile Turkish ones so a man could do some business.

'I was disgusted with myself,' he said in Greek, 'but what could I do? The money had almost gone. I could never repay it. I was trapped. I was scared, but I promise you it was not until we were returning from our second trip that I found out what I had done.

'I did not dare leave the water of the cave. Outside the sun shone but I had to stay hidden. I could see Turkish ships and boats out at sea and I was afraid. I wanted to leave but remembered that Ghillyand had hidden something Turkish on my boat. If I could have found it, I would have gone. I spent two days looking but could not find it. So I waited.'

Christos paused to allow Edith to finish translating.

'Ghillyand boasted to me of his success,' he continued. 'He told me that he had at last used the Rouget Corporation properly. That he had sold its secrets to the East, so he could get what was rightfully his. He said he had rebalanced the power. I could not believe what I was hearing. I had betrayed my country and England. England, who helped us so much in the war, and who was now providing much work for my people on Kalymnos.'

At this point Christos broke down into noisy sobs and wails of self-reproachment. Edith and Rose tried to soothe him but it didn't help. It wasn't until they promised not to tell his family or the police, assuring him it was so long ago that they wouldn't be interested, that he finally began to calm down.

'Besides,' added Dan with a degree of irony, 'science has moved on so far since then, it wouldn't be worth much anyway!'

Alex had remained silent as she listened, taking hold of Dan's hand halfway through the long translation.

After expressing his relief that he had finally confessed, but also his deep shame and embarrassment, Christos eventually excused himself and left.

'David was a spy.' Alex shook her head in disbelief. 'The manipulative bastard was a spy!'

'Jesus Christ! No wonder poor old Christos had a thousand blue fits when he saw your name. He must have thought it had all caught up with him. Poor old sod.' Dan was as vehement in his exclamations as Alex was quiet in hers.

Edith and Rose looked from Alex to Dan and began whispering to each other.

'Come on, girls,' said Dan. 'You might as well finish the story – there's obviously more.'

'We didn't know about *that*. Honestly, Alex, we didn't. We knew Christos had been involved in something, but he would never tell us what, any more than we told him about you.' Rose looked pinched and frail as she sank back into her rocking chair.

'I'm sure you didn't, Rose.' Alex stroked the old woman's wrinkled hand. 'Look, I'm not after revenge. I just want to know what happened, that's all.'

*   *   *

250

When David returned from his trip, Elizabeth greeted him with evident affection. It crossed his mind that something was different about her, but the lure of a bath and clean clothes meant that he didn't pay as much attention to her as he would have done normally. Which was why, when, over dinner, she casually dropped her bombshell, he was quite unprepared for it.

'Thank you, Anna. I shall serve Dr Ghillyand tonight.'

Anna placed the platter of succulent lamb in front of Elizabeth and handed her the silverware. Concentrating hard, Elizabeth selected the choicest slices of meat to put on her husband's plate. As the light twinkled on her diamond earrings and necklace, David let the effect of the wine mingle with his exhaustion to create in him a restful contentment.

'So, darling,' she began in a conversational tone, 'how was Turkey?'

David spluttered as his wine went down the wrong way.

'Just because I'm stuck here, don't think I don't know what's going on. I hope you were paid a good price for the Corporation's work? After all, it would be a shame for you to go to all that trouble and no doubt take many risks if it wasn't well rewarded, wouldn't it? More meat, or is that enough?' She held the plate up for him to see before setting it before him.

David thought rapidly. Was it worth denying it, telling her she was imagining things? What would she do? If she told Cecil it might be the end of everything, but could he bluff it out? Could he really make Cecil believe that Elizabeth had finally succumbed to the mental illness he has so carefully hinted at over the last few weeks? It was too big a risk.

David set his glass back on the table. 'I had hoped you wouldn't find out . . . but *c'est la vie*. What do you want, Elizabeth?'

Anyone listening to their conversation would have heard a cosy chat between a married couple. The implied threats came not from the tone but from the content of their words. Neatly Elizabeth cut up her meat and popped a small morsel in her mouth, delicately lifting her napkin and dabbing it at her lips. She smoothed it back on to her lap and picked up her knife and fork.

'What I've always wanted – you. Not just in name, but all of you.'

Abruptly Elizabeth almost threw her cutlery down on her plate and went to kneel beside David, her full skirt billowing out

251

behind her as she grasped his arm and looked up at him with naked desire.

'You know I've always adored you, but no matter what I do it's not enough. I've given you everything you wanted – money, privilege, status. But all you do is throw it back in my face. You need me, and whether you like it or not you also love me. Now I want to see that love, and I want everyone else to see it too. It's not so much to ask in return for my loyalty, is it?'

David tucked his hand under her upturned chin and bent down, placing his lips on hers to kiss her tenderly. 'No, it's not, sweetheart.'

'I think we need a fresh pot of tea.' Edith got up and went into the kitchen, making an excuse for a break after Christos' revelations.

Dan followed to lend a hand. 'Edith, I know there's more, but please don't keep any of it back. I know it's difficult for you and Rose to go over all of this, but please do it. Please tell Alex everything.'

'You love her very much, don't you?'

To his amazement, Dan felt himself blush beneath her direct gaze. 'Yes, I do. I think she loves me, but she's still too scared to tell me. To actually say it. Edith, I don't want to hurt her – hell, I'd do anything to protect her – but do you really want her to spend the rest of her life not knowing the truth? With the same sort of fear and doubts you and Rose have had? You obviously gave her a lot of love when she was a baby. Prove you still love her by telling her all the facts now. Please?'

Edith nodded slowly. 'We don't know all of it . . . that's the trouble. We can only tell her what we saw and heard.'

'That's all I'm asking.'

Once they had seated themselves again with cups of tea, it was Rose who began speaking first. 'After his trips finished, things seemed to settle down more. It was like it was when we first arrived, with David coming home for lunch each day. Elizabeth stopped creeping around and almost became nice all the time.'

'That one was never nice unless she got something out of it!' Edith snorted disdainfully.

'Exactly. So, although it was lovely that everything seemed

252

happy, it was odd. You have to admit, Edie, it was odd . . . and it got odder the night she died.'

Without realising they were doing it, both Alex and Dan leaned forward slightly in their seats as once again Edith dovetailed her account with Rose's.

Elizabeth was having a wonderful time. She stood at the bow of Maria's yacht, legs braced as she held on to the rail, her arms straight and her head flung back while the wind sent her hair streaming out behind her. The boat rode the water magnificently, rising on the crest of a wave before dropping down the other side to smack against the sea, sending the spray up into her face.

'David! Come and join me! This is heaven!'

To everyone's surprise, David put down his book and went to stand close to his wife, his left arm wrapped tightly round her waist, drawing her towards him, his right hand next to hers on the rail. Aware that he was being watched, he bent his head and nuzzled Elizabeth's neck. William found the raw sexuality in the air uncomfortable; she reminded him of a sleek cosseted cat.

'It is a change, is it not, William?' Maria commented in her clipped tones. 'But a good one to see. My darlings – lunch is ready!' she called across to the couple, who, laughing, made their way hand in hand to the buffet laid out under the awning on the rear deck. 'Having fun?'

'Oh, Maria, it's wonderful. I can't remember the last time I enjoyed myself so much. The sea makes me feel totally overawed but at the same time as if I'm in control, taming it. It's a feeling of freedom and I love it!'

She picked up a chicken leg and sank her teeth into it, wrenching the meat off the bone with a greedy delight before licking her lips to remove the last traces of spices. Again the image of a cat sprang to William's mind.

'But sweetheart,' said David smoothly, 'you're always in control – we all know that!'

The group laughed, yet more than one person there felt they were watching a charade.

'It's as if they're playing a very sophisticated game, but only they know the rules,' commented one of Maria's friends later that afternoon as she painted her nails while keeping a surreptitious eye on the Ghillyands.

'Yes,' agreed Maria. 'And I would not mind. But we are losing!' It was a shrewd comment.

Since confronting David, Elizabeth had indeed been controlling him. If she wanted something, she got it. Whether it was a trinket, an outing or attention in bed, it was hers. They had been married for two years, in Greece for barely six months, and at last she was enjoying herself. It was as if she were back home wrapping her father around her little finger, with everyone bowing to her every whim. It was a feeling she relished. At last the picture she had created of herself and David as a loving couple was a reality. Everything she had worked for was hers, and as far as Elizabeth was concerned she *had* worked hard to fulfil her ambitions. The combination of a husband who clearly appreciated and adored her, a baby she didn't have to worry about and all the trappings of wealth, which she had always taken as her right, were rewards for her efforts.

Elizabeth Ghillyand was definitely having the time of her young spoilt life; but not so her husband.

From the first moment he had become aware of her as a woman, David had been both attracted to and repelled by Elizabeth. He had seen her ambition as clearly as if he had been looking in a mirror, and he had been drawn towards it. Despite the rows and fights he knew that they were a well-matched pair; until recently, that is. So long as he had been in control he could continue to play Elizabeth's games, but the power had shifted and someone else was now pulling Dr David Ghillyand's strings. He did not like it.

How Elizabeth had found out about his trips didn't bother him. That was over and done. All that mattered was that she had something to use against him, to make him do as she wanted, and it was a tool she was not afraid to use. For the first time in his life David was being manipulated as he had manipulated others. If his situation hadn't been so precarious he would have appreciated its irony; in a dangerous game, however, it was a luxury he couldn't afford.

Initially David had objected to playing his role at home, preferring to make it merely a show for public outings, but Elizabeth had made it clear that the attention she was demanding was for

254

her benefit in private too. If he did anything that displeased her, a carefully worded comment about midnight boat trips, or a remark that it was a shame the political situation prevented them from visiting Turkey, or other apparently innocent asides, made him realise that Elizabeth required obedience twenty-four hours a day.

As she forced David to perpetuate the myth of the loving couple, Elizabeth seemed to forget that the face they were presenting wasn't all that it appeared. She had soon deluded herself into believing, like everyone else, that her marriage was secure and happy. But the more Elizabeth controlled David the more frustrated he became.

David walked down the gangplank from Maria's yacht as Elizabeth jumped lightly off it. 'Catch me, David!' Obligingly he did so, his hands gripping her waist beneath the shirt which she had knotted above her shorts. For a moment, out of sheer malice, he was tempted to drop her but instead gave her a kiss before setting her feet on the ground.

'We dine together tonight?' It was a generous invitation from Maria, considering they had been her guests all day on the yacht.

'I want to eat alone with you,' Elizabeth hissed in David's ear, and gave his earlobe a none too playful nip.

'Maria, it's kind of you . . . but I really feel Elizabeth and I shouldn't abuse your hospitality any further. Besides, it's our wedding anniversary, and I'm sure you understand.'

'Oh, David – I thought you'd forgotten!'

Maria didn't mind. After all, it wasn't as if she personally had to prepare the food; it was just a question of telling her cook how many people to expect for dinner and it all miraculously appeared. They said their farewells, and David led the way back to the car, which he had parked on the waterfront that morning.

'Of course I've not forgotten. How could I?' He reversed the car along the quay before taking the road to Elies. 'I have plans to take you dancing to a wonderful place. It's close to the sea and under the stars.'

'I knew you'd eventually enjoy our new arrangement,' Elizabeth said. 'It's much nicer, isn't it?' With a contented sigh she rested her head on his shoulder, which was just as well, for it meant she couldn't see the stony expression on his face.

When they got home Elizabeth called to Anna that since David was taking her out somewhere special she and Spiros could have the night off. Bouncing up the steps under the burgeoning vines on the arbour, she saw Edith and Rose sitting on blanket with Alex between them.

'How is my darling today?'

She scooped the baby up and tossed her into the air before dangling her above her head. Alex stared down with limpid eyes at Elizabeth before bursting into noisy tears. It was the sort of gesture that infuriated the two nannies but they dared not say anything, so Rose quietly took the infant back to hold and soothe her again.

'She's cutting another tooth, Mrs Ghillyand, and it's making her fractious.'

'Poor darling. Rub whisky on it – there's plenty in the drawing-room. It's what my nanny used to swear by. It might not work, but after a while Alex will get so tipsy she'll fall asleep and it won't matter, will it?' With a giggle she continued on into the villa to prepare for her special evening out.

That night she dressed with particular care, choosing a full-skirted, calf-length, vivid green silk dress that tied under her neck to reveal her elegant golden back. At the last minute she swept her hair on to the top of her head before grabbing a light shawl to drape over her shoulders.

It was a long time since she had made an entrance. Tonight she waited until the setting sun was at just the right angle to throw its reddish-tinged hues across the doorway to the terrace. David heard the rustle of her skirts and involuntarily rose to his feet as she appeared, hesitating for a moment in the doorway so he could fully appreciate the effect. Although the circumstances were different, he suddenly recalled how Elizabeth had looked, standing in the sunlight at the top of the stairs the day she had been presented at court.

Gallantly he offered her his arm and escorted her to the car, ensuring she was comfortable before walking round to the driver's seat. They set off, not, as Elizabeth expected, towards Pothia, but in the opposite direction, towards the village of Myrties.

'David, where on earth are we going?'

'I told you – somewhere special. No, don't be impatient, sweetheart.'

The road began to rise up the hill until it reached the top and began to climb down the other side. Although not a tarmacked road, it was the main route linking the northern villages to the capital in the south, and as such was better than most of the tracks; at least it had a level, if somewhat erratic, surface. They had wound carefully round a few bends when David pulled over to the side of the road. Although they had been descending there was still a sheer drop down to the right beside Elizabeth. To keep her mind off it she gazed across to the little island of Telendos. The sun had now set and the sky blazed in a multitude of colours in the afterglow. The rough sea of the morning had settled and on the horizon they could see the large Athens ferry steaming on its way.

'Why have we stopped?' Inexplicably Elizabeth suddenly felt nervous. Maybe it was the precipice by her right shoulder, or maybe it was the sudden gust of wind; whatever it was, she didn't like it. 'David?'

'I want to give you my anniversary present now, by the light of the setting sun.'

Elizabeth felt foolish. She took the flat box that David held out to her and snapped open its clasp. Inside lay a gold necklace with five long links on either side that resembled the buds of an exotic flower. In the middle was set the blossom in full bloom and at its centre lay a perfect emerald. Inside the circle of the necklace lay a matching bracelet and earrings. It was an exquisite and stunning collection.

'My God, David, it's beautiful.' For once Elizabeth was lost for words, but not for long. 'Here, help me put it on.' She wriggled round so he could fix the clasp at the back of her neck, while she removed the bracelet and earrings she was wearing to clip the new ones into place. 'Isn't it lucky I chose to wear green tonight?' she purred, and gave him a thank-you kiss.

David let out the clutch and the car continued round the bends and down the hill. Small trees grew along the roadside and they had barely reached the edge of the village before David again pulled over and parked the car. He helped Elizabeth out and led the way down a few steps into a courtyard. In the centre stood a gnarled olive tree around which were set tables and chairs, many already filled with people chatting as they ate. Each table had a number of candles on it that twinkled away as if in competition with the stars now appearing overhead. At the back of the courtyard a trio of men were softly playing bazouki, but not loud enough to drown out the gentle swoosh of the sea as the waves lapped against the shore. The whole scene was enchanting.

They were shown to a table but not presented with a menu, since Nikos, the proprietor, fed his customers with what he considered to be the best selection of dishes. David, however, drew the line at relying on the owner's choice in wine and called him over to ask if he had any champagne.

'How extravagant, but delicious!' Elizabeth exclaimed, over-joyed at David's sudden expansive mood.

It took some time for Nikos to find the champagne, for although he had a few bottles available it wasn't something often ordered. While they waited, David ordered them both a glass of Metaxa, which they had almost finished when the champagne arrived.

'You had better put two more bottles of this on ice, just in case,' he instructed Nikos, who gave him a huge grin, displaying a mouthful of silver teeth, as he recognised customers with money to spend. 'Oh, and you might as well bring us the Metaxa bottle as well as some sugar.'

'Sugar?' queried Elizabeth.

'I'd ask for Angostura bitters but I know they won't have them, so we'll just mix our champagne cocktails without.'

Elizabeth gave a squeal and clapped her hands with delight. David sprinkled the sugar in the bottom of their glasses before adding the brandy and champagne. Elizabeth didn't notice him pour a lot more brandy into her glass than his and took an appreciat-ive sip while they waited for Nikos to bring them their food. She had finished her first drink before David had started his, and she held out her glass for a refill. Silently David did as he was told, again adding an extra measure of brandy. Elizabeth drunk was easier to control than sober.

The food appeared dish by dish at a leisurely pace, and as Eliza-beth finished each champagne cocktail David refilled it for her. Soon she was so inebriated she didn't notice that he was no longer drinking. As the evening wore on, the bazouki players became more boisterous until, at last, the men stood up from their tables to dance. Arms resting across each other's shoulders they began to snake their way slowly around the floor, moving from heel to toe and back again, slapping first this foot and then that. David found himself thinking of the Zeybek dancers he had seen in Tur-gutreis, and how similar were the dances of these two nations that so hated each other. Elizabeth simply observed the men, mesmerised by their movements, watching their feet as they flashed in and out and moved with ever-increasing speed. The onlookers stamped their feet and clapped their hands in time to the music.

David barely had time to notice her get to her feet before she had run out to the centre of the courtyard to join the dancers. Uncertain what to do about the woman among them, the men stopped their dancing and the players stopped strumming.

'I want to dance!' Elizabeth stamped her foot in rage. 'Come on, I want to dance!' She held her shawl up by its corners and began to dance. 'Come on! Come on!' she urged.

She had obviously been studying the men closely because, even without the music, everyone could see she was performing the right steps. Slowly one of the players picked up his instrument and began playing. The others quickly followed and before long the dancers had also decided to break with centuries of tradition and allow this strange but beautiful woman to dance with them. However, they did refuse to hold her hands, using their handkerchiefs instead to form the chain. Once Nikos and his customers realised there wasn't going to be an unpleasant scene, the atmosphere again picked up, and a few other women even stood up and joined in.

'That was fun! I'm thirsty. I need another drink.'

David emptied the last dregs of their third bottle of champagne into her glass. She knocked it back like lemonade, no longer tasting it, nor aware of its effect.

'Let's do it again . . . Come on, David – you too.' She stood in front of him and took his hands, trying to pull him to his feet.

'No, Elizabeth, you've had enough. I think it's time we went home.'

'I'm not going home! I want to dance and I'm going to, whether you want to or not! And I won't need these.'

So saying, she kicked first her right, then her left leg into the air, sending her shoes sailing skywards. Deftly David caught them as she reached up and released her hair from its pins. She shook it loose and lightly dodged her way back to the dance floor. David watched her, exchanging sympathetic glances with the other customers. Finally he settled their bill, got to his feet and made his way to join her.

'Put these on, sweetheart – we're leaving.'

'*No!*' she shouted, '*I'm not going!*'

She turned to look round the restaurant but everyone was torn between seeing the spectacle she was making of herself and not wanting to catch her eye in case they got drawn into what was obviously going to be a huge marital fight. Elizabeth turned round in the middle of the dance floor a few times, making herself dizzy, and then stopped as suddenly as she had started, throwing her head back and laughing loudly.

'You all think he suffers because he's married to me, don't you?' she yelled at no one in particular and everyone in general. 'Well *I'm* the one who has to suffer, not him. And do you know why I suffer? It's because my husband, my wonderful husband, is a spy. You think he's helping give your men jobs but he's not. He's using them and he's using me. You know what's he's doing?'

By now the customers had stopped pretending they weren't interested. All eyes were fixed on Elizabeth, who stood shouting in the middle of the restaurant.

'Well, I'll tell you. He's stealing from his own family and he's stealing from *you*. You know why he's stealing from you? Well, I'll tell you. He's stealing from you because he's taking secrets and selling them to –'

'*Elizabeth, that's enough!*' David roared over her.

Despite the noise she was making, David's voice drowned it out. She stopped and looked at him. His face was pinched and his lips drained of colour as unflinchingly he returned her stare.

'You are very drunk and very embarrassing. Either you leave now, with me, or . . .' He left the threat hanging in the air.

'Or what?' She didn't feel as defiant as she sounded.

'Or this.' And he bent down, wrapped his arms round her knees and virtually flung her over his shoulder.

There was a round of applause as they left, even though Elizabeth was screaming that she wanted to stay and drumming her fists hard against David's back, much to the amusement of the other clients. He dumped her unceremoniously in the back seat of the car, tossing her shoes and shawl in after her; and amid loud cheering from the men drove off back towards the villa.

Elizabeth sat next to him and sulked. 'You always spoil my fun. I get little enough of it and when I get it you spoil it. I want to go back.' She twisted round in her seat to gaze longingly over her shoulder at the receding lights.

David drove in stern silence. She had nearly ruined everything. If anyone found out, he would be dead, such was the hatred between Greece and Turkey. He glanced sideways at Elizabeth, who was now waving her arm out of the window, trying to make the light from the headlamps catch the stones in her bracelet.

When they arrived back at the villa, David had difficulty getting Elizabeth out of the car. In the end he prised her out and, holding on to her firmly, half led and half pulled her up the flight of steps. As they emerged from under the arbour he was surprised to see Rose walking up and down holding Alex, who was grizzling away. 'What are you doing up? And why isn't Alex asleep?' he demanded.

'She's teething and won't go down. Edith has taken up Mrs Ghillyand's suggestion and gone to get some whisky to rub on her gums. I hope you don't mind.' Rose felt she was letting Elizabeth down. She willed Edith to hurry up. As if in answer to her silent plea, Edith appeared round the corner clutching the bottle from the drawing-room.

'Here we are, Rosie – oh!' She stopped as she saw David and Elizabeth.

'Oh good – whisky! Let's have another drink!' Elizabeth lunged for the bottle.

David pushed her away. 'For goodness sake, Edith, pour some into a glass. Give me the bottle and do whatever is needed to stop that infernal row. All right, Elizabeth, you can have a drink. Just stop nagging.'

'Do you think she should have another? Hasn't she had –'

'Edith, just do as you're told and let me take care of Elizabeth. Thank you.'

When she finished replacing the cap he snatched it from her. Elizabeth was still trying to wrest it from him as they went into the villa. She let herself drop into a chair and David poured her a drink, which she tossed down in one gulp.

'Sweetheart, I think you need sobering up a bit before you go to bed. How about a walk? It's such a lovely night.'

Elizabeth thought about David's suggestion before answering. 'I'm not drunk, just tipsy,' she said. She had problems picking her words and spoke slowly and precisely. 'But a walk in the starlight with you would be so romantic.' She bent down and pulled her shoes on.

David crossed to the bureau and took out a torch from the top drawer. Elizabeth swayed to her feet and, grabbing David's hand, dragged him back outside. Edith and Rose were still trying to get Alex to sleep, but David pointedly ignored them as he helped a befuddled Elizabeth down the marble steps. At the bottom he firmly took her hand and, without her knowing it, guided her back along the road to Myrties.

Away from the village the lights quickly disappeared and David turned on his torch.

'David, I want to go back. I'm tired.'

'Oh no, sweetheart, we're going on. I thought you wanted to go dancing again. Let's go back to the dancing, shall we?'

Elizabeth let go of his hand and began to dance her way along the road, singing to herself and not noticing as it began to rise before winding down the other side. David followed her, letting the beam from his torch light the way in front of her. She played with the light, hopping in and out of it, letting her body cast shapes across the road. David joined in, shining the torch first here and then there. Elizabeth ran after it like a kitten trying to catch a ball of wool. Eventually they reached the spot where, earlier, David had pulled over and given Elizabeth her present. He still made the light bounce from one side of the road to the other and Elizabeth kept following it, twirling this way and that as she tried to find it.

Suddenly the light went out.

'It's gone. Where's it gone? Turn it on, David. It's dark.' Elizabeth's voice echoed through the blackness at him. 'David, where are you? I don't like this. Turn it on.'

He could hear the rising note of hysteria in her voice but he stood still, allowing his eyes to grow accustomed to the gloom. He could just make out Elizabeth's shape against the skyline, and gently he called to her.

'Elizabeth, over here. I'm over here, sweetheart.'

Holding her hands out in front of her, she stumbled towards his voice, but just when she thought she would reach him it was behind her, again calling her. 'Here, Elizabeth, I'm here.' She spun round, the movement increasing the giddiness from her excessive drinking earlier, and again tried to follow his voice. She began to get frightened.

'David! David, where are you? I can't find you. *David!*' Her panic was increasing.

David moved up and down the road, from one side to the other, constantly teasing and calling her, aware of the hem of her silk skirt brushing against his legs as he weaved this way and that, leading her round in circles.

It didn't occur to her to stop and make David come to her. She was terrified. Where was he? He was there, no, there, all around her but she couldn't reach him. It was like a horrible nightmare. Again she tried to follow his voice; she was sure he was to her left. She could feel the breeze on her face. There he was – she was close to him. Eagerly she ran towards him, certain that this time she would find him. Reaching out she went to grab him but she missed. Feeling herself pitch forward she moved her hands down to brace herself against the road but instead of solid ground she found nothing. She was falling through the air, the scrub and bushes ripping her clothes as she plunged through them, the rocks bruising her as she crashed down. By the time she hit the bottom she was already dead.

The last sound David heard Elizabeth make was a terrified scream as she propelled herself head first over the edge of the road and down the mountainside. He took out a cigarette and lit it, slowly dragging on it, its tip glowing red in the night. It wasn't until he had ground it out and tossed it after Elizabeth that he turned on the torch again. He crouched down and methodically swung the beam down the mountainside. It was the glint of the light on her gold necklace that showed him where she lay, her head twisted at an impossible angle, her limbs oddly askew, and the green of her dress blending in with the undergrowth.

He stood up and began mechanically to walk home. This time the villa was in silence; obviously Alex had finally gone to sleep. Once inside he poured himself a large whisky from the bottle he had taken from Edith and Rose and wearily made his way upstairs. He shrugged himself out of his jacket, loosened his tie and sat down on the edge of his bed. As Elizabeth had done earlier, he tossed back his whisky in one gulp, feeling it warm him as it went down. Suddenly he began to shake uncontrollably, as the realisation of what he had done hit him with full force. He flung himself backwards on the bed, one arm bent across his eyes, as he tried to put his thoughts in order.

Christ, what have I done? Elizabeth, I'm sorry, but you gave me no choice. We could have been so happy if you had just stayed out of it. With a sickening jolt he realised that he loved her. That he was responsible for the death of the one person he loved. Maybe she

263

had survived. Maybe she was lying there in a coma and he could still go back and save her?

No! the voice in his head screamed at him. *Do that and you're back where you started. Come on, man. You haven't gone through all of this to toss it away. You can't afford feelings. Feelings get in the way of logical thought – you know that. So ignore them and think.*

She was drunk. She wanted to go back to the dancing. I went to bed and she slipped out . . . Yes, that will work. Enough people saw her, heard her. It was an accident. A post-mortem will find all that alcohol. Suddenly his eyes snapped open. *Christ, no! They saw both of us go out. Those sodding women again. They'll know we both went out again. Think, man. Think!* He got up and began pacing up and down the room, making and rejecting plans as he went. As the light outside began to soften, he knew he had worked out how to silence them both.

At first he had been concerned that they would object, but in the end it had been quite easy, especially with William there, ostensibly as his legal representative, but in truth as much in his control as the others. William explained that the document they were signing would, on paper, make them powerful and wealthy women, but in reality would give them a regular income until they died. David explained the terms of the trust, and what would happen to them if they did not sign. Spiros and Anna were then called in to witness the signing of the documents; Edith and Rose added their names above those of David and William. This done, they were again shown out of the room. David picked up the papers and began blowing on the ink to help it dry.

'Of course, should you decide to tell the police the truth after we've left, then I will inform them that you, with Spiros and Anna, forced me to draw this up. It would be a pity to implicate two such nice, innocent people . . . don't you think?'

Edith glared at David but all he did was hand her a copy of the papers they had signed.

'Let's keep this all above board, shall we? There's your copy. William will keep mine, and if anyone asks we shall all say it was a gift from a grateful employer. Well, go on . . . take it.'

Edith did as she was told and put an arm round a statue-like Rose to propel her out of the room.

*   *   *

Edith turned to Alex, interrupting Rose's account. 'You see, because you were cutting your teeth and having a bad time of it, poor lamb, we were both awake. Which is why we saw them come in and go out again. It was about three hours later – you wouldn't settle, you know – when Dr Ghillyand came back by himself. I think he was surprised to see both of us, and he certainly wasn't happy to have you crying at him, but he told us that if anyone asked we had seen them come in together and that they had both gone to bed. And that was all.'

'It was awful, Alex, just like the night Robert and Sally died. He started threatening us again.' Rose's comment overrode Edith's voice.

'So what happened?' asked Dan.

Edith continued, without looking at Rose. 'We did as he said. When the police asked, we told them we had seen David and Elizabeth come in but hadn't heard anyone go out again – which, strictly speaking, was true, because the noise you were making, Alex, was enough to mask any sounds. But it didn't seem right. The next day they found Elizabeth's body halfway down the mountainside on the road to Myrties. Other people confirmed she'd been drinking a lot, and David said she must have gone out again and in the dark, being drunk, missed her footing and fallen off the edge of the road. He told the police she'd been under a lot of strain and suffered from mental illness. I have to admit, that with the way she'd been creeping round the house' – 'We now know why,' mumbled Rose – 'and eavesdropping on David,' Edith went on, ignoring Rose's comments, 'we sort of agreed.'

'You don't believe that, though, do you?' Alex heard herself asking.

'Something happened, something bad, but we can't say what. We don't know.'

'What do you *think* happened, Rosie?' Dan spoke in a soft, encouraging voice.

Rose pondered before answering, and even then it sounded as if she were talking to herself instead of the people around her. 'I don't think he pushed her, exactly. Believe it or not, I think he did care for her – in his own way that is. But I don't think he tried to stop her, either. I think she knew what he'd done – it would explain all that snooping, wouldn't it? – that he had sold something and she was sort of using it against him.' Rose gave a little shudder.

'No, he didn't actually push her, but he was definitely responsible.'

'But there was something he didn't want us to know.' Edith's voice seemed to boom in contrast to Rose's softer one. 'You see, early next morning he arranged for William Smythe to come by the villa. He had some papers drawn up which he made us sign. He said he'd be going back to England and taking you with him. That we were to stay here and he'd ensure we'd have enough money to live on. It was horrible, but we had to sign the paper. It was a trust that David and William controlled.'

'We did try not to sign it, honestly,' Rose said, agitated, 'but he told us that if we didn't he would say we'd been blackmailing him. Can't you see we had no choice?'

'No, I don't suppose you did.' Dan began to walk up and down the small veranda. 'The name William Smythe seems to weave in and out of all of this. I don't suppose he's still around, is he?'

'No. His drinking got worse and worse. Maria went back to Athens, and soon after she left in 1959 he shot himself. There was a lot of fuss. Do you remember, Edie?'

'Oh, yes. They found he'd been embezzling and cheating people, and he owed a huge amount of money, some of it linked back to the Rouget Corporation. I must admit, we were quite pleased when he died because we hoped it would release us, but it didn't. The money kept coming in until David died earlier this year – and then it stopped.'

'Oh, but you don't have to worry. It was always more than we needed. We've put a bit by each month and can live on that very easily. We're good at budgeting.' The air of independent pride in Rose's voice betrayed her longing to redeem herself and Edith in the eyes of Alex and Dan.

'Dan, do you think it was William Smythe who owned that unaccounted-for block of shares?'

'I think it might have been. What I don't understand is, if William and David held the trust jointly, it should have reverted to David in full after his death. In which case it should have all been there for you to inherit. Thirty per cent of Rouget stock should have been waiting for you. I don't understand where the missing fifteen per cent has gone.'

'We don't understand money, do we, Rosie?'

Was Alex imagining it, or was there a warning note in Edith's voice as she said this?

Rose shook her head, examining her fingers as they lay interwoven on her lap. 'No, we don't.' It was an odd reply, considering her previous boast about being good at budgeting.

The little group fell silent, each following his or her own thoughts; Edith and Rose reliving the past, Alex and Dan trying to piece it together. That gaps remained there was no doubt, but Alex knew she had enough details to fill in the spaces – that after all these years she could begin to make sense of her background and the relationships that had formed her. Dan was still considering the matter of the trust. Despite his earlier plea to Edith, he felt the two old women were still keeping something back, that there was yet one more piece of the jigsaw they were keeping hidden from them. Instinctively he also knew that it wouldn't be worth pushing them for this piece of information. Like everything else, it would have to come out of their own free will. Edith and Rose were mentally sorting through past images, faded images relating to events long ago which over the last few days had suddenly become alive and vivid again.

Alex couldn't believe how exhausted she was. The facts she had learned over the last few days had emotionally drained her and she withdrew into herself, shutting Dan out. That night she couldn't sleep and finally gave up trying. She eased herself out of bed, trying not to disturb Dan. She put on her thin cotton dressing-gown and crept out of the door on to the patio. Silently she stood there, her arms wrapped round her and her shoulders hunched.

'Alex, what's up?' Dan appeared behind her.

'What do you think?'

'Sorry, it was a stupid question – but standing out here isn't going to help. Come back to bed and get some sleep. It'll be better in the morning.'

'Christ, you can be so bloody insensitive sometimes – you know that?' Alex exploded at him, taking her feelings out on him again. 'In the last few days I've had everything – *everything* – that I accepted as being me shoved on the rubbish tip. The people I thought were my parents aren't. The man I spent all my life believing was my father was a spy and as good as a murderer. The woman I thought was my mother was a manipulative, neurotic, spoilt brat. I feel as if someone has kicked a hole in my guts, and you tell me

267

to get some sleep. Just piss off and leave me alone!'

Dan's jaw set in a rigid line. Marching across the patio towards her, he grabbed her by the shoulders and spun her round, forcing her to look at him.

'Now it's my turn. You were the one who wanted to find out what it was all about. No one made you do it. I've been as supportive and helpful as I know how. I've also been walking on fucking eggshells trying to keep up with your moods and tantrums. Well, you've got the answers, so now you have a choice. Either you carry on lugging that bundle of misery around with you, or you finally let it go and start living. We've got four days of this holiday left, and *I* intend to enjoy them. And that's with you or without you. It's up to you. I'm going back to bed.' He stomped back into the apartment.

Alex seethed as she watched him go but as he reached the door she could not help herself and a huge gale of laughter erupted from her, pushing her rage away. Puzzled, Dan looked over his shoulder at her.

'What the . . . ?'

'I shouldn't laugh, but it's sight of your bare white bum glowing in the dark against your tan. It somehow takes all your dignity away.' She giggled again, her mood changed as she became aware of the odd intimacy of the situation. 'I've been a pain in the arse, haven't I?'

Dan nodded. 'Yes. Now will you come to bed?'

Still giggling, she gave his rear a proprietorial pat as she went past. 'I'm an ungrateful bitch. You've been wonderful and I've taken it all for granted. It's just that it's been difficult keeping it all in perspective. I'm so sorry.'

After their outbursts both Dan and Alex tried to show more consideration for each other, and Alex made an effort to enjoy the rest of their holiday, which wasn't as difficult as she thought. Their last few days trickled by. Most of the time they were like any other holiday-makers, although they did make a few attempts to explore old records, to try to track down information about William Smythe.

A number of documents signed and authorised by him were lodged in the records department of the police station, but these gave them no more information about the man. A few of the older policemen they talked to vaguely remembered him, but no one knew anything definite – just the occasional allusion to his 'special' relationship with the local police force which Dan and Alex, rightly, assumed referred to various deals (to which the authorities turned a blind eye in return for some of the proceeds) to allow certain goods in and out of the country.

It would seem that William Smythe had spent much of his life keeping one step ahead of everyone else, but had lived and died a man who was accepted only because of who he knew, and seldom for himself.

'It's rather sad, really, isn't it?' Alex said, closing a ledger with a bang, sending up a small shower of dust from its old pages.

'What is?' asked Dan from the other side of the desk, where he was studying one sheet of yellowed paper after another.

'That he was obviously a clever man but there's nothing left of him. Nothing of note, nothing to show he actually existed, apart from a signature here and a vague memory there.'

'Alex, I'm bored with this. We're not going to find anything we don't already know, are we? How about calling it a day?'

Alex agreed, and Dan took the pile of papers from the right-hand side of the portfolio to place them on top of those on the left that he had yet to sort through, unaware that just two papers lower in the pile was the copy of the trust deed that David had entrusted to William the day after Elizabeth had died.

They spent their last full day on Telendos, a peaceful companionable silence between them as they sat and read or dipped in and out of the sea. As usual they had lunch at the taverna on the top of the hill. Wistfully Alex gazed across the sea to Myrties and Massouri. So much of her history was wrapped up here that she seemed to belong to this little corner of Greece. She wanted to tell Dan how she felt, but somehow couldn't find the right words.

Dan sat with his chin in his hand observing Alex gazing out at the scenery, trying to guess what she was thinking. Her expression gave little away, though he could tell that, whatever it was, it wasn't painful. He still felt guilty about his attack on her the other night; when they had gone back to bed he had lain awake for some time, trying to imagine what it must feel like to have your life turned upside-down.

He had never had to question his parents' or sisters' love, and coming from a close-knit family had accepted the family support system – encouragement, delight in successes and commiserations at disappointments – as his right. His family was a demonstrative one; his father was the sort of man who was not afraid to give his grown-up son a hug or peck on the cheek when he saw him, and his mother the sort of woman who would call to have a cosy chat with her children without them feeling she was prying into their lives. Dan had tried to imagine what it must have been like for Alex, but it was something beyond his comprehension.

'I love you.' For a moment Dan wasn't sure whether or not Alex had heard him, but he then realised she was struggling with herself. *Go on*, he urged her inside his head. *I know you love me, but I want to hear you say it. Tell me you love me, Alex. Say it. Trust me with those feelings.* He waited for her reaction, almost holding his breath, certain she could hear the silent plea. When she opened her mouth he fully expected to hear her say it. Instead she just said, 'I know', and squeezed his hand. Dan sighed, beaten again by her fear of revealing too much of herself to him, even after all this time.

That evening they spent their time saying their goodbyes. They started with Manolis and Diane. Alex promised she would come back, and although she refused to tell Manolis what she had discovered she did at least confirm that she had found what she had been looking for.

They hesitated about going to see Christos, but in the end Alex insisted, and darted into the factory to scramble over the still-large pile of sponges round the old man's feet to give him a kiss before darting out again. He never did manage to explain it to his daughter.

They also managed to see Papas before leaving. 'You talked to Edie and Rosie, then.' His use of their pet names indicated that he knew the women well.

'Papas, why didn't you tell us you knew them?' Dan sounded hurt.

'It might have hurt them. They had to tell you of their own free will what they knew. I could not be a part of that. What they tell me is between them, me and God.'

Again Alex experienced that sense of honesty she had felt when visiting the little church on the hill, and found herself respecting the man she had disliked when she first met him.

'Papas.' She used his name for the first time. 'Look after them for me. They're very special people.'

Finally they went to see Edith and Rose themselves, and took with them the present of a small music box that played the Brahms lullaby, which they had found in one of the side streets of Pothia.

'It's silly, really, but it's my way of saying thank you.'

Rose held the box, opening and closing it, listening with delight to the tune before Edith took it away from her to stand it in pride of place in their small living-room. Alex and Dan gave them both a hug, and the last they saw of them was Edith standing next to Rose's rocking chair when they turned at the curve in the road to wave.

The next day they stood on the little stone jetty like the other passengers with their luggage stacked around their feet as they waited for the ferry. When it arrived they scrambled aboard, and once again Dan ran up the stairs to secure them a place on the top deck. Alex heaved the luggage aboard before joining him. As the ferry's engine sprang into life they heard a yell from the quayside.

'Dan! Alex!'

They both looked down to see, much to their surprise, Papas standing there with a bulging holdall gripped firmly in his pudgy fingers. 'Here! This is for you!' The gangplank had already been raised but Dan hurried down the steps and leaned over the stern of the boat.

'Throw it!' he yelled over the roar of the engines.

Stepping back, Papas swung his arm behind him to bring it forward, sending the bag somersaulting through the air, where Dan, leaning over the rear rails, just managed to catch it. Downstairs he waved to Papas, then Alex did the same on the top deck. Pushing past the huge pile of luggage, and tripping over other people's legs, he made his way back to his seat next to Alex.

'What on earth is it?'

The ferry was picking up speed and the wind blowing straight into their faces as together they looked at the rather plain bag resting on Dan's knees. Dan pushed the handles to one side and opened the zip. As he did so the contents began to spill out and the wind caught the bits of paper, hurling some of them behind them into their wake and others across the deck. It was only as their fellow passengers began to scrabble around trying to pick it all up that Dan shut the bag and gave a low whistle.

'Alex, it's money! It's thousands, if not millions and millions of drachmas!'

271

Passengers were coming up to them, giving them back the crumpled high-denomination notes, which Alex accepted and thanked them for, scrunching them even further in her fists. Shielding the bag from the wind, Dan opened it again for Alex to stuff the money back inside it, so that she saw the neatly bound piles of notes under the loose ones on the top. She shoved her hands down to push it all in and then wriggled them out. As she did so she dislodged an envelope with her name written on it in a vaguely familiar, neat copperplate hand, which had been taped inside the top of the bag. Aware that their fellow passengers were staring at them with open curiosity, they twisted round to open and read its contents by themselves.

My dear Alex,
Forgive us for not contacting you and telling you the truth sooner, but while David was alive we were too scared to do it. Which is why we have asked Papas to give you this, as by rights it is yours, and it is our way of saying we're sorry.

We told you most of the truth about what happened, but not all of it. You see, that trust David made us sign gave us half of his shares in the Rouget Corporation. That was $7^1/_2$ per cent each.

We didn't want it, but as the trust deed said David would keep all the voting rights, that all dividends would go to him and that *he* would pay us a monthly sum, we felt it was removed from us. We always knew they were our shares, that they would ultimately give us a lot of money and a lot of control in the Corporation, but we could pretend it was nothing to do with us. We didn't want it then and we don't want it now.

When we heard that David had died we gave instructions to sell the shares. Alex, we are old women, and while David was alive we were forced to live a life that was not truthful. Finally, now he is dead, we can be free, which is why we want you to have the money. There's a lot more, ever such a lot more, but this is all the bank had. We will send the rest to you as soon as we can.

Thank you for coming to find us, for giving us the chance to be honest at last. We're not bad people, just cowardly ones.

God bless you and that nice young man of yours.
In gratitude
Edith Jones (Miss) and Rose Haggerty (Miss)

PS: We're really not *that* stupid with money after all. Our copy of the trust deed is enclosed so you can see it for yourself.

272

Dan was the first one to speak. 'The missing fifteen per cent. It was *theirs*, not William's. Christ, but whatever you say about him, David Ghillyand was a clever bastard!'

'Dan, I can't take this money. I want *them* to have it. They deserve it.'

'Alex, are you sure? It's a hell of a lot. Well, *you* know that – look what *your* fifteen per cent is worth, add this to it, invest it properly, and you could be getting close on a million quid a year. Think about it before you toss it back to them.'

Alex looked up from the trust deed she had been scanning while Dan was speaking. 'I'm not tossing it back. Look at the terms of this trust and tell me if I've understood it correctly.' She handed Dan the paper.

It was cleverly written. Reading through all the jargon Dan discovered that, while the shares had been fully and properly assigned to Edith and Rose, the terms of the trust stipulated that David retained the full voting rights of the shares and that the full dividend from them would be paid on a quarterly basis to David. He, however, would transfer on a monthly basis a fixed, index-linked, sum to Edith and Rose. Inevitably it was far less than the full value of the dividend. The shares were non-transferable and would revert to David Ghillyand on their deaths, unless he should predecease them, in which case they would own the shares outright.

'God, it was so simple! No one would be able to trace the ownership of the shares. To all intents and purposes they were still under David's control during his lifetime. And after his death he didn't give a shit, did he?'

'Nope. So you can see why I don't want it. David screws up their lives, makes them into criminals, blackmails them, effectively banishes them from their home to a strange country and controls their purse strings. No, Dan, they deserve this.'

When they reached the airport Alex bought a small padlock while Dan went to find Christine. 'I know it's your busiest day, but I did this really stupid thing. I picked up someone else's bag by mistake. I know who it belongs to, but as they're back on Kalymnos I was hoping you might be an absolute angel and return it to them. Please, Chris. Would you?'

While Dan was pleading with Chris, Alex had returned with the padlock and had managed to find a piece of paper and an envelope. She quickly scribbled a note.

Dear Edith and Rose,

What can I say? Except I can't keep it. David left me the rest of his shares, and it's more than enough. Anyway, as you know, all those years when David was transferring a monthly sum it was less than the dividend. He was stealing from you what was rightfully yours.

No, my mind is made up. It's yours. I can see why you don't want it but Dan agrees with me. You truly have earned it, so enjoy it. Please.

Alex

By the time she had written this, Christine had agreed to take the bag back for them. 'Dan Westbury, you get worse and worse! OK, give it here!'

Dan handed the now padlocked bag to Chris and gave her a kiss. 'See you next time round. 'Bye.'

Before she could say anything else Dan and Alex had disappeared through passport control and into the departure lounge.

'I knew he was a crook!' Jen whooped ecstatically. She was sitting crossed-legged on Alex's floor, listening enthralled to the account of the holiday, making Alex feel as if she were telling a story from an old schoolgirls' annual.

Alex laughed and hurled a pillow at her head. 'A crook! He was worse than that. A crook makes him sound like a lovable rogue. Just think, I wasted all this time hating the man, when in fact I didn't have to worry about him.'

'Well, we've been through all that,' Jen said, waving Alex's last comments aside with her long, fluorescent-pink nails, dismissing the talk of David, Elizabeth, Robert and Sally that had so far dominated their evening. 'What I want to know is, what about the lovely Dan?'

'What about him?'

'Don't you go all defensive on me, hon – I know you better than that. What happened between you two?'

'Well, you know, the usual . . . We lay in the sun, ate a lot, drank far too much, slept a lot and . . .'

'Let's go back to the sleeping bit . . .'

'Jen, it's none of your bloody business whether I euphemistically slept with him or *slept* with him.' But Alex was laughing as she said it. 'If you must know, we did both, and that's all I'm saying on

274

the subject. Another coffee.' Alex tried to get up and change the subject but Jen wouldn't let her.

'Come on, hon,' she said, pushing her glasses up her nose, a sure sign that she was about to get serious. 'This is me, your old mate Jen. I reckon he's in love with you, but what about you? Do you love him?'

'Oh, Jen! He's away covering a story for a couple of days and I can't tell you how much I miss him.' Alex sank back into the sofa and ran her fingers through her hair. 'He's told me he loves me and I believe him. I also know I love him, really love him. The idea of Dan not being a part of my life any more is unthinkable. He makes me feel like . . .' She stopped, trying to find the right words. 'When I'm with Dan I feel as if we've fitted inside each other, that there's someone who makes me feel complete and whole. Does that make sense?'

'Have you told him you love him?

'Not yet. I know he knows that I do. But every time I try and say it, the words stick. It's stupid, isn't it? Inside my head I can yell it as loud as I like. *Daniel Westbury, I love you!* I just can't take that final step and say it to *him*.'

'Alex – a word of advice from your Auntie Jen. Stop thinking about it and just say it. For once in your bloody life, let go.'

Alex smiled to himself. For a moment she wondered what Jen would say if she discovered how much she had let go in Greece, even to the extent of making love on the beach in broad daylight. But there were certain things not even your closest friend should know about.

They had had an evening in and were sitting in Dan's flat after supper when he fetched the letter to show Alex. The envelope bore a Kalymnos postmark and was heavy, with something large and flat in the bottom. She was going to fish it out, but Dan made her read the letter first.

Dear Dan,
I am sorry to have to write this letter, but I know you and Alex would want to know. Edie died in her sleep on September 24th. It was very peaceful and Rose said how pleased she was that they had been able to set the record straight before it was too late.
I went to see Rosie every day and she managed quite well for a

while, but she told me a few weeks after Edie died that without her there to look after and to share things with she had decided that she wanted to go too. Rose was always more determined than you would imagine and I was not surprised when she also died in her sleep a few days later.

Both were contented when they were laid to rest as they felt they had finally righted the wrongs that had been forced upon them. I know they have left everything to Alex, but there is one final personal gift that they wanted her to have and I have enclosed it with this letter.

May the Good Lord and the Virgin protect you.

Papas

Alex ran her fingers over the paper, as if trying one last time to touch the two old women. Dan didn't stop her now when she peered into the envelope at the object weighing it down. In the bottom was a rolled-up piece of tissue paper. Carefully she took it out and unfolded it. Inside was a large, old-fashioned, filigree-worked locket on a gold chain.

Alex turned it over in her hands, her fingers fumbling with the catch. It opened easily. Inside on the right was a small but nevertheless clear photograph of a man and woman holding a small baby. The man had unruly hair and was grinning widely, and Alex could tell by his expression it was something he did quite often. He was perched on the edge of a bed with one arm protectively round the shoulders of a pretty plump woman. She too was smiling and facing the camera, and in her arms was a very young, wide-eyed baby. The man's other hand was stretched across the woman to help her to hold the baby.

On the left-hand side of the locket a faded note said: 'Robert, Sally and Alex. 10 November 1952.'

Dan, looking over Alex's shoulder, felt his throat constrict and fully expected Alex to cry as well. Instead she gazed silently and lovingly at the locket, a faint smile on her lips, before angling it so that Dan could have a better view.

'Dan, I'd like you to meet my parents – Dr Robert and Mrs Sally Ghillyand.'

It was some time after she received the locket that Dan fired the shot across her bows. She had had a particularly trying day. Once again Alex's submission to Vickie's board of trustees for the fund-

276

ing for a new CAT scanner for the department had been rejected. It was the third time the papers had gone in and she had been sure that on this occasion she and Edward had presented a conclusive argument that would mean the equipment would be sanctioned. Although it wasn't necessary, Sam had also got involved in the presentation, despite the fact that he was studying for yet another set of exams.

'I know I should be swotting, Alex, but this is important. I want the department to have that equipment as much as you do. After all, it's enlightened self-interest, isn't it? I want to have the best department in London when I take it over in a few years' time, don't I?'

Alex had given him the figures and she had to admit that he had managed to pull them into a better shape than she had.

Apart from her own feelings, it was for Sam's sake that she was so angry. She clattered around in the kitchen getting supper ready while Dan set the table.

'Honestly, Dan, they couldn't agree to give funds for a new CAT scanner but they *have* allocated money to refit the Prince Consort Wing. I know private patients are important – I've heard the arguments often enough about needing more fee-paying patients to help support the NHS side – but talk about getting your priorities wrong. Can't they see that, without decent equipment, we won't even get the NHS patients as referrals, and then what will happen to their precious ratios and quotas?'

'Have they really turned it down?' Dan hooked his notepad out of his briefcase.

Alex looked out of the kitchen door. 'Oh no, you don't. Just because I have a moan it doesn't give you the right to start creating headlines about it. I didn't say it, but I should have done. It's off the record, Dan! It's a bit much when I can't even sound off after a bad day without you taking notes. Just leave it, Dan, please?'

'OK. Anyway, there's something else I want you to read.' He took out a large brown envelope and handed it to her.

'What's this?' She put the tea-towel over her shoulder and came into the living-room.

'Open it and see. I need your opinion on it. Just to check I've got the facts right.'

Curiously she opened it and pulled out a sheaf of paper. It was headed 'AN ACCIDENTAL DAUGHTER'.

No matter how hard they try, every big corporation has at least one skeleton in its cupboard. The Rouget Corporation is no exception. After the death of eminent Nobel nominee Dr David Ghillyand earlier this year, the bones began to rattle so loudly that they have finally had to emerge. It's a fascinating tale of espionage, manipulation and murder that can only now be told.

Alex didn't read beyond the introductory paragraph but began to shuffle through the pages, scanning the odd paragraph here and there, a look of mounting disbelief and rage on her face.

'Dan, what *is* this?'

'It's my feature for the *City* about David. I admit it was originally meant to be about why there was that sudden surge in the market in Rouget stock after he died, but to explain it came from two old women in Greece dumping unwanted shares on the open market I have to explain how and why they had them in the first place, and why they didn't want them any more. It's a question of working backwards.'

'And you honestly expect me to read this . . . and do what, Dan? Give you a gold star, or a tick? Nine out of ten, could do better? Who the hell gave you the right to tell the world about me and my family? Whatever they did, and whoever they were, they are all still a part of *me*! I honestly thought I meant more to you. Do you know, I actually believed we had something going between us. Well, it only goes to prove that you're never too old to be taken for a ride. I actually thought you helped because you cared, but you didn't, did you? It was all a ploy so you could get another fucking byline. Get out.'

Dan couldn't believe her reaction. 'Hey, come on, you knew why I was interested. You knew I was working on a feature. I thought it didn't matter any more, that now you knew the truth you didn't care. It's not as if David's your father, is it? Look, if you don't want me to submit it, I won't, OK?'

'I told you to get out. Now will you leave my flat, or do I have to call the police?'

'*Alex!*'

She made a move towards the phone and Dan quickly gathered his things, stuffing his briefcase closed. He made a move to kiss her but decided against it. When he shut the door behind him she was standing with the phone in one hand and his sheaf of papers in the other.

278

He tried to call her at home and hit the answering machine every time. After a few days he stopped leaving messages; it was obvious she wasn't going to return his calls. He tried calling her at Vickie's, but on the one occasion he was actually connected she hung up on him. He even went so far as to book an appointment in her clinic, hoping to corner her in her office, but she had come out of the room before his appointment and seen him in the waiting area.

'Sam, please could you check who the man in the brown cords and leather jacket is waiting to see me, please?'

Sam had been about to object that it wasn't part of his job, yet Alex had been in such a bad mood the last few days he decided it was easier to do as he was asked. 'Mr Haggerty is a new patient and he's one of yours.'

'Haggerty? I thought I knew him. The Haggertys are old family friends. Well, I don't believe in treating people I know – the emotional side gets in the way. Even if he has got a direct referral to me, can you have him changed to Clive's list, please?'

Again Sam thought it better not to object and scurried off to do as he was asked.

When the nurse explained that unfortunately Dr Ghillyand would be unable to take his case and he had been transferred to Dr Fiordi's list, Dan told her not to bother and walked out of Vickie's feeling beaten and dejected.

Although he had been surprised at the vehemence of Alex's reaction, he had to admit that maybe she did have a point, and in deference to that doubt he hadn't submitted the feature. Anyway, with Christmas so close, the *Citadel* was, like every other paper, running the usual silly-season copy and his piece wasn't missed. Dan had always enjoyed Christmas and this year had been looking forward to taking Alex to his parents and show her what a real family Christmas was all about. Now he felt cheated. In an attempt to cheer himself up he entered into the round of Christmas parties with a vengeance, which meant that on more than one occasion he was nursing a sore head the next morning.

Alex was also feeling miserable. She wanted to phone Dan to tell him she was sorry, but as ever her pride got in the way. That, and her belief that she was right. Dan had led her on, had made her believe he really loved her. Without realising it she began to scan the pages of the *Citadel* each day, looking for the feature and waiting for the reaction, but as the feature never appeared the reaction didn't either. Slowly she began to realise that Dan had kept his word and hadn't submitted it.

Since the night she had thrown him out, Alex hadn't read the full manuscript, but had banged it down among the piles of old magazines by the telephone. It was only when they grew too high and finally toppled over that she found it again. Sitting down on the floor she raised her legs and, using them like a lectern, began to read. When she had finished it she read it again. Much as it galled her to say it, it was a very well-written piece. Dan had presented the facts without over-dramatising them, and in his reporting of her own feelings had been sympathetic and supportive. When the phone rang shrilly in her ear it made her jump, and she answered it without thinking to listen to the machine first to check that it was not Dan.

'Hello?'

'Alex? Malcolm Bratby.' Alex groaned to herself and raised her eyes to the ceiling but kept her voice light as she greeted him. 'Just wanted to check you're still on for the annual Christmas bash here at the Corporation? You haven't forgotten, have you?'

'No, of course not.' It had completely slipped her mind. 'But I must admit I've only just got in, so I'll be a bit late. I'm looking forward to it,' she lied as she hung up the phone.

Alex looked down at herself in her favourite old leggings, sweater and the large hiking socks she was wearing to keep her feet warm. The last thing she felt like doing was getting tarted up and going out to Elstree, but she had promised. With a sigh she rose to her feet and went to run a bath. As it was filling she began to go through her wardrobe looking for something to wear. She caught sight of the green and gold outfit and, in an attempt to cheer herself up, decided to wear that, telling herself that at least she'd look festive, even if she didn't feel it.

By the time she arrived at Elstree, the party was in full swing. She had barely got through the door before Malcolm was beside her, fussing around and getting a drink and something to eat. Various people came up to talk to her and she made polite conversation, listening to people again saying what a sad year it had been with her father dying. Finally she could take no more of the small talk and, telling Malcolm she needed to go to the loo, she excused herself and left everyone else dancing.

Instead of going upstairs she pushed her way out of the main door, smiling at the security guard as she went. 'Slight headache. Need some fresh air,' she explained unnecessarily. Once outside she inhaled, and watched her breath mist the cold night air. Not quite sure where she was going, she began to walk round the building. To the right was the research administration wing, which used to be the old Clinic. Since the mid-seventies it had no longer been viable as a medical facility on site, especially with the BUPA hospital up the road, so the building had been converted. Externally it looked much the same as it had in the fifties.

Alex walked up the steps, wanting to go in and wander around, but the doors were locked. She continued round the building, following the tarmacked road to the houses that residential staff called home. Although she didn't know which one had been Robert and Sally's, it was interesting to look at the cottages. For a moment she toyed with the idea of walking down through the woods to the bridge over Tykes Water, but decided it was too cold and too far to go.

Slowly she made her way back into the main building and up the stairs. 'Toilet,' she said again, feeling the need to explain herself to the man at the reception desk. Almost as if she were justifying her actions she did go into the loo; however, instead of coming straight downstairs again, she carried on along the corridors, trying to envisage the Manor House as it must once have been. Not knowing why, she tried the door of her father's old office. To her surprise it opened. The glow from the security lights outside bathed the room in an eerie light, but she could see that, apart from having been cleaned, it hadn't been touched since the day she had finished clearing David's things away. She made her way to his desk and pulled out the high-backed leather swivel chair. She ran her hands over the top of the desk, feeling the patina under her fingers.

She swung the chair round to look out of the window and could see the mist rising off the grass. In the distance the lights of the cars snaked their way as usual along the M1. In some respects hardly anything had changed since the last time she had sat in this chair; in others, changes so enormous had taken place that it was almost impossible to comprehend them. In her mind she reread Dan's feature, and began to accept that all she had discovered during that year actually had very little to do with her.

I'm still me, aren't I? Still Alex. The same Dr Alexandra Marie Ghillyand who cleared this desk out. All that's changed are the facts

281

around me, and the history, but I haven't changed, have I? I'm still the same person.

No, you're not, said the little voice in her head. *You're nicer. Less fraught, and calmer – and that's because of Dan.*

Without switching on the desk light, Alex turned back to face into the room and pulled the phone towards her. She hesitated before dialling his number, fully expecting him to be out and not sure what message she would leave on his answering machine. But Dan himself answered.

'Dan, it's Alex. I wanted to let you know you can publish the feature. It's good. Very good. How do you fancy dinner tomorrow? My treat. I'm sure Ari could fit us in.'

She listened as Dan replied, accepting her invitation. He said he would book the table and they agreed to meet at eight o'clock.

'Alex, I'm glad you called.'

'Good, and Dan – I also wanted to say I love you.'

At his end of the phone Dan triumphantly punched the air.